THE LEGAL CONCEPT OF ART

THE LEGAL CONCEPT
OF ART

PAUL KEARNS

B.A. (Oxon), LL.M. (Cantab), Ph.D (EUI), Barrister

·H A R T·
PUBLISHING

OXFORD

1998

Hart Publishing
Oxford
UK

Distributed in the United States by
Northwestern University Press
625 Colfax, Evanston
Illinois 60208–4210 USA

Distributed in Australia and New Zealand by
Federation Press Pty Ltd
PO Box 45, Annandale
NSW 203, Australia

Distributed in the Netherlands, Belgium and Luxembourg by
Intersentia, Churchillaan 108
B2900 Schoten, Antwerpen
Belgium

Hart Publishing is a specialist legal publisher based in Oxford, England.
To order further copies of this book or to request a list of other publications
please write to:

Hart Publishing, 19 Whitehouse Road, Oxford, OX1 4PA
Telephone: +44 (0)1865 434459 or Fax: +44 (0)1865 794882
e-mail: hartpub@janep.demon.co.uk

British Library Cataloguing in Publication Data
Data Available
ISBN 1–901362–50–7

Typeset in 12pt Sabon
by Hope Services (Abingdon) Ltd.
Printed in Great Britain on acid-free paper
by Biddles Ltd, Guildford and King's Lynn.

Preface

When law operates on art various specialised problems arise, and art law, as a distinct legal subject area, is now well-established in the United States of America. The task of this book is an analysis of the treatment of the concept of art in legal culture and, to this end, a range of traditional legal subject areas have been chosen as models in accordance with their particular relevance to artistic subject matter. The bold title *The Legal Concept of Art* is intended to indicate that the enquiry is about how law (in a variety of its established categories) constitutes definitively its notion of art. It is not, of course, intended to suggest that the same legal idea about art prevails in all legal contexts.

As art, the author has limited his analysis to non-motion visual art and creative literature.[1] Although creative literature can, of course, be distinguished from the visual arts, many of the legal problems cut right across the distinction. This analysis focuses, then, on permanent media, including paintings, photographs, sculpture, monuments, architecture, the novel and poetry.

For the convenience of the reader the text is presented in a single language, with the author's own translations provided. England, France and the United States of America, as well as housing the three leading art markets, have always had a prominent profile in the arts, and in this respect, as well as in presenting three different types of legal system,[2] are

---

[1] This was a necessary delimitation for reasons of time and space. Though accommodating a large range of art forms, dance, film and press literature, for example, are excluded from the analysis. In the chosen field of non-motion visual art and creative literature, there is much variance in definition of individual art forms. Moreover, the motion/non-motion art division is not always clear-cut. Artist Damien Hirst, for example, used Malaysian butterflies hatching from chrysalis form as part of his art exhibition "In and Out of Love" (July 1991, 2–3 Woodstock St., London W1). The creative literature/non-motion visual art distinction is also traversed, for example, in the *"livres de luxe"* (beautifully illustrated literary works) and concrete poetry (poetry expressed in a visually attractive way in physical objects such as stone or a series of stones). This text in part examines the legal setting of bounds to such categories.

[2] Common law, civil and federal. The EC also presents a federal model in Chs. 7 and 8. England and France present, respectively, a classical opposition between common law and codal systems. Although historically a common law system based on English law, the United States of America, unlike England, provides for the judicial review of the constitutionality of its legislation. Whereas the judicial review of the constitutionality of legislation also

particularly appropriate jurisdictions for this analysis. *A fortiori*, it is considered that a comparative analysis best facilitates ascertainment of a unitary[3] sense of law's treatment of art. However, this is not a comparative study where all jurisdictions are necessarily given the same depth of analysis. The focal point remains the English law.

When writing more generally about legal culture, the term "the law" is used for convenience's sake, and this may refer to the judiciary, legislature and/or the constitution, depending on the context. In the course of the text, the term "American" refers only to the United States of America and never to Canada, and in the tradition of A.V. Dicey,[4] the author refers to English law, as opposed to British or United Kingdom law. By the term "English law", the law applicable to Wales is commonly understood to be included. When the law does apply to the whole of the United Kingdom, such as the Copyright, Designs and Patents Act 1988, the term "English law" is retained merely for expositional consistency and convenience, and not out of any jingoism.[5]

It is perhaps not essential for a work of this kind to be as up-to-date as possible but the text nevertheless traces developments up to May Day 1998, though it has been possible at various proof stages to take account of some later developments. Policy on art law is particularly changeable in the field of the public funding of the arts, for example, and in this area it has therefore been particularly desirable to keep abreast of the most important recent developments.

The purpose of this text has necessitated the isolation of art-related material within a range of legal areas whose main focus is not necessarily art (some of which do not even recognise art as a specific cultural category). The distinctive way in which art is treated in each legal area has necessitated the choosing of an appropriate methodology for each (in each chapter), and the text may be regarded as a series of exploratory essays linked by the core theme of the legal treatment of art, rather than as simply a text-book monograph on art law *per se*.

It is hoped that in all areas the text and its conclusions will help improve the understanding of the art-law relation, and, as a result, ultimately help improve the law internally, and its image from with-

operates in France, it is restricted there to the examination of new bills. My field of enquiry covers only established statutes.

[3] See, further, more generally, K. Zweigert and H. Kötz, *An Introduction to Comparative Law* (2 vols., trans. Weir, 2nd edn., OUP, Oxford, 1987) (especially vol. 1 at 3).

[4] See A.V. Dicey, *Introduction to the Study of the Law of the Constitution* (10th edn., Macmillan, London, 1964).

[5] The author is himself Welsh.

out (especially in the eyes of the art-concerned), as well as foster the fairest possible treatment of art by law.

There is a main thesis plus appendix contributions. The reader does not necessarily have to read the latter but they are offered as forms of extra insight into the art-law relation based on themes of the main text.

Thanks are due to many. The idea for this book emerged from a "Law and Culture" research programme spearheaded by Professor Bruno De Witte who provided seminal guidance in the art-friendly environment of the European University Institute, Florence. Pascale Lorber, a colleague at the University of Leicester, was most helpful in elucidating French law when this proved difficult, and Bela Chatterjee, my research assistant, was commendably assiduous in verifying all my footnote references. Rachel Armitage and Jo Goacher endured the task of much typing conscientiously and with good humour, and the Art Law Centre, Geneva, and the Institute of Art and Law, Leicester, gave me support at various points in the evolution of my project in this fascinating area.

Grateful thanks are due to three law journals which have permitted the reproduction of material previously published in them, namely *The International Journal of Cultural Property*, *The Maastricht Journal of European and Comparative Law* and *Art, Antiquity and Law*, for material in Chapters 1 and 6 originally published in *IJCP* No. 2 Vol. 1 1992 at 383, *MA* Vol. 1 No. 3 1994 at 307 and *Art, Antiquity and Law* Vol. 1 Issue 1 February 1996 at 5, respectively.

The present era, in particular, has witnessed the radicalisation of art, and it has not been easy to juridify. In this text, the author has adopted the role of defence counsel for art, even when it may appear that the art is in bad taste. It will become apparent to the reader that freedom of artistic expression is preferred to art's heteronomous status in the legal arena where it may be abused. The author here declares his interests as a creative writer and essayist as a possible reason for his sometimes impassioned art sympathies, and for what some see as art's idealisation via a Christian hermeneutic.

A final note of thanks is due to my publisher, Richard Hart, and to my father, both of whom have in different ways been habitually kind and supportive during the gestation period of this colourful and extensive enterprise.

PAUL KEARNS
May Day 1998
University of Leicester
England

Contents

Introduction

For legal purposes, objects of analysis tend to be viewed through legal lenses dispassionately and it is arguable that art, in particular, requires a response from the viewer or reader as a whole man not just as a legal functionary. The courtroom may then be seen as a place inhospitable to art appreciation. However, in certain situations art has been deemed subject to legal regulation, sometimes for its own purposes, as in the case of copyright, but mostly for other reasons, by the legislature as well as by courts.

Like law, art was once a rule-based activity. In classical antiquity, the word "art" (Greek, *"tekne"*, Latin, *"ars"*) was the name given to any activity governed by rules.[1] An absolutist attitude is that there are certain immutable principles for determining what is art. However, such approaches find little support today. A typical postmodern stance is that art is all that self-termed artists claim to produce, such is the current era's emphasis on self-legitimation.[2]

Recognisable[3] art exists, but the absence of rules or principles for its recognition beyond the undefined rudimentary standard now established will be found to be unhelpful for a controlling mechanism like law, and the imposition of its minimal æsthetic criterion is

[1] This was also the case in the Middle Ages—see Umberto Eco, *Art and Beauty in the Middle Ages* (Yale UP, Princeton, NJ, 1986), 92: "Art was a knowledge of the rules for making things . . .". Contrast the postmodern statement by Colin Wheeler in *The Independent*, 21 August 1990, at 25: "There are no rules in art".

[2] Jürgen Habermas's theory of modernity built upon Max Weber's conception of the "differentiation of the spheres". He discerned "independent logics" in the value-spheres of science/technology, morality/law and art. In premodern societies, the autonomy of spheres was inhibited by cosmological world views, including religion, against whose terms value was forced to legitimate itself. In the present study, law provides the system in which the inherent meanings of art struggle to preserve ontological self-definition in the course, and with the backcloth, of legal process. Nietzsche suggested that existence can be understood and justified only in æsthetic terms; and his ideas can be considered to mark the advent of postmodernism. See, further, H.G. Gerth and C.W. Mills (eds.), *From Max Weber* (Routledge, New York, 1946), 323–59, and Habermas's *The Philosophical Discourse of Modernity* (MIT Press, Cambridge, Mass., 1990), at 83–106: "The Entry Into Postmodernity: Nietzsche as a Turning Point". On postmodernism, see Appendix, Essay 1, below.

[3] The rule of recognition is difficult to pin-point in law as it is in art, but recognisable law and art nevertheless exist.

difficult to make generally acceptable, especially in legal contexts where the legal personnel are often conservative and not appropriately specialised in artistic matters.

The main chapters of this work treat convenient models of the art-law relation: it is impracticable for reasons of time and space to incorporate all possible options. The legal areas chosen were selected for their pertinence to the theme and their representation of varied legal policies: a function of copyright law is the protection of creative originality; artworks are exempted from customs duties; obscene art is regulated for public-morality reasons; in the competitive area of the public funding of the arts, the issue becomes less "what is art?" than "what is the best art?"; in the law of charitable trusts, purposes including the artistic are assessed for charitable status in accordance with what they advance for the public good; in the law of defamation, the transmutation of real-life characters to ones in art finds unclear demarcation for the purpose of protection of reputation; the international movement of art reveals, *inter alia*, the "cultural heritage" and "cultural property" dichotomy as another issue of definitional concern apart from that of art.

Ineluctably, politico-legal questions of freedom of artistic expression emerge in the course of an enquiry into legal conceptualising about, and policies towards, art. Questions of constitutional law then become important. These are treated implicitly in this work. Whereas the United States of America and France have the benefit of written constitutions which protect freedom of speech, Britain currently does not. However, this formal difference may not have much significance for the substantive matter of the protection of specifically *artistic* liberty, in view of the consideration that artistic expression is expressly constitutionally protected in neither the written constitution of the USA nor that of France.[4] Existing constitutional provisions, and the law that has developed upon them,[5] tend to protect speech primarily, and only secondarily expression, the point being that the right to usually non-political, and sometimes non-cognitive expression, such as is involved in the essence of art, is comparatively neglected in all three states in favour of speech that has political or at least cognitive import. Having said this, art is protected under the

---

[4] Some constitutions uphold a right to specifically artistic expression. See, e.g., German Basic Law, art. 5(3).

[5] See, further, the terms of the US First Amendment and art. 11 of the French Declaration of the Rights of Man and the Citizen, and any subsequently evolved "constitutional bloc" of principle.

speech principle to varying degrees in each state, and the nature of this variance will become apparent in this book.

The object of the legal critiques that follow, on the operation of various branches of law on art, is intended to elucidate the results achieved when legal culture that demands solution treats another that defies definition. One presupposition may be that art has the tendency to engender grey areas of law resultant upon the complexities involved for law in operating on art's elastic discourses and definitions, sometimes irreducible to the neatness of finite conceptual clarity that law requires for a practical result. Law, on the other hand, may be seen as the oppressor of art's distinctive character in the interests of its own and society's sense of social order based on priorities insensitive or antipathetic to art. The following study will confute or confirm any such caricature impressions of the art-law relation.

An abiding theme of the text is art's allegedly ineluctable transgression of traditional general social norms of a given society because it looks outside or beyond immediately surrounding social mores, not in a specialized experimental way, necessarily, but in a search for "truth" in a less social context-dependent sense than that to which contemporary law tends to be adhered.

One can look at it, like Habermas,[6] as follows: all systems, including art, are environments that amplify the more general environmental complexity, and are there for the mutual benefit of particular environments within that whole; but to modify Weber[7] slightly, if law is coercion to bring about conformity, art, which by its nature is in its many parts unique, may be intrinsically unable to follow a prescribed legal object set i.e. may be unable to conform with the uniformity that law seems to anticipate. The interaction of two cultural tectonic plates may therefore become collision rather than harmony, and the art-law interface highly protean.

---

[6] J. Habermas, *The Philosophical Discourse. Twelve Lectures* (MIT Press, Cambridge, Mass., 1987), 371.

[7] M. Weber, *Economy and Society* (University of California Press, Berkeley, Cal., 1978) and *On Law in Economy and Society* (Harvard University Press, Cambridge, Mass., 1954).

I

The Legal Regulation of Art

". . . the greatest interest in free speech should be sacrificed only when the interest in public safety is really imperilled, and not, as most men believe, when it is barely conceivable that it may be slightly affected" [Zechariah Chafee Jr., "Free Speech In The United States" (*Harvard University Press*, New Haven, Conn., 1946, 35].

"All art is at once surface and symbol. Those who go beneath the surface do so at their peril" [Oscar Wilde, in the prelude to *The Picture Of Dorian Gray*].

INTRODUCTION

The undertaking of this chapter is a comparative analysis of the operation of English, French and American public morality laws oriented to the proscription of the obscene, with particular reference to their regulation of art. Public morality law is not just art-oriented. Consequently, the law presented here has been specifically selected according to its particular relevance to art (cleaved from a broader dimension). It adumbrates the legal mechanisms for regulating potentially offending art and, for the sake of conciseness and clarity, does not focus on the particular facts of the art law cases. Rather, the judicial approach to art is examined thoroughly in Chapter 2. The object of the French law of "outrage of good morals" is broader than obscenity *per se*, so, unlike its English and American equivalents, it cannot accurately be placed under the narrower category of "obscenity law", though in practice obscenity is indubitably its central concern.

In 1957, in *Roth* v. *United States*,[1] the US Supreme Court established for the first time as a matter of federal constitutional law a

---

[1] 354 US 476, 1 L Ed 2d 1498, 77 S Ct 134 (1957). *Roth* is not hereafter footnoted because reference to it in the text is constant. The *Roth* test is "whether to the average person, applying contemporary standards, the dominant theme of the material taken as a whole appeals to prurient interest".

standard of obscenity applicable in both federal and state courts that
rendered invalid any more stringent statutory or judicial standards. It
is on this dominant standard that my study of American law will
focus. In addition, state statutes regulate obscenity in every individual American state,[2] and between 1842 and the *Roth* decision, for
example, 20 federal obscenity laws were enacted by Congress[3]; following *Roth*, both state and federal laws have to conform to a constitutional standard that embodies the maximum permissible in
proscriptive force—the constitutional standard is the most severe
standard of obscenity state or federal American law can impose. This
maximum limit inaugurated by *Roth* is designed to secure greatest
national freedom of expression (while proscribing the obscene) and
to encourage a certain uniformity of standard beneath its top one.

French "outrage of good morals" and English obscenity law are
not complicated by a comparable constitutional, federal and state tier
system. Broadly speaking, the French law developed by legislative
enactment, with a minimum of judicial creativity, based on article
283[4] of the penultimate penal code, this article being the most important with respect to art. The new penal code entered into force on
1 March 1994, emergent from 1992 and 1993 laws. The old code
article 283 (ff.) became article 227–24 of the new code. Because of
this correspondence, the case law based on the old article 283 is still
relevant and that article treated in this chapter as the important provision in the history of the offence. The new law appears only to
embody provisions respecting minors, and, with the arrival of violent
"messages" to join pornographic ones as illegal in this area, the law is
not now confined to matters of sexual immorality. Exactly where that
leaves obscenity and adults is a matter of conjecture. It is the old

---

[2] Many states attempt to protect freedom of expression by specifically exempting either
art or art institutions from their obscenity statutes. The Iowa legislation produced a novel
style of exemption, its statute providing that "[n]othing in this chapter prohibits the attendance of minors at an exhibition or display of works of art . . ." (Iowa Code Ann. 728.7
(West 1979)). Colorado exempts from the ambit of its statute "[t]he exhibition . . . by any
accredited museum . . ." (Colo. Rev. Stat. 18–7–104 (a) (Supp. 1985)). More usually, works
are either deemed to have sufficient artistic value, for which evidence is frequently deemed
admissible, to be exempt from the statute's operation (as in Montana) or the institution, or
individual working with that institution, is likewise exempted (as in Nevada).

[3] 5 Stat. 548, 566; 11 Stat. 168; 13 Stat. 504, 507; 17 Stat. 302; 17 Stat. 598; 19 Stat. 90;
25 Stat. 187, 188; 25 Stat. 496; 26 Stat. 567, 614–15; 29 Stat. 512; 33 Stat. 705; 35 Stat. 1129,
1138; 41 Stat. 1060; 46 Stat. 688; 48 Stat. 1091, 1100; 62 Stat. 768; 64 Stat. 194; 64 Stat. 451;
69 Stat. 193; 70 Stat. 699. (Stat. indicates Statutes at Large (USA), an official compilation of
the acts and resolutions of each session of Congress published by the office of the Federal
Register in the National Archives and Records Service).

[4] See nn. 5 and 6, below.

code's article 283 that generated law related to art, and the change of emphasis in the new code provisions means that it is to the former article 283 that we must turn for specifically art law content. The new code article so far only has potential in this area, of, it would seem, a limited nature (for example, if a question arose about the attendance of children at an exhibition of Mapplethorpe's "sado-masochistic" photographs in France). The degree to which lack of a system of precedent will affect matters is also one of personal opinion. Chronologically cumulative "outrage of good morals" legislation is interpreted in the individual case without the harness of precedent: the law in France traditionally lacks the judicial thematic development of rules that characterises English common law.

In England, the emergence of an obscenity statute is followed by court-to-court judicial rule development, though the latter has not always been reliant on the former as determinative guide: in the absence of statute, the earliest English obscenity cases emerged from judicial common law.

In America, the constitutional law standard begun by *Roth* governs legislative enactment; in England, common law co-operates with the 1959 and 1964 legislation; in France, the penal code and ancillary legislation provide the law that judges apply directly to the immediate case.[5] The nature of the dominant law is therefore different in all three of the jurisdictions treated.

FRENCH AND GENERAL MECHANISMS OF CONTROL

(i) *The notion of outrage*

The French have rarely been happy to confine their obscenity law to that name. Whereas it is inappropriate in the present legal analysis to attempt to explain this by expanding on the political and historical context of eighteenth and nineteenth century legal measures, of central legal interest is the fluctuation of the legal criteria by which offending art has been prosecuted. Unlike in England and America, obscenity has not been the prevailing concept in the French

---

[5] The American standard is found in n. 1, above, and the English legislation is the Obscene Publications Act 1959, as amended by the Obscene Publications Act 1964. In France, art. 283 of the penal code and ancillary legislation pertaining to the outraging of good morals provided the law that judges apply directly to the immediate case, which is still a rule.

legislative censure of obscene art. Although statutes of 19 and 22 July 1791 and 2 August 1882 suppressed only the "obscene", a more pervasive French criterion for the suppression of art on moral grounds is that of "contrary to good morals" which featured in article 287 of the 1810 penal code, the statute of 29 July 1881, the decree-law of 29 July 1939 (and its prototype of 18 April 1930). Sometimes, both criteria were employed, as in the statutes of 29 December 1875, 16 March 1898 and 7 April 1908. The criterion of "outraging public or religious morals" (in a statute of 17 May 1819 and orders of 2 and 21 February 1852) does not find favour in twentieth-century law, whereas the criterion "contrary to decency" is a peculiarly twentieth-century formula. As previously stated, by far the most important French provision affecting the moral content of art was embodied in article 283[6] of the old penal code, other articles not having art as a direct focus and affecting it only marginally[7] or incidentally.[8]

(ii) *The Old Article 283*

In article 283, French law was distinctive in making criminal not only publications but, more widely, all propaganda in favour of immorality. Publication, a word that dominates English legislation in particular, is not favoured by the French, who employed an enumeration technique in article 283, detailing as many activities as could feasibly involve the offensive material's dissemination, with the notable omission of the term publication. The list of disseminating activities is not

---

[6] The precise provisions of this art. can be found in every major textbook dealing with French obscenity law and are discussed here thematically. For present purposes, the most pertinent part of the old penal code's art. 283 read as follows: "[w]hoever has done one of the following will be punished by imprisonment from one month to two years and a fine of 360 to 30,000 francs:

> Made or had in possession with a view to trading, distributing, renting, putting up in poster form or showing;
> Imported or had imported, exported or had exported, transported or had transported knowingly to the same ends;
> Put up as a poster, exposed or projected within the vision of the public;
> Sold, rented, put up for sale or renting, even not publicly;
> Offered, even with free title, even not publicly, in some form albeit directly or indirectly;
> Distributed or set in motion their disribution in whatever manner:

All printed matter, writings, drawings, posters, paintings, photographs, films or negatives, matrixes or photographic reproductions, emblems, all objects or images against good morals."

[7] E.g., old penal code, arts. 284 and 285.

[8] E.g., outrage of decency law (*"pudeur"* as opposed to *"bonnes mœurs"*).

exhaustive, and its purpose is to clarify particular aspects of dissemination proscribed. In developing the constitutional standard of obscenity definitionally, the American Supreme Court has been less concerned with the law governing the publication element of the crime.

The publicity element of the offence detailed in the old article 283 was specified in the term "cast for public view" but the phrase "even not publicly" was appended to certain acts of dissemination mentioned, obscuring the basic degree of publicity required for the crime in general: the phrase "kept with a view to doing business" demonstrated that the publicity was not an absolute requirement for its commission. This latter-mentioned phrase is parallelled in section 1(1) of the English Obscene Publications Act 1964, the French phrase entering the law virtually simultaneously with the English formula "[any person who] has an obscene article for publication for gain". In English law, the gain is specified as not needing to be for the gain of the person so acting. The English phrase is further elaborated upon in the 1964 Act,[9] the English legislation defining its terms much more conscientiously than the French article 283. This can be explained by the fact that French "outrage of good morals" is really made up of lots of possible crimes under one convenient title, as opposed to one crime with many detailed facets. Article 283 listed a variety of possible crimes starkly, and was therefore less dense than its English legislative counterparts which elucidate one basic offence's elements. It is not that the French provision was more concise, it was that its cataloguing function was simpler.

In accordance with this function, article 283 enumerated possible forms the offensive material can take. English legislation simply employs the word "article" and only incidentally particularises types of object susceptible of prosecution; the American constitutional law governing obscenity does not use lists, but neither does the constitutional standard prevent any state or federal statute from employing them, providing they abide by the import of that standard.

What of the defendant's intention? English law excludes intention as an element of its obscene publications offence; American constitutional law surprisingly does not pronounce on it; and French law specified it in the single word "knowingly" in the context of "had

[9] S. 1(5) of the Obscene Publications Act 1964. This reads "[r]eferences in Section 3 of the Obscene Publications Act 1959 and this section to publication for gain shall apply to any publication with a view to gain, whether the gain is to accrue by way of consideration for the publication or in any other way".

transported knowingly". English obscenity law's position here is tortuous: the crime is one of strict liability, which is bizarre in itself for English law (which generally requires *mens rea* as a necessary element of a crime); moreover, evidence of the defendant's artistic intention *is* permissible in English obscenity law if the defence of public good is raised. It is an anomalous arrangement.

The requirement of intention in the French law was easily satisfied: "[t]he knowledge of the offensive character of the object presented to the public suffices, in effect, to constitute the intention".[10] It has been otherwise simply expressed as "the consciousness of the act".[11] In all three countries, the defendant's intention is a very weak factor in "obscenity" law, always totally eclipsed by the obscene matter's judged effect (immorality in France, prurience in America and corruption in England). However, intention is permitted to play a role in English and American defences of art, and in French law, although intention was not to be confused with motive (for example, "the cover of a claimed artistic vocation"),[12] genuine artistic purpose was differentiated from calculated arousal of unhealthy curiosity.[13] André Vitu has written that it is certain that writings, designs or objects which are exclusively and truly of the artistic order do not outrage good morals even when they impinge on sexual matters.[14]

(iii)   *The Nature of the Evil*

Theoretically, French "outrage of good morals" is said to be wider than obscenity,[15] but until the new code in practice it was even more confined to sexual matters than English obscenity law. Perhaps, though, it is a misassumption to equate obscenity with the sexual. Whatever the semantic point, Michèle-Laure Rassat has recently written: "[i]t is thus unanimously acknowledged today that outrage of good morals must relate uniquely to what has sexually moral features".[16] In practice, "outrage" traditionally relates exclusively to sex in one way or another, and the nature of the cases before the new

[10] Cass. Crim. 13 Mar. 1956.

[11] Cass. Crim. 17 July 1903.

[12] Trib. corr. Seine 21 Oct. 1964: *Gaz. Pal.* 1964, 2, 439.

[13] Michèle-Laure Rassat, "Outrage Aux Bonnes Moeurs", *Juris-Classeur Pénal*, Vol 2, at 8.

[14] André Vitu, *Traité de Droit Criminel: Droit Pénal Spécial* (CUJAS, Paris, 1982), at 1530.

[15] *Ibid.*, at 1531.

[16] *N.* 13 above, at 7.

code reinforces this view. In the leading American Supreme Court case of *Miller* v. *California*[17] it was held that the permissible scope of state regulation must be confined to works which depict or describe sexual conduct, and that the constitutional standard had been developed exclusively with attention to what gives offence in the sexual realm, with emphasis in *Miller* on "appeal to the prurient interest". In England's obscenity law corruption is not restricted to the sexual: the promotion of the delights of drug-taking is within its sphere,[18] as is the conditioning of children to engage in violence.[19] The law ignores the fact that art is not conative.

(iv) *The Difficulty of Assessment of the Evil*

The notion of "good morals" in French law is notoriously variable: it is a "customary" notion.[20] Contradictions in its interpretation abound. The Paris Court of Appeal considered that a luminous statuette, on one side a clothed woman, on the other a detailed erect penis, did not violate good morals.[21] Less than two months later, a Bordeaux judgment pronounced criminal an album of pornographic photographs.[22] The inconsistencies emerge from differing inferences of community standards and, perhaps, differing community standards.

In England, France and America this fluctuation of standards is recognised and accommodated by the law. In *Miller*,[23] the American Supreme Court held that in a prosecution under a state's obscenity laws, the contemporary standards of the state, as opposed to national standards, are constitutionally adequate to establish whether a work is obscene. The American constitutional law accommodates not only a chronological changing in national "moral" standards but also a constantly shifting regional multiplicity of such standards. In practice, France and England tolerate regional divergences too because the deciding tribunal's ideas of community standards—particularly a jury's—will reflect, at least in part, prevailing feeling in its particular geographical location.[24] In all three countries community standards

[17] 413 US 15, 37 L Ed 2d 419, 93 S Ct 2607 (1973).
[18] *John Calder (Publications)* v. *Powell* [1965] 1 All ER 159.
[19] *DPP* v. *A. & B.C. Chewing Gum Ltd* [1968] 1 QB 159.
[20] There is very extensive case law on the concept of "good morals" that charts its vacillating content.
[21] Paris Court of Appeal, 30 Apr. 1974.
[22] Bordeaux, 19 June 1974.
[23] N. 17 above.
[24] See Dennis Barker, "Obscenity—Where to Draw the Line", *The Guardian*, 13 Mar. 1971.

on a national level are changing with time and are different from one another. This complicating diversity apart, gauging community sentiment is a difficult matter in itself and one which all three countries choose to treat unscientifically (without the use of referenda) and somewhat artificially (expecting members of a tribunal correctly to infer a community standard from their own experience in society, though Frankfurter J in *Smith* v. *California*[25] espoused the view, never adopted by a majority of the Supreme Court, that experts for the defence could be called to enlighten an American judge or jury on prevailing moral as well as artistic standards).

In all three countries, reference is made to the feelings of ordinary members of society as those which are to be protected and respected. This is done by different terminology in each country. In France and America there is "the average man" (*"l'homme moyen"*),[26] whereas in England there is "the ordinary decent citizen".[27] However, in England the average member of the sector of society that would be likely to have contact with the material[28] is the test of the power of depravity and corruption of the material, whereas the community standard of ordinary decent citizens is that which the jury is exhorted to bear in mind when determining obscenity.[29] This is an artificial and confusing distinction. American law experiences similar difficulty: the "average" person excludes a particularly susceptible or sensitive person or a totally insensitive person, but does not preclude the determination of obscenity by reference to the prurient-interest appeal to specific groups, such as sexual deviants or minors, as distinguished from "average" adults.[30] French law experiences the difficulty common to all three systems of never being certain of the unanimity of so-called "public opinion" or the capacity of the members of any tribunal for beginning to assess it by reference merely to their own social experience. A specific assessment of the public's art awareness in a moral context is ignored.

[25] 361 US 147, 4 L Ed 2d 205, 80 S Ct 215 (1959) (for prosecution right to bring such evidence see *Miller*, text to n. 23, above).

[26] To be more exact, "average person" in American law—*Mishkin* v. *New York* 383 US 502, 16 L Ed 2d 56, 86 S Ct 958 (1966).

[27] See Lord Reid, *Knuller* v. *DPP* [1973] AC 435 at 457.

[28] The jury must also be satisfied that a significant proportion of the likely readership would be corrupted: *R.* v. *Calder & Boyars* [1969] 1 QB 151, at 168.

[29] N. 27 above.

[30] *Mishkin* v. *New York*, 383 US 502, 16 L Ed 2d 56, 86 S Ct 958 (1966).

(v) *Experts*

It is at least arguable that juries are better able to judge contemporary community standards in the realm of public morality than are judges or magistrates taken from a relatively narrow class of society. In England, trial by jury is available only at Crown Court level, and in France only in the Assize Court where the composition includes a professional element (the court of three judges) and a lay element (the jury of nine members chosen from a list for the session, by lot, for each case). The latter is a court of first and last resort from which there is no appeal because of the presence of the jury. This is not the case with the Crown Court in England where there is more scepticism about the conclusive correctness of jury decision. Whether or not one agrees that obscenity cases should always come before juries depends largely on one's faith in juries to appraise issues of sexual morality and, where relevant, art. In French practice, the most usual court for deciding "outrage of morals" cases is the Correctional Tribunal which is a court of first instance that contains no lay element, and the jury has remained much more relevant in America than in England because, as far as federal courts are concerned, the seventh Amendment to the American Constitution guarantees its retention. US federal courts can be seised in cases involving obscenity by dint of the latter's relation to freedom of expression which rests on constitutional provision. However, when federal courts can be so seised, their jurisdiction is not exclusive: the parties can still resort to the state rather than the federal courts. In the latter eventuality, an appeal may be possible to the US Supreme Court from the final decision rendered by the state court. The US Supreme Court has no jury but the option to have a trial by jury in state courts is widely admitted in numerous states.[31]

A major difference of approach in France rests in the nature of its manner of reception of experts to inform the law, for example on art. The French Code of Penal Procedure[32] (hereinafter referred to as the CPP) regulated expert evidence in its articles 156 to 169.[33] In France, regulating expert evidence is a preliminary matter the function of which is the gathering of information for ultimate use by the case-trying judge.

[31] See, further, P.G. Kamper and F.X. Beytagh, *Constitutional Law: Cases and Materials* (Little Brown, Boston, Mass., 1980), at 1359–410.

[32] Statute of 31 Dec. 1957 and ordinance 58–1296 of 23 Dec. 1958.

[33] Some amendments of arts. 156, 159, 164 and 167 entered into force in Mar. 1993 by statute of 4 Jan. 1993.

Before the CPP, it was the established practice to use only one expert except for very difficult matters. The CPP approach to experts was deficient in two major respects: first, expert evidence plays a part in so many different realms that it is extremely ambitious to establish, as the CPP attempted to do, a regulation perfectly adapted to all types of expert evidence; instead of the uniform regulation that the code provided for, without doubt it would have been preferable to organise distinct procedures. Secondly, the CPP allowed for the parties to discuss the chosen expert, and the job which he was enlisted to do, and to demand a second expert from the official lists to be chosen by the defence: a sort of co-expert's opinion arose, each of the experts paradoxically giving his own opinion after working as a team.

Ordinance 58–1296 of 23 December 1958 amended the expert procedure before the CPP came into force. It withdrew the right of the defence to name a second expert and accentuated the character of co-expert evidence by demanding that the examining magistrate use as least two experts each time (article 156, paragraph 2, thus amended). An ordinance of 4 June 1960 arranged yet a third solution which brought a system into practice differing very little from that followed before the CPP arrangement. *In toto*, French law in this realm lacked careful thought.

The experts attended to their role under the control of the examining magistrate (article 156, paragraph 3, of the CPP). If they wished to ask the defendant a question, they had to have it asked for them by the magistrate in their presence (article 164, paragraph 2, of the CPP, amended by Ordinance 58–1296 of 23 December 1958). Instead of the blatant adversarial model operational in England and America, experts in France are there essentially to inform *per se* and not to inform for one party. Moreover, there is much more co-operation on an equal basis between the examining magistrate and the expert in the French "preparatory" procedure than in England and America where the case-trying judge merely receives into his constant control the expert (as he would any other witness). The French system of dealing with evidence in the pre-trial procedure is the root source of the different treatment of experts there from in England and America. In England and America there is emphasis on regulating the substantive issue of what the expert can and cannot say, rather than on a practical procedural dichotomy because of the fact of the expert evidence. The different nature of the role of the expert in the French system was indicated in particular by his independent initiative there: for example, if an expert himself spontaneously wished to be informed on a certain point by an expert from another discipline, he needed only to ask the examining magistrate to authorise him to incorporate such-and-such a person (specially qualified by his competence) named by him (article 162, paragraph 1, of the CPP). In effect, it was provided that experts personally carry out the work that has been allocated to them as they see fit (article 166, paragraph 1, of the CPP). Such autonomy and such a major active role are denied experts in an English or American court where they are procedurally treated merely as ordinary witnesses who happen to be experts (though there exists a body of sophisticated rules on what they can actually say and be asked). In English and American courts, the role of the expert giving oral testimony is essentially passive, in that he simply gives the information asked of him in the line of direct questioning by judge or counsel. In France, a specific mission to provide expert evidence was conferred on an expert and he virtually independently fulfilled it in accordance with what the court wanted: he worked with the court on a much more active and equal basis.

In the new penal code that came into force on 1 March 1994, there is a special section IX on expert evidence commencing at article 156. This more explicitly schematises the process and is clear and manageable. In essence, it improves rather than removes old rules. Article 162 may have a valuable part to play in the instance of any allegedly "morally outrageous" art case. It provides that if the experts called desire a point to be illuminated that is beyond their realm, the judge can authorise them to have the assistance of someone specially so qualified. Art experts, for example, may wish to consult someone who is a specialist in the art-law relation. However, experts are not used as often, or in as many contexts, or in as many numbers in individual cases, in France: expert evidence is only sought when it goes to the heart of the crime in issue. "Outrage of good morals" is not a realm where expert knowledge is usually imperative for determination of its basic issues, in comparison to criminal areas which may require information that is only scientifically discoverable, such as the forensic determination of the age of teeth in a badly burnt corpse in a murder case.

Similarly, in America, the Supreme Court has held that there is no constitutional need for expert evidence on the question of obscenity of the material involved when that material itself is placed in evidence, but that the defence is free to introduce evidence on the obscenity question by calling a qualified expert.[34]

---

[34] *Infra*, n. 35 below, and see G.K. Whyte, Jr., "The Use of Expert Testimony in Obscenity Litigation", [1965] *Wis. L. Rev.* 113.

Kaplan v. *California* [35] is the leading American case on the use of expert evidence on the question of obscenity. In a state criminal prosecution under the state's obscenity laws, the court held that there was no constitutional need for expert evidence on behalf of the prosecution or for any ancillary evidence of obscenity once the allegedly obscene materials were placed in evidence. The court indicated that though the defence was free to introduce any appropriate expert evidence, the prosecution need not. The court referred to the dicta of Frankfurter J in *Smith* v. *California*[36] (which views have never been adopted by a majority of the Supreme Court). Included in his opinion was the uncontested statement that there is a right for the defence to enlighten, through experts, the judgment of a tribunal regarding prevailing moral and literary community standards. In the same case, Harlan J expressed the view that the US Constitution does not require that oral opinion evidence by experts be heard, even though expert evidence may be the most convenient and practicable manner of proof. Nevertheless, he viewed a conviction for violation of an obscenity statute fatally defective where the trial judge persistently refused to accept the defendant's attempts to introduce such evidence. Whether he would extend this to one judicial refusal to permit expert evidence is not clear.

In *Miller* v. *California*,[37] the court ruled that the state's expert witness was qualified to give evidence on the state's "community standards" on obscenity, and that permitting such expert evidence was not constitutionally erroneous where the witness was qualified as an expert. However, it is noteworthy that in *Miller* defence counsel never objected to the giving of such evidence and this lack of objection was a factor in encouraging the court's pronouncement. In *Paris Adult Theatre I* v. *Slaton*,[38] the court rejected any constitutional need for expert evidence on behalf of the prosecution, and in *Hamling* v. *US*,[39] the court made clear that expert evidence is not necessary to enable a jury to determine the obscenity of the material in issue, and that if an expert happens to be heard a jury is not bound by his view.

In English law, there is the public good defence which provides unqualifiedly for the prosecution and defence to call experts.[40]

[35] 413 US 115, 37 L Ed 2d 492, 93 S Ct 2680 (1973).
[36] N. 25 above.
[37] N. 17 above.
[38] 413 US 49, 37 L Ed 2d 446, 93 S Ct 2628 (1973).
[39] 418 US 87, 41 L Ed 2d 590, 94 S Ct 2887 (1974).
[40] Obscene Publications Act 1959, s. 4(2). S. 4 reads: "(1) A person shall not be convicted of an offence against section two of this Act, and an order for forfeiture shall not be made

However, where no public defence is raised juries must rely on their own unaided knowledge. Under the public good defence, no evidence may now be proffered of the therapeutic value of pornography, but expert evidence on the literary, artistic, scientific or other merits of an article is not confined to a consideration only of content: the evidence can also indicate how publication of the given work would serve or defeat intellectual or æsthetic values. The holding in *DPP* v. *Jordan*[41] that expert evidence on the therapeutic value of pornography (previously given to effect in *R.* v. *Gold*[42]) is inadmissible has no basis except in a firm prejudice against pornography. As a result of this sort of attitude, the most striking feature of the English defence of "public good" as evolved by the common law is a vital lacuna—even if pornography were an excellent thing, which it arguably may be, there is no provision that it can be said to be so by qualified experts or that it has any recognised worthy means of defence. Can this unsubstantiated prejudice really be enforced by the law of a democratic society? Moreover, it is precisely pornography that may now need a defence in days when the freedom of all that is clearly art is virtually completely secure.[43]

(vi) *Distinctively French Legal Mechanisms*

It remains to note two features of the French law of "outrage of good morals" that do not appear in Anglo-American law. The first goes to the heart of the degree of legal enforceability of the judicial appreciation of art in public morality cases,[44] the second is a procedural and institutional idiosyncrasy confined to the crime in relation to certain types of book.

(i) French *jurisprudence* has long held that a judge must state precisely in what way an allegedly offensive item is contrary to good

under the foregoing section, if it is proved that publication of the article in question is justified as being for the public good on the ground that it is in the interests of science, literature, art or learning, or of other objects of general concern. (2) It is hereby declared that the opinion of experts as to the literary, artistic, scientific or other merits of an article may be admitted in any proceedings under this Act either to establish or to negative the said ground." S. 2 sets out the penalties possible for publishing an obscene article.

[41] [1976] AC 699.

[42] See Geoffrey Robertson, *Obscenity* (Weidenfeld & Nicholson, London, 1979), at 146 (case of 1972).

[43] See *Wiggins* v. *Field* [1968] Crim LR at 503.

[44] See Ch. 2.

morals. Whereas this prescription does not ensure that a judge pay particular attention to art, as opposed to any other item, it does ensure that adequate attention is paid to it as an item.

(ii) Article 289, paragraph 3, of the old penal code prescribed that:

> "when the offence will have been committed by way of a book bearing the name of the author and indicating the editor, and having been the object of copyrighting in a regular way, the prosecution can only be carried out after the opinion of the special commission."

The composition and operation of this commission have been fixed by articles D.8 to D.13 of the old penal code.

This commission, which meets at the Ministry of Justice, is composed of a judge, actively or honorarily of the highest court of appeal, who assumes the presidency of it, and six members including a judge, actively or honorarily of the court of appeal, a law professor, a representative of the Society of Men of Letters, a representative of associations constituted for the defence of public morality, a representative of the Union of Family Associations (each of these personalities being replaceable by a substitute with the same purpose), and, an officer of the Ministry of Justice who fulfils the functions of secretary.

The terms of reference of this commission, as they are laid down in articles D.11 and D.13 of the old penal code, codified by the decree of 20 June 1961, are very simple. Every offence of outrage of good morals committed by way of a book is, before all proceedings and with the surveillance of the Attorney General, brought to the attention of the Minister of Justice, who alerts the President of the Commission, who in turn convenes a meeting of the members. At least four members in addition to the President must attend and the decision is a majority one, the President having the casting vote in the event of equal division of votes. The report containing the Commission's opinion is conveyed to the Minister of Justice, who in turn conveys it to the relevant public prosecutor.

The consultation of the Commission is obligatory before all proceedings within its ambit. A book does not fulfil the requirements for being examined by the Commission if it fails to bear the name of the author and editor and has not been made the object of copyright in recognised manner. Each of these requirements must be fulfilled. It does not suffice for the identification of the author for the book to bear only a forename, initials or a pseudonym.[45] Obscene illustrations

---

45 Cass. Crim., 10 July 1973.

accompanying non-obscene words in a book do not admit of the Commission's opinion.[46]

The Commission is restricted in a number of ways—by the material it can deliver opinion on and by the fact that its opinion has to be directed to whether a criminal prosecution should be begun: "underground" books and all periodicals are outside its ambit, for example, and the Commission complements the prosecutor's presumed inadequacy as a judge of literature, not the trial judge's. The Commission is only consultative: its opinion is only an opinion, is not legally binding, has no teeth. Established at the request of the Society of Men of Letters, it provides a useful safety-valve for serious literature to avoid completely thoughtless prosecution but beyond this is of limited efficacy.

AMERICAN PUBLIC MORALITY DOCTRINES[47]

The earliest obscenity case on record in the United States of America occurred in Philadelphia in 1815 and involved art. There were then no obscenity statutes, so it was of necessity a common law action. Jesse Sharpless was convicted of exhibiting, for financial gain, a painting "of a man in an obscene, imprudent and indecent posture with a woman". In 1821, the first case involving creative literature was prosecuted, again under the common law. Peter Holmes was convicted in Massachusetts for publishing the book *Memoirs of a Woman of Pleasure*, more popularly known as *Fanny Hill*.

The first state laws against "indecent" literature were adopted by Vermont in 1821, Connecticut in 1834 and Massachusetts in 1835. At a federal level, in 1842, the US Congress, undeterred by the first amendment, adopted section 28 of the Customs Law, prohibiting the importation of indecent and obscene paintings, lithographs, or other forms of pictorial art; later amendments added printed literature to the list. A federal law of 1865 provided criminal penalties for sending obscene literature through the US mail, although no power was given to in the Post Office Department to stop such mail. This omission was corrected in 1873 with the adoption of the famous long-standing Comstock Act, named after Anthony Comstock, leader of the Committee for the Suppression of Vice. In 1896, New

[46] Crim., 3 Mar. 1955.
[47] In France, as indicated above, there are no set doctrines and standards in obscenity evaluation, hence there is no sub-section on France.

York publisher Lew Rosen was one of the first to be convicted under it at Supreme Court level.[48] The trial court judge defined obscenity for the jury in terms if what came to be known as the "*Hicklin* rule". This rule had been formulated in the 1868 English case of *Regina* v. *Hicklin*,[49] obscenity defined as material with a "tendency to deprave and corrupt those whose minds are open to such immoral influences".

The stubborn rule of *Hicklin* that was to dominate English law for nearly a century had crossed the Atlantic to be of equally dubious benefit there. In America, though, the first amendment posed an interesting obstacle to proscriptions on expression, but what was its impact in the realm of obscenity in its early days? Did it contain an inherent *ab initio* distinction between types of expression, as Brennan J later suggested in *Roth*, below?

That obscenity statutes existed at the time of the framing of the first amendment would not prove a conscious purpose to exclude that type of "speech" from protection; the fact that advancement of the arts was definitely in the minds of the framers is historically evidenced by the letter of the Continental Congress to the inhabitants of Quebec. Even if the problem of obscenity had been a developed issue at that time, which it was not, and even if the framers were uniformly wholly intolerant of obscene expression, which they were not, the scope of the first amendment, including as it undoubtedly does a belief in the advancement of the arts, cannot realistically be tied to any late eighteenth century restrictive moral tastes.

The primary test of obscenity, first enunciated as a matter of federal constitutional law in *Roth* v. *United States*, is "whether to the average person, applying contemporary standards, the dominant theme of the material taken as a whole appeals to prurient interest". *Roth* is the central case in American obscenity law. In holding obscenity outside the protection of the first amendment, the Supreme Court asserted two strangely conflicting doctrines: first, that because obscenity lacks idea or social value it is not communicative speech but, secondly, that the first amendment protects communicative speech unless it impinges on the "limited area of more important interests". The conflict lies in the fact that, if obscenity is never protectable communicative speech, the second doctrine is superfluous in relation to it. Only if the second doctrine is considered as affecting

---

[48] *Rosen* v. *US*, 161 US 29 (1896).
[49] (1868) LR 3 QB 360.

the determination of obscenity can a balancing mechanism be set up legally to perceive it.

In England at this time a different balance was developing, made manifest in the Obscene Publications Act 1959, section 4, whereby obscenity was balanced against a justification of the offending object as being for the public good. If we accept that *Roth* created a balance, it is of a very different genre, being a balance to ascertain obscenity rather than to make possible its redemption.

Under English law, obscenity is first tested and, if confirmed, is balanced against the obscene matter's qualities for the public good to determine the obscene matter's legality or illegality. Under *Roth*, alleged obscenity, with or without artistic merit, is balanced against public decency which is used in the constitutional law not only to help ascertain obscenity but, if ascertained, outlaw it because it outweighs it in social importance and renders it unprotectable by the first amendment.

The American formal constitutional right of freedom of speech should place obscene matter in a stronger position than in England, where such a right is not part of the formal legal framework. However, in practice, American constitutional law leaves allegedly obscene matter to battle against public decency which seeks to repress it, whereas in England, that battle lost, obscene matter can be redeemed by its positive qualities—an arrangement American constitutional law only provides for in defining obscenity and then not specifically, with much less emphasis on the matter's positive worth. There is a schism, then, between American theory and practice. The first amendment, designed to protect expression, has no real teeth in the obscenity arena because the constitutional law does not provide in its formulae for obscenity a practical protective mechanism for certain forms of expression. In theory, American law does not have to provide a redeeming *schema* for any expression because the onus is on the suppressive force to justify circumscription of freedom, not on any form of expression to have to justify itself. In practice, though, expression is not favoured, the struggle of obscene matter to survive being much more difficult under *Roth*-initiated American constitutional law than in an English system, which also determines its evil but then provides a legal avenue for its merits to redeem it.

In a nutshell, artistic merit evolved as an indirect definitional factor in American obscenity cases as a judicial response to philistine enforcement of obscenity statutes. The substitution of "the average conscience of the time" for the *Hicklin* "most susceptible person" was in response to the condemnation of such works as *Hagar Revelly*. The substitution of the "dominant effect" on the normal man for the practice of excerpt judging was to avoid the condemnation of a work like Joyce's *Ulysses* on the basis of the "coarse, blasphemous and obscene" passages it was conceded it contained. The restrictive definition adopted by *Roth* and subsequent constitutional cases is, in part, a composite of these changes.

Any judicial protection of works of literary repute is not attributable solely to the appropriately-termed reformed standards. Co-extensive with their exercise, the same courts somewhat illogically but effectively affirmed that a work of artistic value was not subject to the operation of an obscenity statute. The first amendment indirectly acquired teeth. So, while the *Ulysses*[50] case is remembered chiefly for the development of the dominant effect rule, the court simultaneously asserted that genuine works of literature were not within the ambit of obscenity statutes. New York trial courts did likewise. In *People* v. *Creative Age Press*[51] it was held that incidental obscenity does not bring literary work within the terms of statute, and in *People* v. *Miller*[52] it was held that statute was not intended to suppress *bona fide* literary effort.

Some means of distinguishing what is artistically worthwhile and what is not is required in this area, and those means have to be within the competence of the courts or a matter of judicial notice. A classic is a work of literary distinction, and since it can be said that it is a matter of common knowledge in the community that a work is a classic, the question whether a given work is a classic is clearly within the competence of the judiciary. This contrasts with the crucial problem of contemporary art: its distinction is a matter of community dispute. Accordingly, the courts turn to contemporary literary and artistic criticism. This reliance involves an element of abdication of judicial responsibility. However, just because judges do not have the means to confute the judgement of critics does not mean that they cannot irrationally refuse to listen to them, especially if they contradict one another.[53] For the most part, though, they attend to them and in so doing abdicate responsibility in another way: they accept, rather than assess, the qualifications of the expert in accordance with the hierarchy of his own discipline. A taste discrimination begins to operate

---

[50] 72 F 2d 705 (2d Cir. 1934).
[51] 192 Misc. 188, 190, 79 NYS 2d 198, 201 (Magis. Ct. 1948).
[52] 155 Misc. 446, 447, 279 NY Supp. 583, 585 (Magis. Ct. 1935).
[53] See Byrne J in *R.* v. *Penguin Books Ltd* [1961] Crim. LR 176.

when a work undefended by an expert is unfairly disadvantaged in reputation before the judge. With this in mind, can equity permit any judicial abdication of taste judgement to critics? Besides, the worth of a work of art depends on its ultimate acceptance by society, not on critical evidence, and critics are notoriously unable to discover the worthwhile creations of their own time.[54] *Jacobellis* v. *Ohio*[55] affirmed that material of artistic value is categorically within the ambit of constitutional protection (though it gave no precise mechanism for its liberty to be ensured). If the right to express freely in the artistic realm depends on the taste judgement of critics, it is arguable that, despite the noble pronouncement in *Jacobellis*, those who are neglected or debunked by critics are denied due process.

In America, the Supreme Court has been looked to as the sole means of protecting worthwhile works from unsatisfactory verdicts. The accepted application of the constitutional fact doctrine to obscenity cases makes it possible for the Supreme Court and all appellate courts to make independent judgments on the issue of obscenity since, under *Roth*, the determination is also decisive of the right to first amendment protection. Harlan J's opinion in *Roth* discloses that independent review was compelled by the likelihood of jury verdicts finding obscene such works as *Ulysses* and *The Decameron*. The fact remains, though, that the right of appeal to a hopefully sympathetic appellate court is far from an efficient means of ensuring the free availability of the artistically enjoyable.

The Supreme Court's internal differences over obscenity questions in the mid-1960s[56] did not prevent it, in 1967, from agreeing to overturn, as a group, obscenity convictions in three different states. Neither is the Supreme Court loathe to reform its own obscenity standard. In *Miller* v. *California*,[57] Burger CJ rejected Brennan J's view post-*Roth* that material must be utterly without redeeming social value to be obscene. The new test was whether material had any serious artistic, literary, scientific or political value. The *Roth* definition was otherwise retained. Regrettably, the *Miller* formula suffers from the same problem as the constitutional law on obscenity in general: it does not knit with the formula for the definition of obscenity but,

[54] E.g., in its formative years the Impressionist School of painting was relegated to the "Salon des Refusés" by French Academy experts.

[55] 378 US 184 (1964).

[56] E.g., in *Grove Press Inc.* v. *Gerstein* (1964) 378 US 577, 12 L Ed 2d (035, 84 S Ct 1909); *Jacobellis* v. *Ohio* (n. 46 above); and the subsequently unfollowed *"Memoirs"* case, 383 US 413, 16 L Ed 2d 1, 86 S Ct 975 (1966).

[57] N. 17 above.

rather, creates an exception without more that eschews the basic problem which is the impossibility of protecting obscene art under a constitutional standard that precludes first amendment protection for obscenity, but which also emphasises obscenity to the degree that the "exception" of art is thrust into a side-channel where it cannot tackle obscenity, or, alternatively, can only weakly bring about changes in the formula for defining the obscene. For efficacy, what must happen is for the first amendment to protect all forms of expression despite conventional acceptability,[58] or for artistic merit to outweigh obscenity in a mechanism that makes the legality of obscene art possible (as in England), or for a tribunal to consider all the issues without reference to strict definitions (as in France). The Supreme Court muddle of criteria and exceptions has only the semblance of efficiency.

Because of the centrality of political expression in first amendment theory, artistic expression has been largely neglected, and in recent years a hierarchy of protected expression has been developed by the Supreme Court with political expression leading the field. Artistic expression has a much more marginal status. Given that the first amendment is to further self-fulfilment, the Supreme Court has given precious few guidelines on the type of artistic value participation in which is legally permissible for legitimate self-fulfilment. What obscenity cases have in common is simply enmity towards some sexual content *simpliciter*, without giving guidelines as to which.

Jürgen Habermas has said "modernity lives on the experience of rebelling against all that is normative",[59] so it is unsurprising that modern art incurs the wrath of law. To demand that it is cognitive before it receives first amendment protection is to ignore the diversity inherent in art, not least its often non-representational aspect. Regrettably, one of the very few 1980s art law cases involving obscenity was so entangled with extra-constitutional considerations that it provided no real guide on the narrower issue of treatment of the artist's right to show his work free of constraint, let alone the broader issue of what is protectable in the artistically valuable, what is unacceptable, and why.[60]

The paucity of case law in the 1980s[61] means the development of

---

[58] In *Grove Press* (n. 47 above), Black and Douglas JJ adhered to their view that even obscene materials are protected by the First Amendment.

[59] In "Modernity—An Incomplete Project" in H. Foster (ed.), *The Anti-Aesthetic: Essays on Postmodern Culture* (Bay Press, Fort Townsend, Wash., 1983).

[60] *Piarowski* v. *Illinois Community College*, 759 F 2d 625 (7th Cir. 1985).

[61] The last obscenity case before the Sup. Ct. of even mild artistic interest involved an application for stay of a preliminary injunction against the showing of allegedly obscene

obscenity law doctrine pertaining to art has remained virtually stagnant since *Miller*,[62] a tailing-off noticeable in England and France as well. Community standards are increasingly judicially inferred to disfavour proscription of the artist in a world where technology and leisure pursuits are increasingly displacing social propriety as a community priority, and conventional acceptability is far from the puritan ethic it was once conceived of as being.

ENGLISH DOCTRINES

The history of English obscenity law is dominated by the notion of corruption, which is emblematic of its close association with the law of blasphemy.[63] The country's first Obscene Publications Bill of 1580 adopted the word, and it still remains implanted in today's ruling statute.[64] The obsession is with the protection of good manners as much as morals, the corruption more disruption of proprietous conduct than a concern for personal moral debilitation. The Licensing Act of 1662, the case of *Curll* of 1727 and the establishment of the Society for the Suppression of Vice of 1802 all played their part in entrenching obscenity law as a persistent though petty aspect of the criminal law. A case was heard by the same magistrate who had issued the summons and the Obscene Publications Act of 1857, hotly opposed by Lords Lyndhurst and Brougham who feared for culture at the expense of prudery, gave rise to the draconian test of *Hicklin*[65] which was adopted in US and English courts alike. Its focus was the prevention of material that depraved and corrupted, verbs preserved by the prevailing 1959 legislation and held to be synonyms.[66] The test of such corruption was the most vulnerable member of society and any isolated passage that aroused sexual desire was enough to condemn a whole work. More than in any other area of English law, the

---

films: *M.I.C., Limited and West Point Drive-in, Inc.* v. *Bedford Township*, 463 US 134, 77 L Ed 2d 1442, 104 S Ct 17 (1983).

[62] N. 17 above.

[63] Blasphemy is ever-diminishing in significance. *The Times* of Thursday, 3 Mar. 1988 reported under "Home News": "Blasphemy should no longer be an offence in English law, the Archbishop of Canterbury, Dr. Robert Runcie, has told the Lord Chancellor, Lord Mackay of Clashfern".

[64] The Obscene Publications Act 1959, as amended by the Obscene Publications Act 1964.

[65] N. 49 above.

[66] *Per* Lord Reid, n. 27 above, at 436.

whole proscription rested on opinion, and the pervading judicial opinion was firmly against erotica, at least publicly.[67]

The public good defence embodied in the 1959 Act was anticipated, ironically,[68] in *Montalk's case*, but despite the progress of time the rule from *Hicklin's case* remained solid, with the Obelisk Press established in Paris in the early 1930s with the object of publishing English books of acknowledged literary merit which had been banned in England. Eventually, the Society of Authors Committee set out fundamental criticisms of obscenity law and a White Paper reflective of these was introduced in 1955 by Mr Roy Jenkins. The 1959 Obscene Publications Act resulted, with emphasis now on the total impact of the work and on the predictable reading public. This was an improvement, but the law still rested on the notion that pornography and literature were on either side of the line determining moral acceptability. Defence of the pornographic was still unthinkable, as it was in America where contemporaneous changes had also taken place in obscenity law with the *Roth* decision of 1957.

Current English law, based on the Obscene Publication Act 1959, is still characterised by the centrality of the "deprave and corrupt" formula. The *"Last Exit"* case of 1967[69] established that "moral corruption" was what obscenity law worked against, and the trial judge's colloquial definitions of obscenity in *"Oz"*[70] were struck down by the Lord Chief Justice. The statutory definition of a word prevails, as it does in America, except that there statutory definitions are all subject to the constitutional standard. In France, the penal code leaves good morals undefined.

England adheres to a policy of relative obscenity now. *R. v. Calder & Boyars*[71] established that the jury must be satisfied that a significant proportion of the likely readership would be guided along the path of corruption. However, relative obscenity is relative only in that respect. No comparison can be made between the material before the court and other material in society. Obscenity is relative to its audience but not to its neighbour, unless the defence of public good is

[67] Victorian England, more than any other epoque, is renowned for its moral, or immoral, hypocrisy.

[68] "Ironically" because the defendant did not benefit at all from the foresight of a dictum that was applied to his own case: (1932) 23 Cr.App.Rep. 182. The Recorder, at 183–4, said "it would be a defence in this case if the thing was done for the public good . . . as an advancement of literature . . .".

[69] *R. v. Calder and Boyars* [1969] 1 QB 151.

[70] *R. v. Anderson* [1971] 3 All ER 1152.

[71] N. 69 above.

raised, when comparisons become admissible. Similarly, the offence is one of strict liability in England unless the defence of public good is raised, which permits attention to the author's purpose. The contradictory nature of what is allowed to be considered for the offence on the one hand and the defence on the other involves the jury in much mental dichotomising: one minute it cannot compare the accused work with other works, the next it can; one minute it is dealing with strict liability, the next it can entertain intention. Attempting strictly to separate artistic merit from the obscenity issue as statute has done inevitably invited legal divisions the common law has been only too willing to provide, but these make the crime as a whole seem a strangely artificial entity.

In England, one charge is usually brought in respect of obscene publications. It is an offence to publish an obscene article contrary to the Obscene Publications Act 1959. However, blasphemous libel is still operative in England and there has been a revival of the ancient common law offence of outraging public decency. An American statute similar to section 3 of the 1959 Act (on powers of search and seizure) which authorised the seizure of pornography from private houses, has been struck down by the American Supreme Court. Dislike of obscenity, *per* Marshall J, provides "insufficient justification for such a drastic invasion of personal liberties . . . a State has no business telling a man, sitting alone in his own house, what books he may read or what films he may watch. Our whole constitutional history rebels at the thought of giving Government the power to control men's minds".[72]

Let us now consider two English case law examples of the application of public morality law to art to illuminate the practical process.

(i) *The Rushdie Experience*

On 13 March 1989, the Chief Metropolitan Magistrate, sitting at Bow Street Magistrates' Court, London, refused to grant the applicant, Abdul Hussain Choudhury, summonses he had applied for against Salman Rushdie, the author, and Viking Penguin Publishing Co. Ltd, the publishers, of a book called *The Satanic Verses*, alleging the commission of the offences of blasphemous libel and seditious libel at common law.[73] The novel won the Whitbread Prize for

---

[72] *Stanley* v. *Georgia* 394 US 557 (1969) at 565.
[73] [1900] 3 WLR at 986–1005.

Literature in 1988 and has been translated into at least 15 languages. It has been banned in all Muslim countries, China, India and South Africa. The applicant sought summonses alleging that the author and publishers had published or caused to be published in the work "a blasphemous libel concerning Almighty God (Allah), the Supreme Deity common to all major religions of the world . . . and the religion of Islam and Christianity" and a seditious libel, in that it raised widespread discontent and disaffection among Her Majesty The Queen's subjects. The relief the applicant sought was an order of *certiorari* to quash the decision of the magistrate and an order of *mandamus* directing him to issue the summonses as applied for. The magistrate had refused to issue the summonses on the grounds that the common law offence of blasphemy was restricted to the Christian religion and the applicant had failed to show that the alleged seditious libel was an attack on Her Majesty The Queen or the State. The magistrate made no finding whether in fact the book was blasphemous of the Islamic religion; he found as a fact that its allegedly blasphemous passages did not amount to a scurrilous attack on Christianity.[74]

Two preliminary general observations must be made about the offence of blasphemy in English law. First, although the law of blasphemy is in theory designed to protect the reputation of God from defamation ("vilification"), the justifications for its existence have become highly secularised. For example, it is said to safeguard "the internal tranquility of the kingdom",[75] to protect "the civil obligations whereby society is bound together"[76] or minors from wrong influences.[77] The importance of God Himself has become in practice subsidiary within blasphemy law in an age when religious matters tend to be treated more hermeneutically, and agnostically, in the "Christian" West, than with serious passionate belief. Secondly, the present case raises the question whether a conscientiously plural society can now justify maintaining a blasphemy law providing such

[74] Consider the possibility of blasphemy of the Christian God by blasphemy of the Muslim God, given the Islamic perception of a single God, with Christ as one of His prophets. Is the Christian God in English blasphemy law interpretable solely with Christian hermeneutics? Should the plurality of Britain's religious groups be supplemented by a better understanding of Islam within the law? See, further, Peter J. Riga, "Islamic Law And Modernity: Conflict And Evolution" (1991) 36 *The American Journal of Jurisprudence* 103.

[75] *R. v. Lemon* [1979] AC 617 at 658.

[76] Ashurst J in *R. v. Williams* (1797) 26 St. Tr. 654 at 714.

[77] See Lord Denman CJ's direction to the jury in *R. v. Hetherington* (1840) 4 St. Tr. NS 563 at 590–1.

selective protection. As it stands, the law indicates the inchoate nature of constitutional protection for minorities in a structure that remains basically "traditional" in its operation; and, as will become apparent below, it is not only with indifference to the views of religious minorities that blasphemy law is at present found to operate.[78]

The Divisional Court established in this case that the law of blasphemy is clear in its protection exclusively of Christianity.[79] It is less definitive about its operation on art. However, it discloses the view that an attitude expressed in the medium of art is not necessarily prevented from being a blasphemous libel simply because of its artistic context, *viz.* simply because the statement is put into the mouth of a character in a novel.[80] This approach has serious implications for art and artists because it ignores not just the autonomy of voices in art but the autonomy of art as a cultural category, and the (only) oblique relation of art to life.[81]

All art is essentially ambiguous in the sense that the interpretation it invites includes an imaginative aspect. Art cannot occur without room in an object's reading or viewing for our own creative activity, making us its internal co-creators. The basis of the crime of seditious libel, i.e. the tendency to excite public mischief, cannot be achieved without an inappropriate relation to the art-work on the part of the reader or viewer. If treated appropriately, i.e. meditatively, by him or her no mischief can result. Any offence for which art is the alleged stimulus is the result of an incorrect psychic approach on the part of the reader or viewer of it (an unhappy situation art education would preclude). In addition, as an acknowledged higher medium of human achievement, at least in modernist and much pre-modern thought, art, especially, should not be condemned for inappropriate relations and responses to it.

The seeming irreconcilability of some types of religion and some art remains a recurrent national phenomenon with which the law fortunately only comparatively infrequently has to deal. In England, Leonard McComb's "Portrait of a Young Man Standing", a statue of a naked youth, was withdrawn from Lincoln Cathedral after

---

[78] See *Lemon*, n. 75 above.

[79] N. 73 above, at 999.

[80] *Ibid.*, at 990.

[81] "The novel is an impression not an argument" (Hardy), "a mirror along a roadway" (Anouilh). See Abraham Kaplan, *"Obscenity As An Esthetic Category"* (1955) 22 *Law and Contemporary Problems*, at 544, and the various works of Stanley Fish (who argues, *inter alia*, that readers themselves construct the texts they read).

complaints that it was indecent for a place of worship.[82] Martin
Scorsese's film "The Last Temptation of Christ" (a controversial portrayal of the prophet or Messiah[83]) narrowly avoided being banned,
whereas a ban on "Visions of Ecstasy", an 18-minute video about the
mystical visions of Saint Teresa of Avila, a sixteenth-century Spanish
nun, was upheld.[84] In *Regina* v. *Lemon*,[85] a poem for a gay or bisexual readership about homosexual acts with Christ was successfully
prosecuted for blasphemy at the instigation of Mary Whitehouse.

The presence of the McComb statue in Lincoln Cathedral has
been defended by Sister Wendy Beckett,[86] a Catholic nun and art
expert, and the Scorsese film has been described by the Bishop of
New York as "Christologically" correct.[87] In relation to "Visions of
Ecstasy", James Ferman, Director of the British Board of Film
Classification (BBFC), said: "[i]t was the general view of the BBFC
that it was invidious in a multi-ethnic society for the law to continue
to give unique protection to the Christian religion, and in particular
to one denomination, namely the Church of England. Nevertheless,
it is up to Parliament to make the law, and as a licensing authority,
BBFC has no choice but to apply it correctly."[88] Regarding the case
of *Lemon*, above, an argument can be put that in a society comprising people of diverse sexual orientation, it is unfair for the law to
impose religious standards allied to heterosexual mores on art for the
particular enjoyment of gay and bisexual people.[89]

The increasing plurality of spiritual, sexual and other belief in
Britain suggests the likelihood of increasing dissatisfaction with the
image of blasphemy while the protected image of God remains
legally contextualised as Christian.[90] However, if the law were
extended to cover a variety of religions without careful thought
about its precise formulation, inter-faith blasphemy proceedings
could, feasibly, occur. Still centred in theory on the reputation of

---

[82] N. 86 below.

[83] His accorded status depending upon which religion's hermeneutics are employed.

[84] *The Independent*, 15 Dec. 1989, at 2.

[85] N. 75 above.

[86] *The Independent*, 9 Aug. 1990, at 15.

[87] *The Observer Magazine*, 1 Mar. 1992, at 9.

[88] N. 84 above.

[89] It would be exceptional for other than gay or bisexual people to subscribe to *Gay News*.

[90] Fundamental constitutional change is rare and takes time in contemporary Britain, and it is therefore unsurprising that the law is slow to accommodate the rapid pace of new soci-ological and cultural trends. At the moment it is straddling between a political consciousness of plurality without corresponding constitutional overhaul; an interim stage?

God, blasphemy law would have to adapt to cover religions such as Hinduism, with its many Gods, and Buddhism, with no God (and the now common stance of atheism would continue to find itself disadvantaged). Enforcing the resulting matrix of protectable religious principle could prove impracticable. Nevertheless, the plural cultural framework characteristic of postmodernism in our society clearly suggests that the current law is unfair, and not just to religious, sexual and other minorities.[91] England's unwritten constitution upholds freedom of expression, and yet its blasphemy law not only permits the silencing of art in favour of enforcing a religious belief, but disfavours art (which is more universally participated in) in favour of what is in practice a small censoring lobby (which happens to be religious in its justification).

Britain is a democracy not a hagiocracy. Freedom of expression is as intrinsic to democracy as freedom of religion, and art, treated as art, in no way rules against the latter, and does not purport to. Art, not necessarily even cognitive, simply offers itself and invites the appropriate meditative (æsthetic) attitude. It is generous, not constricting, and is not the exertion of the will that its contemplation results in real-life disaccord. Art is an option for its reader or viewer, not an imposition.

If a publication is couched in decent and temperate language, it cannot, according to current English law, constitute blasphemous libel.[92] The publication of opinions hostile to the Christian religion is insufficient for the offence; the test to be applied is as to "the manner in which the doctrines are advocated and not as to the substance of the doctrines themselves".[93] There seems no good reason why the manner should not cover the (artistic) medium. If coarse and scurrilous attitudes are expressed in the medium of art, can it be realistically and reasonably said that the art (or its maker) is scurrilous, indecent or intemperate? Shakespeare, for example, presumably did not posit either the views or tones of his characters as either his own or correct: rather, they were conceived within his exceptional artistic frame of thinking that produced each of them as authentic for the purposes of art.

Voices from the artist are from him but not necessarily of him. Even in non-fiction in the first person, the "I" of the author is (only)

---

[91] The ideal postmodern democratic society would ensure the legal equivalence of that society's self-classifying groups; to use a mathematical metaphor, it would guarantee the legal equivalence of all sub-sets in the set.

[92] N. 73 above, at 995.

[93] *Stephen's Digest of the Criminal Law* (9th edn., Sweet & Maxwell, London, 1950), 163.

the "paper-I".[94] *A fortiori*, to talk of art attacking something coarsely or scurrilously is to ignore the specifically artistic *modus operandi*. The art may reflect the artist's own views, but enquiry into the precise form and extent of this reflection (if it exists at all) is a complex enquiry even for an expert biographer or literary psychologist and, in *R. v. Chief Metropolitan Stipendiary Magistrate, ex parte Choudhury*, an oneirocritic specialising in the interpretation of dreams in works of fiction (because the alleged instances of blasphemy occur in the dreams of one of the two main protagonists) and another specialist in the discernment of a writer's own real beliefs given alleged intertextuality between his fiction and sacred lore.

The writer of a blasphemous libel and his publisher are strictly liable: following the majority decision in the leading case of *Lemon*, above, there is no *mens rea* requirement as the law stands, save that the writer and publisher intended to publish the words complained about. This puts the artist and his publisher in a position whereby the very nature of the cultural exercise they are fostering precludes just process: the law will not consider the writer's culturally distinctive artistic intent, in effect not just depriving art of a defence but ignoring its own necessary and ineluctable ontology. In the cognate offence of obscene libel, (statutory) provision is at least made for a defence of public good on the grounds of the artistic merit.[95]

The creative writer's intent is to create a work of art. This is not malice. Moreover, any possible ulterior or sub-intent is subsumed under the artistic intent, the dominance of which is proven by the artistic character of the product.

God's approach to art is a central theme in neither Islamic nor Christian tradition. This is interesting because it would be logical for a creative God to favour creativity,[96] and yet surprisingly sparse mention is made of this in existing sacred literature. It would be helpful not just for ethics and knowledge but also for peace among Her Majesty The Queen of England's subjects if God's wishes for Man's artistic creativity were more closely considered by theologians, not least as a value relative to God's perceived interest in His own reputation. Linked to this consideration is the thought that it is not just in

---

[94] I am grateful to the scholarship of Roland Barthes for this particularly neat term for the entity in the first person that appears on paper. Jacques Derrida maintains that it is a mistaken assumption that behind every literary work there is an authoritative speaking voice that tells us things.

[95] S. 4 of the Obscene Publications Act 1959 (as amended by the Criminal Law Act 1977).

[96] Created, we emulate our Creator and create.

the ontogeny and product of artistic genius that we sometimes witness religiously iconoclastic tendency. Many now established religions are based on the teachings of prophets who radically altered existing religious practice following inspiration subsequently accepted as of God's volition.

Islam is a younger religion than Christianity and it acknowledges Christ in its hierology, the Koran equitably voicing the contribution of Christ as well as Mohammed to God's truth. This equity does not find reflection in the exclusively Christian English law of blasphemy. Neither is there equity, if political sense, in the selective non-prosecution of certain members of society for incitement or conspiracy to murder (a novelist).[97] Such sad circumstances deeply threaten the rule of law and illustrate the highly inconsistent enforcement of "Christian" principle within the English legal system. Within that system neither Mohammed nor art nor the individual human life is held sacred, and it is arguable that they all should be. Efforts in this direction will have to be based on more subtle intellectual considerations than are currently revealed in English legal practice if they are to result in the desired reconciliation of what are currently seen as competing claims.[98]

(ii) *The Fœtus Earrings Case*

On 30 January 1989, at the Central Criminal Court, Richard Norman Gibson and Peter Sylveire pleaded not guilty before Judge Smedley QC and a jury to an indictment containing two counts. On a charge of outraging public decency, contrary to common law, Gibson was fined £500 with 28 days' imprisonment in default; Sylveire was fined £350 with 21 days' imprisonment in default. On the second count, which had alleged a public nuisance, they were acquitted by direction of the judge.[99]

---

[97] The God of love in neither Islam nor Christianity encourages the violation of the sanctity of human life.

[98] Consider the view of the poet and scholar Kathleen Raine, starting the Temenos Academy in London, that knowledge and the arts have traditionally grown from some sacred vision, in the *"temenos"*, or precinct, of a sacred place, inspired by some tradition of spiritual knowledge, whether Hindu, Muslim, Buddhist, Jewish or Christian; and that without such a centre we are lost. (Interview with *CAM*, Spring 1992, at 34).

[99] [1990] 2 QB 619, [1990] 3 WLR 595.

(a) *The Facts*

The facts of the case are *prima facie* simple. Sylveire ran an art gallery called the Young Unknowns Gallery at 82, The Cut, London SE1. He selected for display at an exhibition there a work created by Gibson, entitled in the accompanying catalogue "Human Earrings". It comprised a model's head, to each ear of which was attached an earring; each of the two earrings was made out of a freeze-dried human fœtus of three or four months' gestation.[100] The general public has access to the gallery and was invited to the exhibition free of charge. Forty-one items had been selected by Sylveire for display out of a much larger number. It was not suggested that Sylveire had taken active steps to publicise in particular the exhibit bearing the fœtal earrings, though Gibson, apparently unknown to his co-defendant, had done some advertising promotion of this particular work, with the consequence that both press and police were in attendance shortly after the exhibition had opened. Sylveire admitted to police that he did not find "Human Earrings" very attractive and that he knew the earrings were in fact human fœtuses. He added: "Why, is that wrong?" The two men appealed against their convictions.

(b) *The Appeal*

In a judgment of the Court given by Lord Lane CJ, the Court of Appeal dismissed the appeal, which was based on three grounds.

(i) On the question whether prosecution was precluded by section 2(4)[101] of the Obscene Publications Act 1959, the Court held that "obscene" had the limited meaning of corrupting public morals as defined in section 1(1).[102] Since there was no suggestion that anyone was likely to be corrupted by the exhibiting of the earrings, the prosecution for the existing common law offence of outraging public

---

[100] Compare the art of Andres Serrano in which he uses his own bodily fluids. One of his most controversial works is entitled "Piss Christ". An exhibition of his work in the Saatchi Collection was displayed without police interference at 98a Boundary Road, London, NW8, in Sept. 1991.

[101] The subs. provides: "[a] person publishing an article shall not be proceeded against for an offence at common law consisting of the publication of any matter contained or embodied in the article where it is of the essence of the offence that the matter is obscene."

[102] S. 1(1), with the heading "Test of obscenity", provides: "[f]or the purposes of this Act an article shall be deemed to be obscene if its effect or (where the article comprises two or more distinct items) the effect of any one of its items is, if taken as a whole, such as to tend to deprave and corrupt persons who are likely, having regard to all the relevant circumstances, to read, see or hear the matter contained or embodied in it."

decency was not precluded by section 2(4).[103] The court applied
Knuller (Publishing, Printing and Promotions) Ltd v. *DPP*[104] and *Shaw* v.
DPP.[105]

(ii) On whether the prosecution could succeed in the absence of
proof of an intent to outrage public decency or an appreciation of a
risk of such outrage coupled with a determination nevertheless to run
the risk, the court held that since the object of the common law
offence was to protect the public from feelings of outrage by such
exhibitions, there was no requirement for the prosecution to prove
that the person charged had an intention to outrage or appreciated
the risk of such outrage and determined nevertheless to run the risk.
It applied *Regina* v. *Lemon*.[106]

(iii) On the question whether the jury was, in the circumstances,
insufficiently directed to consider the element of publicity required
to constitute the offence, the Court of Appeal held that the jury had
been correctly directed. There was no requirement that the second
appellant should have drawn particular attention to the exhibit before
he could be convicted.

(c) *Comment*

This appeal raises many points of interest, not least for the art community and those concerned about it.

The Court of Appeal chose not to designate Gibson an artist for his
work in the language of its judgment. This is important because it
indicates that the offending enterprise was not treated as purporting to
be of particular cultural value and significance. If a prosecution is
brought under the Obscene Publications Act 1959, the legislative provision of the defence of public good[107] on the ground of artistic merit

---

[103] On this point, the Court of Appeal was probably correct. It seems logical as a matter
of statutory interpretation that the "test of obscenity' set out in s. 1(1) governs the meaning
of obscene in s. 2(4). If this were not the case, it would mean, *inter alia*, that in s. 2, where
the word "obscene" is used three times, on two of those occasions the restricted meaning
would obtain, and on one of them, namely in s. 2(4) alone, would the meaning be quite different.

[104] [1973] AC 435, [1972] All ER 898, [1972] 3 WLR 143.

[105] [1962] AC 220, [1961] 1 All ER 330, [1961] 2 WLR 897.

[106] [1979] AC 617, [1979] 1 All ER 898, [1979] 2 WLR 281.

[107] S. 4 provides: "(1) A person shall not be convicted of an offence against section 2 of
this Act, and an order of forfeiture shall not be made under the foregoing section, if it is
proved that publication of the article in question is justified as being for the public good on
the ground that it is in the interests of science, literature, art or learning, or other objects of
general concern. (2) It is hereby declared that the opinion of experts as to the literary, artistic, scientific or other merits of an article may be admitted in any proceedings under this Act
either to establish or to negative the said ground."

ensures that the particular cultural status of the defendant(s), and of the offending item, is recognised. The prosecution of the defendants in *Gibson and Sylveire* on the common law charge of outraging public decency, where no such legislative provision obtains, made it possible to minimise the significance of the art issue. This is what the Court of Appeal chose to do. It could have chosen otherwise.

It is not made clear in the Court of Appeal's judgment in *Gibson and Sylveire* that the leading authority on the crime of outraging public decency is *Knuller. Lemon* is less persuasive authority because it treats only the related crime of blasphemous libel.

In *Knuller*, the appellants published a magazine, *The International Times*, which contained on inner pages columns of advertisements headed "Males". Most of the advertisements were inserted by homosexuals for the purpose of attracting persons who would indulge in homosexual activities. The appellants were charged on two counts. The first count alleged a conspiracy to corrupt public morals. The second alleged a conspiracy to outrage public decency by the publication of the "lewd, disgusting and offensive" advertisements. No argument for the applicability of the public good defence on either count was submitted and yet the appeal on the second count was allowed.

It seems anomalous that in subsequent proceedings involving a conspicuous art element, where a defence of public good (on the grounds of artistic merit) is more obviously relevant, appeals against conviction for outraging public decency should be dismissed. The Court of Appeal in *Gibson and Sylveire* chose not only to dismiss the appeals but to consider, *obiter*, that the availability of the defence was "unlikely",[108] without citing any authority to support that view.

In *Knuller*, Lord Simon of Glaisdale[109] made clear that outraging public decency goes considerably beyond offending the susceptibilities of, or even shocking, reasonable people. He affirmed that "public" is used in a locative sense and was of the opinion that the jury should be invited, where appropriate, to remember that they live in a plural society, with a tradition of tolerance towards minorities, and that this atmosphere of toleration is itself part of public decency. Lord Kilbrandon[110] expressly agreed with Lord Simon. Lord Diplock[111] emphasised that the courts should be the vigilant guardians of the liberty of the citizen, and Lord Reid[112] held the view that the offence

[108] [1990] 2 QB 619 at 625.
[109] [1972] 2 All ER 898 at 936.
[110] *Ibid.*, at 938.
[111] *Ibid.*, at 923.
[112] *Ibid.*, at 906.

of outraging public decency was "new" and should not be recognised. Only Lord Morris of Borth-y-Gest[113] would have entirely dismissed the appeal.

The Court of Appeal in *Gibson and Sylveire* in effect affirmed the
less liberal approach of Lord Morris of Borth-y-Gest on the second
count (dissenting), which their other Lordships in *Knuller* emphatically contradicted in their majority result. The Court of Appeal in
Gibson and Sylveire should have paid more attention to the majority
of their Lordships in *Knuller* so as to allow the appeals, and to distinguish clearly a case involving art in accordance with the more liberal
reasoning and policy established by the majority of their Lordships in
that leading case.[114]

There is little hope of a fair defence for an artist and art gallery
curator on a charge of outraging public decency if no provision is
made for the consideration of the distinctive ontology of art. If the
mens rea requirement is as narrow as decided in *Gibson and Sylveire*
(cognate with that for the offence of obscene libel[115] and amounting
to strict liability), the availability of a defence accommodating the
specialised nature of artistic intent is essential. If the Court of Appeal
had framed its judgment mindful of this, the long considered importance of art as a cultural phenomenon, and the concomitant importance of artistic freedom, it could have indicated the following *inter
alia*, to distinguish art's position from that of other facts[116]:

1. That artistic intent is not usually considered base[117] (but,
    rather, noble) and is not a singular[118] attitude but one

---

[113] *Ibid.*, at 914.

[114] If a Court of Appeal decision cannot stand with a decision of the House of Lords, the
Court of Appeal decision should not be followed (*Young* v. *Bristol Aeroplane Co. Ltd* [1944]
KB 718). Since Lord Denning's retirement, the Court of Appeal appears to have adhered to
this traditional doctrine.

[115] [1990] 2 QB 619 at 628.

[116] This is not to forget that the primary duty of finding the appropriate material for the
particular case in issue rests on the respective counsel for the parties.

[117] Prosecuting counsel in *Gibson and Sylveire* pointed out that if the defendant's state of
mind is a critical factor, a man could escape liability by the very baseness of his own standards. See [1990] 2 QB 619 at 627.

[118] Lord Russell of Killowen said in *Lemon* (n. 8 above, 657 (AC), applied by the Court
of Appeal in *Gibson and Sylveire* [1990] 2 QB 619 at 629):

> "The reason why the law considers that the publication of a blasphemous libel is an offence is that
> the law considers that such publication should not take place. And if it takes place, and the pub-
> lication is deliberate, I see no justification for holding that there is no offence when the publisher
> is incapable for some reason particular to himself of agreeing with a jury on the true nature of the
> publication."

common to artists and approved of by the art-appreciating
community.

2. That reasonable members of the public would approach an
art-work meditatively and respond to it suitably contempla-
tively.

3. That an inappropriate social response to his art-work is not
something an artist should reasonably have to consider.[119]

4. That reasonable people know that art can (or even must)
shock, and that an art gallery is a particularly likely place to
discover and view art.

5. That it is impossible for outrage to be an effect of art except
if the viewer receives it inappropriately, i.e. without the
appropriate psychic distance involved in an æsthetic attitude.

6. That since the publicity requirement in the offence of outraging public decency is locative, the fact that the object is art
and appropriately displayed in an art gallery is particularly relevant.[120]

On 3 June 1964, the Solicitor-General[121] gave an assurance,
repeating an earlier assurance, that a conspiracy to corrupt public
morals would not be charged so as to circumvent the statutory
defence in section 4 of the Obscene Publications Act 1959. This
undertaking did not explicitly apply to the offence of outraging public decency. It is a matter of some concern that lack of such formal

---

[119] Instead, the Court of Appeal adopted the following approach, [1990] 2 QB 619 at 629:

"[O]nce the outrage is established to the satisfaction of the jury, the defendant is scarely likely to
be believed if he says he was not aware of the danger he was running of causing offence and outrage to the public."

[120] From "Human Earrings" we see the reality of the cheapness of life, used as a mere
ornament in the cosmetic age of postmodernism. The already dead beings tell the world of
their thorough abuse. It is a selfish public that wishes to protect its own sensitivities above
recognition of the awful truth of this sculpture and the plight it reveals. There is no such
outrage at the arguably less moral exposure of human tissue of once-mummified Egyptian
pharaohs (which exposure to the Ancient Egyptians would have been clearly sacrilegious).

Religious relics, including parts of the human anatomy, rarely raise contemporary public
indignation, even if vile to the eye and mere curiosities as opposed to art. In art "the problem of ugliness dissolves; for pleasure and prettiness neither define nor measure either the
aesthetic experience or the work of art. The pleasantness or unpleasantness of a symbol does
not determine its general cognitive efficacy or its specifically artistic merit. 'Macbeth' and
the Goya 'Witches' Sabbath' no more call for apology than do 'Pygmalion' and the Botticelli
'Venus' " (Nelson Goodman). See, further, Nelson Goodman, *Problems and Projects* (Hackett
Publishing Company, Indianapolis, Ind., 1992), at 103–19.

More difficult art to legitimise in solely the name of art would be portrayals on grounds
of *abuse* of the subjects *whilst they are alive.*

[121] Hansard, HC, vol. 695, col. 1212.

assurance could jeopardise the basic trend of public policy followed by Parliament at that time. Without doubting that the common law offence of outraging public decency is judiciously administered, it is suggested that, instead of relying on such assurances, Parliament should take a necessary legislative step to provide incontrovertibly that a defence of public good based on literary, artistic or scientific merit obtains in the common law offences cognate with obscene libel. A matter of more general social concern is that the legal notion of a reasonable member of the public following *Gibson and Sylveire* is of one who, having decided voluntarily to enter an art gallery, is incapable of responding to something purporting to be art in a manner appropriate to art, even when it is explicity exhibited as art in the traditional artistic context of an art gallery. It is in accordance with this standard of ignorance that art is here condemned.

Returning to statutory obscenity trials, juries are exhorted to "keep in mind the current standards of ordinary decent people"[122] (America's "average person", France's *"homme moyen"*). Instead of asking the jury to hypothesise about the standards of a dreamt-up Mr Average, perhaps it would be better to ask a juryman to follow his own standard since he is a member of the jury precisely because he is one element of the community that makes the community standard: all 12 jurymen in conference should separately voice their own standard and the community standard is that of the 12, who reflect, as well as anything could, the general community standard. This approach also avoids the problem that the view given must be the current view, because whatever forms the jurymen's view is currently voiced by him, and even if he is unmodern-minded, he is allowed to be, for this is an ordinary and decent mental attitude and perfectly consistent with how one component of a community standard would really and naturally operate. To ask jurymen to express their own standard is more realistic than to make them perform an exercise in amateur sociology.

The item-by-item approach of evaluating obscene matter's effect, established in section 1 of the 1959 Act, has caused a number of problems and is the result of the legislation having been too tightly worded. The undefinitional French approach in Article 283 incurs no such pitfalls. The English disjunction in section 1 ". . . or . . . the

122 N. 27 above.

effect of any one of its items" was interpreted in *"Oz"*[123] as meaning that one tiny item of a magazine could be excerpted and, if in isolation obscene, could contaminate the entirety. The question "what constitutes one distinct item?" has been left unanswered; likewise the question, "would an expert, for the purposes of the public good defence, be confined to evidence on the one obscene item?".

Despite possessing some technical faults, English law has finally come to realise that art and literature must not be sacrificed for the sake of possible harm to an abstract notion of social morality: in *Wiggins* v. *Field*,[124] the Divisional Court discouraged the prosecution of genuine if *avant-garde* literature. The prosecution of Baudelaire had discouraged the French in this respect over a century earlier.[125]

Rules on experts called for the public good defence have been developed by the common law.[126] These are lenient. In England there is no limit to the number of experts who can be called; they can testify on authorial intention, literary reputation and historical placing; they can contextualise the work in world art or literature. One obvious restriction is that they must be *bona fide* experts, a crucial one is that they cannot express any opinion on the balance that is the prerogative solely of the jury i.e. whether the value of a work outweighs its tendency to deprave and corrupt.

Comics of the underground press were accepted as "art" for the purposes of a section 4 defence in both *"Oz"*[127] and *"Nasty Tales"*.[128] Though copyright protection is readily given in England to the most pedantic writing, it would seem that the standard for section 4 literature and art is somewhat higher, one commentator suggesting that excellence of sorts is required to redeem a tendency to corrupt.[129] It is doubtful whether the *"Oz"* and *"Nasty Tales"* comics possessed any form of excellence, but for the purposes of a section 4 defence they could be regarded as "art". Since section 4 provides a classification and divides literature and art there must be a judicial temptation to place, for the purposes of its defence, a given work into one of the categories statute provides. My suggestion is that a given work is fitted into a convenient category for defence purposes rather than having its qualities determine its cultural identity independent of the

---

[123] N. 70 above.
[124] N. 43 above.
[125] See "Conclusions", Ch. 2.
[126] Primarily by Byrne J, n. 53 above.
[127] N.70 above.
[128] Robertson, n. 42 above, 171.
[129] *Ibid.* above.

established classification. The question of its merit comes after its categorisation and this need only be obvious enough to outweigh the degree of its obscenity. It would be illogical if public "good" required the higher requirement of "excellence".

The public good defence has facilitated the implementation of part of the prelude to the Obscene Publications Act 1959 "to provide for the protection of literature[130] and to strengthen the law concerning pornography". In England and America fewer and fewer conceivably genuine art works are prosecuted, and in practice only pornographic films and sex toys came before French courts under the old penal code article 283.

In September 1997, the English Royal Academy took the unprecedented step of making one of its galleries an "adults only" space for its exhibition of *avant-garde* young British artists, "Sensation". The room, to which those under the age of 18 were not admitted, featured, *inter alia*, the brothers Jake and Dinos Chapman's work "Zygotic Acceleration", which comprises androgynous children with aroused genitalia instead of faces. Other controversial works were on general view, including a portrait by Chris Ofili of the Virgin Mary surrounded by explicit photographs from hard-core pornography magazines, a Matt Collishaw canvas showing a bullet hole in a human brain in extreme close-up to resemble female genitalia, and a Marcus Harvey painting of the Moors murderer Myra Hindley composed of child's-hand prints. Purchasers of tickets were warned that some of the artworks could be considered "distasteful" and that "parents should exercise their judgement in bringing children to the exhibition". It was perhaps on the grounds of such warning, unique in the Royal Academy's 230-year history, that criminal prosecution was avoided, and a judgment of legal immorality consequently eschewed.

In Chapter 2, a survey of the judicial approach to art in the morality law context is intended to reveal the variety of judicial taste that has contributed to the fate of allegedly immoral art in particular cases. As perceived from the present chapter, the exercise of judicial taste is not provided for in any of the pertinent English, French or American law. This is unsurprising because formally it is forbidden.[131]

---

[130] The public good defence had a resounding success in its debut in the *"Lady Chatterley"* trial, n. 44 above.

[131] Robertson, n. 42 above, at 156: "In strict legal theory, an obscenity jury cannot be a mechanism for enforcing the aesthetic taste or moral judgment of the ordinary man". *A fortiori*, judges cannot exercise their own taste. As Stable J said in his *"Philanderer"* direction [1956] 2 All ER 683: "[w]e are not sitting here as judges of taste. We are not here to say whether we like a book of that kind."

CONCLUSIONS

In law governing the publication of matter considered offensive to public morality in England, France and the United States of America, the presiding concern is the protection of what is legally perceived as society's accepted morality. Art is not its central concern and the establishing of quality standards on art is relatively peripheral in its everyday working. The system whereby artistic merit is used to off-set a charge of obscenity results in a challenge to the simple accep-tance by law of an accepted morality. The art factor here performs what can be described as a critical moral role. It challenges the foist-ing of a single moral stance on an involuntarily-subjugated culture with a contrasting morality or, in the case of art, a morality necessar-ily outside that of accepted morality. One function of art is the provocation of new moral insight by the presentation of new artistic visions of the world. This prevents accepted morality from stagnating or atrophying, and is a useful tool in its development.

The US constitutional provisions for the protection of speech, and their subsequent development, have not protected art appropriately. It is submitted that a system preferable to the one seen to have devel-oped, would be to say of obscenity: (i) it *is* speech, and then to ask (ii) should it be prevented because it adversely affects matters consid-ered more important? It is arguable that the second consideration should not necessarily be influenced by a populist criterion, especially in the case of art, which is a specialist realm with its own very pecu-liar relation to society, often popularly perceived as antagonistic (a judgement made without due attention to the very valuable heuris-tic nature of its ontology and its role of catalyst in relation to the development of society mores). The English provision of a defence of artistic merit to outbalance a charge of obscenity at least ensures that art is seen as an autonomous culture with its own values beside those of accepted morality, which can displace that morality by a higher (or at least other) value. The contemporary French tendency not to prosecute art for outraging public morality illustrates a civilised approach to the matter by an art-appreciating culture.

The prosecution of art for in some way offending public morality has not, of course, disappeared with the advent of postmodernism. Postmodern art, moreover, in particular, tends to react against any demand of seriousness or traditional value.[132] Tests such as that set in

---

[132] See, further, Amy M. Adler, "Postmodern Art and the Death of Obscenity Law" (1990) 99 *Yale Law Journal* 1359. See, also, Appendix, Essay 1, below.

Miller v. *California*[133] protecting sexually explicit art only if it demonstrates "serious . . . artistic . . . value"[134] then become obsolete and threaten contemporary art by maintaining a standard that art seeks to defy. Because art, by its nature, calls into question any set definition, and will always violate standards set, the most obvious conclusion is that either art as a whole is protected *or* "society" is protected from "obscenity". If standards imposed were undone, art might react by becoming less seemingly anti-social, and the problem would resolve itself.

[133] 413 US 15 (1973).
[134] N. 17 above, at 24.

2

The Judicial Approach to Art

"Those who find ugly meanings in beautiful things are corrupt without being charming. This is a fault. Those who find beautiful meanings in beautiful things are the cultivated. For these there is hope" (Oscar Wilde, in the preface to *The Picture of Dorian Gray*).

"The artist can express everything" (Oscar Wilde, in the preface to *The Picture Of Dorian Gray*).

"Oscar Wilde—And I? May I say nothing my lord? [his lordship made no reply beyond a wave of the hand to the warders, who hurried the prisoners out of sight]" [from H.M. Hyde (ed.), *The Trials of Oscar Wilde* (Dover Publication, New York, 1974), at 339].

"It would be a dangerous undertaking for persons trained only to the law to constitute themselves final judges of the worth of pictorial illustrations, outside of the narrowest and most obvious limits. At one extreme some works of genius would be sure to miss appreciation. Their very novelty would make them repulsive until the public had learned the new language in which their author spoke. It may be more than doubted, for instance, whether the etchings of Goya or the paintings of Manet would have been sure of protection when seen for the first time." [Holmes J in *Bleistein* v. *Donaldson Lithographing Co.*, 188 US 239, 251 (1903)].

INTRODUCTION

The basic focus of this critical survey is how judges approach and describe art in public morality law cases. The individuality of judicial *dicta* on art and the fact that in a given case the judge does not necessarily reveal the degree of his powers of artistic appreciation mean that the achievement of a definitive pronouncement on a single or general judicial concept of art is not scientifically possible. The study here focuses only on what is observable before the court i.e. the descriptive attention judges pay art as art and their discernible sensitivity to artistic concerns, e.g. in a case with art at the centre, what is the extent of judicial use of art criticism's typical modes of expression? Trends in judicial attitude are witnessable here, and any generalisations made are based on a survey of all available relevant judgments. A particular preliminary reference is made here to the trial of D.H. Lawrence's *Lady Chatterley's Lover* which warranted singular treatment because of the celebrity of the case, and choice from much judicial comment available was determined in accordance with its illustrative pertinence to a point established.

Historical in part, this analysis treats the appreciation of non-motion visual art and creative literature by judges and magistrates in the context of certain public morality laws. Within the wide ambit of public morality laws, the following are discussed: English obscenity law, French "outrage of good morals" and the law in the USA pertaining to obscenity that has accrued primarily under the First Amendment[1] constitutional standard of the Supreme Court.[2] Because English obscenity law has been so closely affected by the law of blasphemy, the latter is discussed where relevant.[3] The trials of Oscar Wilde, involving indecency, not obscenity *stricto sensu*, are nevertheless alluded to because of their centrality to art as well as public morality.

THE CASE LAW

The following brief résumé of the prosecution of D.H. Lawrence's *Lady Chatterley's Lover* is confined to its English setting, where the novel was confronted by Byrne J, who was particularly antagonistic to it. It was a seminal case under the then relatively new Obscene Publications Act 1959, and the judge's summing up was over two days. His approach was a caricature of the judicialisation of art's worst features. Despite the statutory right to call experts, Byrne J advocated ignoring a specialist view of the novel. He wanted the jury to assess the book immune to the influence of those who correctly put it in an artistic context. He told them that they were not addressing their minds to questions of taste but to those of moral standards. They were to consider the novel dispassionately bearing in mind that morality

---

[1] Art. 1 in addition to, and in amendment of, the Constitution of the United States of America, proposed by Congress, and ratified by the legislature of the several states pursuant to the fifth article of the original constitution: "Congress shall make no law abridging the freedom of speech, or of the press; . . ."

[2] US obscenity law is prescribed by state and federal statute under the guiding and dominant influence of a constitutional standard developed by the Sup. Ct.

[3] They are cognate crimes.

was fundamental to the well-being of the community and must prevail over the desire for self-expression. The judge then paid little attention to the novel's details, though he did acknowledge, paradoxically, that D.H. Lawrence was one of the great authors of the twentieth century. Clearly operating in the socio-moral dimension, Byrne J focused on whether promiscuity was condemned in Lawrence's book and was affronted by artistic realism. For example, he did not approve of Lawrence using words as a gamekeeper might use them. In his view, "marriage" in a non-legal sense could never be "sacred". In response to Dame Rebecca West's evidence, he intoned: "[t]hat was her view, for what it is worth". He continued by doubting whether sex was discussed on a "holy" basis, suggesting disparagingly that the main protagonists were "merely having sexual intercourse and enjoying it", as if that were self-evidently gravely reprehensible. Somewhat ironically, the jury responded to the judicial tirade against the novel by returning a verdict of not guilty. Byrne J was clearly out of touch with the public's moral outlook and under-estimated general reverence for literary art irrespective of sexual content.

As displayed in the *Chatterley* case, judges eschew their own or a jury's taste as a determining factor in public morality cases. In his *"Philanderer"* direction,[4] Stable J said: "[w]e are not sitting here as judges of taste", and in the Supreme Judicial Court *"Tropic of Cancer"* case[5] it was stated that "[i]t is not the function of judges to serve as arbiters of taste". In the *"Madame Bovary"* judgment,[6] mention was made of pictures of which good taste disapproves whilst Douglas J in *Paris Adult Theatre* v. *Slaton*[7] was keen to point out that the American Constitution makes the individual, not the government, the keeper of his tastes.

What degree of artistic merit or taste, then, must a creative work possess to escape the punishment of public morality laws?[8] In France, articles 283 and 284 of the old penal code set out the basic law of "outrage of good morals" but it is well established that the offending image or writing need not have had obscene content to be convicted. It was thus broader than obscenity law *stricto sensu*, but often involved the regulation of obscenity, in practice if not always in name. The

[4] R. v. *Martin Secker & Warburg* [1954] 1 WLR 1138.
[5] Per R. Ammi Cutter J.
[6] *Gazette des Tribunaux*, 8 Feb. 1857.
[7] 413 US 49 (1973).
[8] Merit rather than taste is claimed to be legally discerned because merit is more suggestive of objective worth.

new code provisions continue this tradition. The French judge focuses on the preservation of good morals whilst acknowledging any artistic worth in the object before the court. The weight placed on each is at his discretion in accordance with the French faith in the judge's intuitive conviction. It is a far less rule-based area than the equivalent laws of England and the USA, where judicial formulae on obscenity evolve to supplement legislation which in England formally sets merit off against obscenity; an equivalent mechanism in the USA depends on the provisions of either federal or state statutes, both ultimately governed by a constitutional standard established in the Supreme Court under the ægis of the First Amendment.

The clumsy balancing formula[9] of the English Obscene Publications Act 1959 sets merit off against obscenity when the two things are obviously not commensurable: an article is judged on its obscenity and, if deemed obscene, there is nevertheless provision for its "justification"—a defence to definite conviction if made out. Merit is the sole statutory defence available, and the degree required is not prescribed in statute but left to be assessed by a jury who only have to determine whether merit is sufficient to outweigh obscenity. It is unknown and a mystery how they manage to make this comparative evaluation. Moreover, we will see that a further difficulty is that, in deciding whether an article is obscene in the first half of the process, attention is bound to be paid to its merits even though this consideration is intended to be reserved for the second half of the process. In theory, and as prescribed by the statute and then the judges, the process should be neatly carried out as follows: is it obscene? If yes, is it justified as being for the public good? If yes, not guilty; if no, guilty.

Contrary to the logical plan of the legislators and judges, given the highly subjective nature of the concepts they have to use and particularly the huge ambit of considerations feasible in adjudging the obscene, the jury will not work as systematically as a machine. It will evaluate merit as part of the obscenity issue—to decide whether object X depraves and corrupts consideration of its good points is ineluctable. The legislators overlooked the fact that the balancing process they set up between obscenity and merit is already intrinsic to the determination of obscenity. Perhaps the legislators envisaged

---

[9] S. 4(1) of the Obscene Publications Act 1959 provides a defence if it is proved that publication of the (obscene) article in question is justified as being for the public good on the ground that it is in the interests of science, literature, art or learning, or of other objects of general concern.

only moral merits being weighed in the determination of obscenity; if they did, they overlooked the highly ambiguous content of a "moral" merit which could easily be confused with, or simply mean, that which is good in something, including its æsthetic worth. If in determining obscenity it was intended that the jury should look only at the object's "immoral" aspects, it would involve them in a very esoteric mechanism indeed: first, viewing the item from the least favourable angle, then, in contemplating justification for it, the most favourable angle, balancing these polarised considerations, then, ultimately, resynthesising a bipolar position by pronouncing an emphatic polarised "yes" or "no" as to the entity's criminality.

The balancing mechanism of the English Obscene Publications Act 1959 treats the jury too artificially in expecting imprecisely, and non-legislatively, defined value considerations to be strictly separated into stated boxes of "obscene" and "meritorious" that are themselves definitionally vague despite judicial attempts to clarify the former. Definitions of "merit" are wrongly left unattempted by the judiciary, presumably on the wrong assumption that its meaning is obvious, which it is not. The issue is further confused by judicial proclamation that it is not personal taste that is exercised here; in practice such proclamation is obviously defeated, humans being psychologically incapable of eliminating their own taste from their value judgements: the judgements they make are ones of their own perception.

In the United States, judicial attempts have been made to specify the type of value, or the quality of value, that renders an object not obscene. Brennan J in *Roth*[10] established the test that material must be utterly without redeeming social value to be obscene. This view was later rejected in *Miller* v. *California*,[11] where Burger CJ established the new test of whether the material has any serious artistic or literary value. The allegedly obscene article always has an uphill struggle—it is obscene *unless* . . . This mechanism is less favourable to the object than those in England and, more particularly, France. At least in England obscenity is an issue to be first determined (*then* merit is considered)[12]; in the USA there is a presumption of obscenity unless there is merit (demonstrable merit of a *serious* value).[13] The First Amendment does not operate in favour of obscenity, so merit is the only hope for the article presumed obscene. In practice, there-

---

[10]   237 F 2d 796 (2d Cir. 1956).
[11]   413 US 15 (1973).
[12]   Obscene Publications Act 1959, ss. 1 and 4.
[13]   From *Miller*, n. 11 above.

fore, the US courts are operating a very conceptually peculiar system: the constitutional standard is meant to protect work from allegedly less equitable state (or federal) standards and yet is a harsh test itself by presuming obscenity till merit is proven, and exempting obscenity from constitutionally protected speech. Where obscenity is concerned, the presumption is *not* freedom.

Unencumbered by this US plethora of different standards (constitutional, federal, state) or the strictures of the balancing mechanism of the Obscene Publications Act 1959 in England, or the constraint of precedent or other judicial decision, the French judge, free from instructing a jury, applies the law of "outrage of good morals" with all the evidential and procedural ease the French legal system allows. With the simple acknowledgement that "good morals" change as society changes, he uses his discretion on a given allegedly offensive work without the tedium of a series of imposed techniques purporting to regulate and rationalise a "moral" issue to a list of optimum legal criteria. It is my conviction that leaving this difficult and highly subjective area to the "intuitive conviction" of one wise man, with the minimum of forced attempts at objectifying the issue, is the optimum system to operate (though a personal doubt is whether it should operate at all). Naturally, some French courts have more than one judge but a corporate judicial decision assessing all merits and demerits of an object *in toto* seems to me an equally effective option, and far preferable to legal systems which try to impose a neat and sophisticated set of rules on a moral realm unsusceptible of such treatment. The objection is not to having rules in this realm—and the French system has them—but to having other than a realistically flexible method of legal approach to an issue ultimately determinable only by value judgements. It does not help the matter to clutter it with *set* formulae and balances which US and English experiences have proved unworkable, as evidenced by the constancy of their inefficacy and the untiring demands for their abolition or reform. The issue is even further confused in America by a political element—some cases such as *Close* v. *Lederle*[14] suggest that for obscene art to be protected by the First Amendment it must have cognitive quality; it must be wanting to *say* something beyond merely presenting itself. This is still the case despite recognition in *Piarowski*[15] that abstract as well as representational art exists.

---

[14] 424 F, 2d 988 (1st Cir. 1970).
[15] 759 F 2d 625 (7th Cir. 1985)

Experts are occasionally called upon to elucidate artistic purpose, whereas judges feel expert enough themselves to speculate about motive. However, receptiveness to experts is not universal and different rules apply to their evidence in England, France and America. Expert witnesses were excluded in *The Well of Loneliness*[16] and *September In Quinze* cases,[17] following the English law of the time with no specific provision for their accommodation and case law favouring exclusion. The Obscene Publications Act of 1959 later provided that witnesses were allowed to be called, if desired by either party, to testify on artistic or literary (or other) merit.[18] The role of experts in the field was still not unqualifiedly accepted as of value by the courts, Byrne J in the English *Lady Chatterley* case[19] of November 1960 being particularly sceptical. "What can an expert do on interpreting a book that a judge or a jury could not do themselves?" is one source of such scepticism, but so is the arguably more important question "[w]ho will best read the book and be affected by it in the way the unspecialised in English Literature will read and be affected by it—an expert, a judge or a juryman?" Whatever the answer to these questions, it is generally accepted that someone with an author's mind is more likely to speculate accurately on an author's artistic purpose than those ignorant of the author. For specific roles, then, such as the giving of insight into the intentions of an artist or author, experts are of undoubted use, leaving their superiority as interpreters of plot still open to understandable doubt. Literary and artistic experts would perhaps be better attended to by judges if their roles in given cases in court were more narrowly defined, confining them to concerns only fully appreciable by the expert and in which they personally *are* expert.

Judges themselves occasionally make brief allusions to other creators or creative work in the course of judging the work before them. Frank J in *Roth*[20] cited Coleridge; Posner CJ in *Piarowski*[21] referred to Aristophanes and displayed knowledge of the history of art; Learned Hand J in *Ulysses*[22] quoted Andrews who alluded to

---

[16] Bow Street, Nov. 1936. See Vera Brittain, *Radclyffe Hall—A Case of Obscenity* (Femina, London, 1968). There was no prosecution of English military hero T.E. Lawrence for his contemporary treatment of male homosexuality in *The Seven Pillars of Wisdom*.

[17] 17 Sept. 1954 at the Old Bailey, London.

[18] S. 4(2).

[19] See C.H. Rolph, *The Trial of Lady Chatterley, R. v. Penguin Books Ltd.* (Penguin Books 1961, Baltimore, Mld., 1961).

[20] N. 10 above.

[21] N. 15 above.

[22] *US v. One Book Entitled "Ulysses"*, 72 F 2d 705 (2d Cir. 1934).

Boccaccio; and Ploscowe, city magistrate, in *People* v. *Gonzales*,[23] made comparisons with Goya and Rubens.

Certain other extrinsic factors sometimes weigh with a judge: the publishers of *The Rainbow* should have attended to the book's adverse press reports, according to the magistrate in that case, and refrained from publishing it; there was a copycat destruction of *Ulysses* by English customs officers emulating their US colleagues; in *Kingsley Books Inc.* v. *Brown*[24] it was said that the conduct of an individual, not the quality of art, should be the issue in obscenity cases. In *People* v. *Gonzales*,[25] there was a suggestion that who buys supposed art is a factor in determining whether it really is art.

Judges are not usually ignorant of general literary forms and major authors. The term "a novel" is commonplace in judgments though it is rarely enriched by adjectives in the fashion of Judge Spalding in the New Jersey *Fanny Hill* case, where he referred to Cleland's work as "a structural novel". Learned Hand J utilised "depiction", one of the critics' favourite nouns, and Judge Manton rather anachronistically referred to literature as "letters" (both in *Ulysses*[26]). *Tropic of Cancer* was neatly defined by Desmond J as "a narrative".[27] Sometimes "material" or "matter" as opposed to "book" is used to differentiate pornography from literature. Sometimes there is no such differentiation, as in the term "pornographic books" in the Paris Cour d'Appel, 11 May 1956.[28] In cases involving pictorial art, judges very rarely use the terminology of art criticism, for example "design", "composition", "colour", "tone", "space", "volume", "shape". However, Posner CJ in *Piarowski*[29] was aware of "representational" and "abstract" art and in *The Philanderer*[30] Stable J addressed the question "[w]hat are the functions of the novel?"

Judges are often aware that a novel needs to be read as a whole for its integrity to be appreciated, for example Learned Hand J in *Ulysses*[31] and Magistrate Greenspan in *God's Little Acre*.[32] In France in

[23] 107 NYS 2d 968 (Mag.Ct. NY County 1951).

[24] 354 US, 436 (1957).

[25] N. 23 above.

[26] N. 22 above.

[27] The New York case of *Tropic of Cancer*: see Charles Rembar's chs. of detailed analysis of this work in his *The End of Obscenity* (André Deutsch Ltd., London, 1968).

[28] Recueil Dalloz-Sirey 1956 Jur. at 376.

[29] N. 15 above.

[30] *R.* v. *Martin Secker & Warburg* [1954] 1 WLR 1138.

[31] N. 22 supra.

[32] For a transcript of the relevant part of the judgment, case of 2 May 1933, see Alec Craig's *The Banned Books of England* (George Allen & Unwin Ltd., London, 1937), 119–21.

the *Bovary* trial,[33] the offending passages were individually and formally cited; in the *Fleurs du Mal* trial,[34] the offending poems were isolated from the rest of the collection. In England and the USA there is no such formal presentation of isolated passages, and although judicial rules have fluctuated, the prevailing approach now is to address the work as a whole, prosecuting counsel drawing attention to gems of vulgarity incidentally as the trial proceeds.

The term "figurative" for art appears in French case law of the early 1970s[35]; Judge Frank in *Roth*[36] refers to "great artistry and charm", Stable J. in *The Philanderer*[37] to "great literature". Judges seldom display an inclination to describe creations before them in other than straightforward terms: there is a noticeable lack of variety of adjectives and adverbs when they describe an art work, the reference in a French case[38] of 19 April 1950 to "an aesthetic, decorative and plastic element" being singularly colourful.

Given a written creative work to assess, English judges are generally inattentive to theme or style but attentive to plot. US judges attend to theme occasionally, but rarely to style. French judges attend to style occasionally, but rarely to theme. French judgments, in generally more succinct than English and US ones, rarely discuss aspects of the plot. US benches join English ones in discussing plot, though also theme. "Subject matter" (as a recognised term in literary criticism) is rarely judicially identified.

Art and creative literature, sometimes distinguished in judicial expositions, sometimes not, are not subject to different public morality legal rules in any of the jurisdictions discussed. Recognised as not necessarily co-extensive by, for example, the English Obscene Publications Act 1959 which separates artistic and literary interest,[39] the judiciary has not always felt the need to so distinguish the two. In the *Madame Bovary* trial,[40] "works of the mind (or spirit)" were distinguished from "productions of fine art" and in the phrase "literature, like art". Judge Frank in the *Roth* case[41] differentiated

---

[33] Trib. Corr. de Paris (6ᵉ Chambre), 31 Jan. 1857 to 7 Feb. 1857.

[34] Gaz. des Tribs., 21 Aug. 1857.

[35] Daniel Bécourt, *Livres Condamnés, Livres Interdits* (2nd edn., Cerclede la Librairie, Paris, 1972), 523.

[36] N. 10 above.

[37] N. 30 above.

[38] Recueil Dalloz-Sirey *"Jurisprudence Générale"* 1950, *"Sommaires"*, at 47 (M.M. Perrier).

[39] S. 4(2).

[40] N. 33 above.

[41] N. 10 above.

"masterpieces of literature" and "the pictorial arts". In *Miller* v. *California*,[42] Burger CJ distinguished serious artistic value and serious literary value. These instances are the exceptions; more commonly, art and creative literature are not differentiated by the judiciary.

Judicial terminology occasionally reveals that similar æsthetic criteria bear upon visual art and creative literature. In the *Madame Bovary* judgement,[43] reference is made to parts of Flaubert's writing as "images" and "pictures"; mention is made of "characters that the author wanted to paint". Similar application of artistic terms to written forms occurs in the *Fleurs du Mal* judgment.[44] The convergence is total in R. Ammi Cutter J's terminology in the Massachusetts Supreme Judicial Court case, *Tropic of Cancer*, of July 1962: he talks of a "literary artist" and "a work of literary art". Intellectual treatment of art and literature involves a similar technique despite the fact that visual art has a visual aspect that creative literature lacks and creative literature has a written aspect that visual art lacks. This is perhaps too easily explained by the generalised nature of vocabulary employed in the arts designed to cover all the media artistically embraced: vocabulary alone does not dictate intellectual approach.

Only very rarely do judges read creative literature aloud in court but Charles J did so in *Wilde*[45]: "In Praise of Shame" (a sonnet) and a few lines from the poem entitled "Two Loves". This reading was not directly in point; sometimes when it would be in point, it is not done, as in *R. v. Lemon and Gay News Ltd.*[46] Nevertheless, judges frequently direct a jury on how to read a creative work—both in *The Philanderer*[47] and *The Image And The Search*[48] cases the jury was sent away with specific instructions to read the work as a whole. Nothing is said of re-reading in any of the cases, despite the argument that re-reading reduces the work's erotic effect and increases the reader's attention to literary merit.

R. v. Lemon (above) is notable not just because it is a somewhat anachronistic blasphemy case: it is unusual for poetry to be

---

[42] N. 11 above.

[43] Gaz. des Tribs., 8 Feb. 1857.

[44] N. 34 above.

[45] 26 Apr. 1895 at the Central Criminal Court, Old Bailey, London.

[46] [1978] 3 All ER 175 C.A. Surely it is imperative for an appeal court to look at the content of a poem *de novo* to determine whether or not it is blasphemous, and not rely on lower court assessment of the matter? It is precisely the content that gives rise to the charge.

[47] N. 4 above.

[48] By Devlin J when the publishers Hutchinson were prosecuted in 1954—see C.H. Rolph, *The Trial of Lady Chatterley* (Penguin, Baltimore, Mld., 1961), 229–30.

condemned before the courts in the context of public morality laws. The famous trial was that of Baudelaire[49] in which the six offending poems of his *"Fleurs du Mal"* were specified as the offending literature but whose offending lines or phrases were not particularised. In the *Count de Montalk's Case*[50] in England, Sir Ernest Wild, presiding, was very disparaging about the self-costuming superiority of poets ("[a] man must not say he was a poet and be filthy"), as well as hard on the offending poet, with a sentence which appalled W.B. Yeats, an influential contemporary poet.[51]

Judicial concepts of art are not, of course, consistent. According to Ploscowe, city magistrate, in the US case of *People* v. *Gonzales*,[52] photography is different from art whereas Lord Denning, in *R.* v. *Metropolitan Commissioner of Police ex parte Blackburn*,[53] refers to "the art of coloured photography". A more nuanced French stance was given in the phrase "photos with artistic character".[54]

In the US case of *Piarowski* v. *Illinois Community College*,[55] stained-glass windows were considered art and "the art of dance" was recognised in a French Tribunal Correctionnel d'Orange case of 19 April 1950.[56] In the latter case, the allegedly offensive poster was not considered a work of art, but there was no indication given that no poster could be art. There is scarcely one reference to artistic movements or genres in pubic morality law judgments involving art save a throwaway French one to "the kind and diversity of schools".[57]

It has been rare for classics to be condemned in the twentieth century, though Voltaire's *Candide* was seized in Boston in 1929 and Swindon magistrates condemned Boccaccio's *The Decameron* as obscene in 1954.[58] In an English trial of 10 October 1934 at Westminster Police Court, Roland Powell discussed classics at length

[49] N. 34 above.

[50] (1932) 23 Cr. App. Rep. 182.

[51] H. Montgomery Hyde, *A History of Pornography* (Heinemann, London, 1964), at 174. In *Ginsberg* v. *New York* (1968) 390 US 629, 20 L Ed 2d 195, 88 S Ct 1274, a publisher's conviction for the publication of a poem entitled "Sex Poem", a frank autobiographical account of sexual intercourse, was reversed, and in *One, Inc.* v. *Olesen* (1958) 335 US 371, 2 L Ed 2d 352, 78 S Ct 364, a poem dealing with the homosexual activities of two English lords was held not obscene.

[52] 107 NYS 2d 968 (Mag. Ct., NY County, 1951).

[53] *R.* v. *Metropolitan Police Commissioner, ex parte Blackburn* [1973] WLR 43, at 46.

[54] Trib. Corr., Seine (10e) 14 Oct. 1949.

[55] N. 15 above.

[56] N. 38 above.

[57] Trib. Corr. Seine (10e) 16 Dec. 1949.

[58] See Norman St. John-Stevas, *Obscenity and the Law* (Secker & Warburg, London, 1956), at 112.

and they were mentioned by Benjamin Greenspan in his judgment of *God's Little Acre*.[59] In the *Roth* case,[60] Judge Frank pointed out how inconceivable it is to deprive the cultivated of works considered classics. To condemn classics is to condemn valuable durable culture, arguably the most irrational of condemnations in the whole artistic field.

Judges vary in their respect for the established reputation of the author of the work before them—Judge Desmond in *Cancer*[61] was unimpressed by Miller's reputation, whereas Flaubert was openly respected in the *Madame Bovary* case[62] and judgment. The good reputation of the work itself was referred to by Judge Hand in *Ulysses*[63] and Judge Cutter in *Cancer*.[64]

Judge Manton in *Ulysses*[65] referred to those "who *pose* as the more highly developed and intelligent" (my emphasis), obviously doubting the authenticity of those involved in quality literature. In contrast, in the judgment of *Madame Bovary*,[66] there was sensitivity to the writer's vocation; reference was made to the literary point of view; and the author Flaubert's own evidence of to his objective was cited and believed. Wills J, in the May 1895 trial of Oscar Wilde[67] doubted whether the letters described as prose poems were really such, but at least attended in this way to the defendant's opinion. All too often the author's voice is ignored, or even shouted down, as in *The Well of Loneliness*[68] where the author, Radclyffe Hall, because her work was the subject of destruction proceedings, was unable to testify at all on her book's purpose or merits and was reproved for her anguished interruption in the proceedings which threatened to vilify her obviously serious novel about female homosexuality.

Judges rarely make distinctions between legitimate erotic work and illegitimate obscene work, but a noble attempt at explaining such a distinction was made in the Tribunal de Grande Instance, Paris, 17th Chamber, 5 October 1972[69]:

[59] N. 32 above.
[60] N. 10 above.
[61] N. 27 above.
[62] N. 33 above.
[63] N. 22 above.
[64] The Massachusetts case of *Tropic of Cancer*. Rembar, n. 27 above.
[65] N. 22 above.
[66] N. 43 above.
[67] N. 45 above.
[68] N. 16 above.
[69] Recueil Dalloz-Sirey 1973 I.R. at 70.

"The distinctive quality of erotic work is to glorify, whilst at the same time obligingly describing, the amorous instinct, and amorous gesture, whilst pornographic works, on the contrary, depriving love rituals entirely of their sentimental context by describing only their physiological mechanisms, contribute to depraving morals if they seek deviations from them with a visible fondness . . ."

But in 1949 Judge Bok in *Commonwealth* v. *Gordon*[70] had defined impurity in literature as "any writing whose dominant purpose and effect is erotic allurement . . .".

In *People* v. *Gonzales*,[71] Ploscowe, city magistrate, asserted "nudity *per se* is not obscenity". "Since time immemorial the nude has been an aesthetic, decorative and plastic thing" proclaimed a French judgment of 19 April 1950.[72] The seemingly objectionable sexual nature of nudity is overcome by art: combining judicial dicta, Bécourt[73] has concluded that "photos with artistic character, although light, did not appear obscene, nor contrary to good morals",[74] from the instant "when they succumbed to retouching whose end was the complete eradication of the sex of the models"[75]: art transforms the sexual to a degree that it eliminates it.

The nudes under scrutiny in *Close* v. *Lederle*[76] were not redeemed: "there is no suggestion, unless in its cheap titles, that plaintiff's art was seeking to express political or social thoughts"; the Court's view of the agent of redemption of art here is that it not only needs to be cognitive to gain First Amendment protection but also, more specifically, to express political or social thought, which is somewhat narrower still. Of course, not all art is cognitive. Some is intentionally not ideaful but simply enjoyable or entertaining: all it wishes to communicate is medium not message. Under *Close*,[77] non-cognitive work—such as certain abstracts—could not enlist First Amendment support against a charge of obscenity. Yet in *Winters* v. *New York*[78] the contrary was recognised: that the entertaining and not just the informing was protected by the Constitution; it need not be "the best of literature". *A fortiori*, it is arguable that some of the best of literature itself

[70] 66 D&C 101 (1949).
[71] N. 23 above.
[72] Recueil Dalloz-Sirey 1950, *"Sommaires"*, at 47.
[73] N. 35 above.
[74] Trib. Corr., Seine (10ᵉ) 14 Oct. 1949.
[75] Trib. Corr., Seine (10ᵉ) 16 Dec. 1949.
[76] 424 F 2d 988 (1st Cir. 1970).
[77] *Ibid.*
[78] 333 US 507 (1948).

is non-cognitive: W.B. Yeats' "Leda And The Swan", whose subject matter can be prosaically described as rape, has arguably not a single "idea" in it. What an idea is is, of course, open to debate.

Why any emphasis on the cognitive function of art anyway? To differentiate it from pornography? In *The Philanderer* case,[79] Stable J said that pornographic books have "no message . . . no thought". However, the cognitive quality of a work is often judicially recognised independently of any issue of pornography—the *Madame Bovary* judgment,[80] for example, refers to "the exposition of theories" and "ideas revealed", and pornography is often distinguished from art on grounds other than lack of cognitive quality: in the Supreme Judicial Court of Massachusetts, R. Ammi Cutter J said in *Cancer*[81]:

> "We think that the book must be accepted as a conscious effort to create a work of literary art and as having significance, which prevents treating it as hard core pornography."

Sometimes a work is stated as being clearly not a work of pornography (e.g. by Magistrate Greenspan in *God's Little Acre*[82]) because it is considered obvious that it is not—no explanations need be proffered. Sometimes, though, the obviousness is not apparent: in *Piarowski*,[83] *Young*[84] is cited which refers to "sexually explicit though non-pornographic art", which is unhelpful as a distinction. In practice, conceptual distinctions between pornography and art are less crucial than a determination at the time of judgment of what is considered offensive to contemporary prevailing social mores.

In *Close* v. *Lederle*,[85] Professor Wright is quoted by Aldrich CJ on the importance of the context of obscene words. In the *Philanderer* case,[86] Stable J acknowledged that coarseness, an aspect of reality, could be artistically portrayed legitimately and in the *Ulysses* case[87] Learned Hand J recognised that the obscene "matter" was relevant to the artistic purpose. Douglas J in *Ginsburg* v. *US*,[88] said that the Constitution protects coarse expression as well as refined, and

[79] N. 4 above.
[80] N. 6 above.
[81] N. 64 above.
[82] N. 32 above.
[83] N. 15 above.
[84] *Young* v. *American Mini Theatres, Inc.*, 42 US 50, 49 L Ed 2d 310, 96 S Ct. 2440 (1976).
[85] N. 76 above.
[86] N. 4 above.
[87] N. 22 above.
[88] 383 US 463 (1966).

vulgarity no less than elegance: "[a] book worthless to me may convey something of value to my neighbour". Judge Harland, in *Cohen v. California*,[89] discussing a notorious four-letter word, observed "one man's vulgarity is another's lyric". Such a recognition of the plurality of taste contrasts markedly with the approach of Sir Charles Biron in *The Well of Loneliness* case[90]: the obscenity in that case, he was keen to point out, emerged not from the treatment of a lesbian relationship *per se* but from the portrayal of that relationship as attractive. The work contained no coarse words.

In the consideration of allegedly obscene creative work there are conflicting judicial attitudes to "realism", and paradoxes emerge such as that the artistic portrayal of something legal in "real life" is condemned as illegal in an obscenity trial: the reflection of an event is punishable where the event is not; imaginative interpretation of an event is punishable where the event is not. The view of Sir Charles Biron in *The Well of Loneliness* case was that literature, especially if well written, could be more offensive and dangerous than the "immoral" real life situation it portrayed, precisely because it could present artistically and, worse, attractively, what in real life was "immoral": artistic realism, in presenting obscenity, was a vehicle for the promotion of that obscenity in real life. The argument is that the artist takes obscenity from life and by presenting it (perhaps as more desirable than in real life) injects it back into real life where real readers are encouraged to perpetuate the obscenity portrayed by emulating it. In the *Madame Bovary* judgment,[91] the book was criticised for "a vulgar and shocking realism"; in the *Fleurs Du Mal* judgment,[92] the six offending poems were chastised for a "vulgar realism offending decency". By contrast, in the *God's Little Acre* judgment,[93] Magistrate Benjamin Greenspan said that "the author has set out to paint a realistic picture", "such pictures necessarily contain certain details", "the court may not require this author to put refined language into the mouths of primitive people." Similarly, Stable J in *The Philanderer* case[94] approved of realism and acknowledged that crudeness in literature revealed an aspect of reality.

Not many judges seem aware of the imaginative element in all art (even in realism). Art is not life; is never precisely it, and never claims

[89] 403 US 15 (1971).
[90] Brittain, n. 16 above, at 129–30.
[91] N. 6 above.
[92] N. 34 above.
[93] N. 32 above.
[94] N. 30 above.

to be; the nearest it comes is being realistic not reality, for art portrays reality in its bounds wherein the stimulus of reality is ordered, determined, by the artist. Charles J alerts us to the dichotomy in one of the *Wilde* cases[95]: "confound no man with the characters he has created".[96] Art is apart. It is also a passive medium in that it is there to be received; it does not inflict, it offers. Even the most realistic art can never offer reality. As Maurice Blanchot has said in the *The book to come*: "[t]o be an artist is to never know there is already an art, to never know there is already a world". Art does not create blood and skin: it is a world of paint or words or some other medium, and any actions in it, such as in dance, are set in that medium, and the audience is invited to view.

Judges frequently pay attention to artistic intent or purpose and less frequently divorce it from motive. In the *Madame Bovary* judgment,[97] we read of "the unique end"; "the end that he [Flaubert] was desirous of reaching". Judge Woolsey in *Ulysses* [98] said that the court's first question was whether the intent was pornographic; whether the book was written for the purpose of exploiting obscenity. Arguably the most prominent characteristic of James Hanley's *Boy* was the serious purpose of the author: when the novel was prosecuted, the court overlooked it.[99] Judge Breitel in a *Fanny Hill* case[100] spoke of "motivation" and Cutter J in *Cancer*[101] spoke of the book's serious "purpose". In *People* v. *Gonzales*[102] it was judicially observed that at least certain books purported to serve the purposes of art. Should that purporting be praised in deciding whether something is condemnable obscenity or legitimate art? To suggest X is an art-work to a degree redeems it by merely that suggestion. In *Piarowski*,[103] mention was made of calculation as opposed to motivation: "art calculated to shock, to outrage, to '*épater le bourgeois*' " whereas in *Ginzburg* v. *US*[104] Douglas J said "a book should stand on its own, irrespective of the reasons why it was written". What an artist intends his painting

---

[95] N. 45 above.
[96] If art is a world of its own, can its author be identified with it and punished for it in the "real" world?
[97] N. 43 above.
[98] N. 22 above.
[99] T.E. Lawrence, author of *The Seven Pillars of Wisdom*, described the book's conviction as "monstrous" in a letter of 5 Apr. 1935 to C.J. Greenwood.
[100] N. 27 above, at 229–306.
[101] N. 64 above.
[102] N. 23 above.
[103] N. 15 above.
[104] N. 89 above.

to be when he sets brush to canvas is vastly different from his motive
for putting the brush on canvas; whether Shakespeare "did it for the
money" or not is a separate issue from his mental attitude as he
worked on the product he was creating. Even if there is an intention
that the created work be shocking, should this derogate from its right
to be treated as much as valid art as a piece not intended to be shocking? Who can decide what was the writer's artistic purpose other than
the artist? Who is qualified to speculate about his motive?

When art is viewed in a law court it is viewed with legal eyes. In
this context, the reader of a literary work, be he a judge or a juryman,
is not a reader for pleasure. To what degree are judges aware that art
is being viewed out of context when viewed with legal vision or at
least in a legal stadium? In *Hannegan* v. *Esquire*,[105] the court was
appalled by the idea of art conforming to the norm of an official. This
sentiment is seldom expressed. R. Ammi Cutter J in *Cancer*[106] said:
"[i]t is not the function of judges . . . to say that an author must regard
vulgarity as unnecessary to his portrayal of particular scenes or characters or to establish particular ideas". In the *God's Little Acre* case
Magistrate Greenspan said: "[t]he court may not say a portrayal of the
sex side of life with brutal frankness should not have been created at
all". No judge has ever simply said "[o]f course, art should not really
be here at all. We have no right to judge it. It is not our world. Art
invites us to go to it. It is not for us to drag it here with antagonistic
hands with an alien purpose."

In England, France and America much judicial attention is paid to
the changing nature of community sensibility. In *People* v.
Gonzales,[107] reference was made to increase in public sophistication;
in *Roth*,[108] Douglas J observed that "the test that suppresses a cheap
tract today can suppress a literary gem tomorrow". In a French case
of 24 November 1981,[109] it was observed that the notion of "good
morals" was "susceptible of evolution", that the "collective conscience" shifts its positions. Paradoxically, judicial views on what
aspect of this conscience can be harmed differ radically. In the
September in Quinze case,[110] Sir G. Dodson voiced acute concern for
the harmful effects of obscenity on the young, "the pollution of the
fountain of our nation blood", whereas Stable J, in a much-cited

---

[105] 327 US146 (1946).
[106] N. 64 above.
[107] N. 23 above.
[108] 354 US 476 (1957).
[109] Cass. 24 Nov. 1981, Revue de Droit Pénal et de Criminologie, Vol. 64, 1984, at 1065.
[110] 17 Sept. 1954 at the Old Bailey, London.

judgment,[111] asked somewhat incredulously whether we were to set our literary standards by the vulnerabilities of 14-year-old girls. The needs of the "collective conscience" are determined without collective consistency by the judiciary.

Bald judicial statements on artistic value are legion but explanations of these evaluations are scarce. In a French case of 10 July 1973,[112] the court was content in condemning the material to say that it was "devoid of all literary value". These dogmatic value judgements without detail are common. Judge Desmond in *Cancer*[113] did explain his artistic appraisal which can be summarised in his poetic phrase "no glory, no beauty, no stars—just mud . . .". Such exercises in quasi-literary criticism are rare for the judiciary. Their absence is particularly anomalous in France where the law requires judges to give reasons in these cases of "outrage of good morals". Occasionally, judges coin specific terms to express art or literature that is allegedly obscene but not yet legally deemed such: in *Roth*,[114] Douglas J refers to "sex literature" and, later, "noxious literature". Posner CJ in *Piarowski*[115] is content to use the term "controversial works of art" whereas in *Roth*[116] we have "the smut artist".

Preoccupied with the limits of decency that art and literature must not traverse, very few judges acknowledge that all art is new. Learned Hand J mentioned the originality of *Ulysses* in that decision,[117] and Judge Frank, in *Roth*,[118] made a plea that is seldom attended to in obscenity cases: "originality, not too plentiful, should be cherished not stifled". This, together with an almost universal judicial non-vocalisation of the need for a plurality of opinions to be voiced for a society to increase in civilisation, is shameful in comparison to the emphasis on cultural richness, diversity and complexity in a society such as classical Athens.[119]

There is a complete lack of judicial pronouncement on the fact that art is always sensuous, if not, of course, sensual, and that a thing called artistic distance exists: art's aim is not to stimulate action but

[111] N. 4 above.
[112] Cass. (Ch.Crim.).
[113] N. 27 above.
[114] N. 108 above.
[115] N. 15 above.
[116] N. 108 above.
[117] N. 22 above.
[118] N. 108 above.
[119] See, e.g., David Cohen, "Law, Society and Homosexuality In Classical Athens", *Past and Present*, Nov. 1987) for details of the accommodation of a multiplicity of sexual tastes in a highly sophisticated legal framework.

foster contemplation. A few voices in the cultural wilderness do however extol the virtues of expressing the truth such as Stable J in *The Philanderer*[120] and Learned Hand J in *Ulysses*.[121] "Truth", said Magistrate Greenspan in his judgment on *God's Little Acre*,[122] "should always be accepted as a justification of literature". It is somewhat ironic that the importance of the spiritual aspect of life that art and creative literature foster is seldom emphasised in law courts, and yet care is said to be taken there of society's collective conscience. There is rarely a judicial acknowledgement that morality and obscenity can be compatible and that there are many more demonstrably harmful "immoralities" to be restrained than the artistic or literary treatment of the basic human act of sexual intercourse or erotic display of nudity.

Very few judges recognise the industry artists and creative writers employ to achieve their creative results. In the *Madame Bovary* decision,[123] the court acknowledged that the novel had been seriously worked on for a long time. All too often, though, judges completely ignore the fact that most creative work is the result of considerable effort on the part of the artist or writer. The judge, moreover, embodying law, can radically circumscribe an artist's life, for his job entails such regulatory power. The artist's vocation calls him to creation, not regulation. In art he expresses and is free until a legal mind, allocated to protect potential viewers of his art, directs the need of society to clamp him down, relying on its own judgment within the bounds of a given legal framework. A judge is allocated the unenviable job of deciding the necessity of society's protection against an allegedly obscene work. Is he to be not only lawyer but psychiatrist, psychologist, moralist, sociologist? If so, it is regrettable he is not more often artist too, and better acquainted with the nature and aims of that which he judges. Replete with newness in the arena of legal consistency and traditions, art is particularly vulnerable in his charge. Why not let it be free to educate and civilise even in its rejection, by individuals themselves, much more vigorous and critical than the abstracted susceptible "collective conscience"?

[120] N. 4 above.
[121] N. 22 above.
[122] N. 32 above.
[123] N. 43 above.

CONCLUSIONS

The general principle that judges cannot be arbiters of taste is central to all Western legal systems.[124] To permit the opposite is to jeopardise the certainty and consistency of the law. This survey has revealed a range of judicial taste on what art is and how to attend to art in a legal arena. The judicial taste observable in this study is never judicially vocalised as taste. Taste is exercised but not admitted. It is inconceivable that there would be no exercise of judicial taste in a legal zone where art-concerns figure. Judicial exercising of taste, patent as it is, should be legally recognised and not illicit.

Judicial art appreciation is not the product of the distinctive national legal system in which it operates but, rather, the product of individuals in the same professional role. There should be undogmatic guidelines on how judges should appraise art to avoid inconsistencies and inequity, whilst at the same time operating a system of public morality law allowing for the broad judicial discretion the subjectivity of the field demands.

The French legal approach of deliberately and openly leaving much within the realm of individual judicial initiative accommodates the highly subjectively-evaluatable components of the law of "outrage of good morals" with a compatibly flexible method of appraisal. This is preferable to the more rule-dominated Anglo-American approach, though it raises fears of judicial despotism in important matters of taste and morality.

The French definitely lead America and England in liberal attitudes to the obscene in art: a century divided the French grand prosecutions of Flaubert and Baudelaire and the English one of Lawrence; moreover, the exoneration of the convicted Baudelaire by a later French age[125] suggests a legal culture not solely preoccupied with the maintenance of consistency of its own mechanism at the expense of appreciation of durable artistic worth.

The greater tradition of art in France is probably the cultural source of judicial sympathy to "obscene" art being in advance of that in England and America.[126] The most conspicuous victim of England's and America's tardiness was clearly the much-prosecuted

[124] In contemporary western-democratic Roman-Germanic and common law families alike.

[125] Dalloz périodique, 1949, I, 348; legislation of 25 Sept. 1946.

[126] French judges are also more inclined to make subtle artistic distinctions than their Anglo-American counterparts.

D.H. Lawrence; his works, like others of authors of widely acclaimed merit, thrived unhindered in France at a time when English law, in particular, was still unenlightened.[127]

The basic problem of the art law/public morality law overlap is the limited recognition of the irreducibility of a complex area to a few finely-chosen legal balances, tests and maxims and the equally limited recognition of the need for reception of non-legal aids to inform the presiding tribunal in matters about which they are inexpert. What is needed in public morality law that has to address art issues is not a search for ideal legal criteria for crystallising the conceptual complexities involved, but an altogether more flexible structure avoiding set criteria and allowing for the airing of specialised opinions in an atmosphere more conducive to justice in the immediate case. The way could be made open for special art-law tribunals, the precise operation of which would require further very careful consideration. They would be consistent with an advanced autopoietic[128] view and foster a more art-comprehending juridification of art concerns in a systematic self-processing.

---

[127] It was not until 1996 that an unexpurgated version of *Lady Chatterley's Lover* appeared legally in Japan.

[128] Gunther Teubner (ed.), *Autopoietic Law: A New Approach To Law And Society* (De Gruyter, Berlin, 1988).

Artistic as a Category and a Criterion

INTRODUCTION

In this chapter, the author examines how the law gives copyright protection to the artistic, with or without resort to specified criteria for determining what is artistic, depending on the area of protection.[1] For comparative purposes I have equated the French "droit d'auteur" with English and American copyright law,[2] as they cover substantially the same subject: for my purposes, intellectual property rights in original artistic work. Throughout, the focus is the interaction of artistic requirements in a legal structure with the functional demands of that structure and the subtle and complex way in which artistic considerations are assimilated into copyright law's basic mechanism, particularly its quality tests that have art at their centre.[3]

Originality is the dominant working concept in the copyright law of all three jurisdictions but is variously defined and applied. In American law it is coterminous with a requirement of creativity and

---

[1] Sometimes artistic character (in addition to merit) is specifically excluded as a matter of judicial notice, e.g. in s. 3(1)(a) of the old Copyright Act 1956 (as amended), referred to in brief form in other Sections of this ch. S. 3(1) reads: "In this Act 'artistic work' means a work of any of the following descriptions, that is to say:

> (a) the following, irrespective of artistic quality, namely paintings, sculptures, drawings, engravings and photographs;
> (b) works of architecture, being either buildings or models for buildings;
> (c) works of artistic craftsmanship, not falling within either of the preceding paragraphs."

[2] The law also pertaining to other areas of the UK is referred to as "English" law to avoid continuous laboriousness of expression (England favoured because Parliament is there). The term "American" law applies only to the law of the USA, in this context federal law (see n. 7, below).

[3] The situation is far more nuanced and less satisfactory than Caroline Carreau's strangely naïve acceptance would have it: "[i]n the name of the harmony which law essentially seeks, in the events and ideas that gave it birth, in the principles that embody it, the legal approach to art corresponds to an eclectic and liberal view of intellectual creation" (Carreau, "Mérite et droit d'auteur", *Revue Internationale du Droit d'Auteur*, Vol. 109, July 1981, at 8).

in French law it requires evidence of the impact of a personality in a created work, hence its use of the term *"œuvres d'esprit"*. In English law, originality is formally divorced from the notion of creation.[4]

With respect to the approach of the law to artistic works, and how they are defined, the English law's primary source was the Copyright Act 1956 (as amended), notably section 3, and the case law under it, which remains highly relevant. In November 1988, the Copyright, Designs and Patents Act was passed in England, the provisions of which have entered into force gradually and not *en bloc*[5]; those provisions supersede those of the 1956 Act. Equivalent in authority in France was the statute of 11 March 1957 and subsequent allied legislation;[6] this law of 11 March 1957 has been codified in the Code of Intellectual Property, which dates from the law of 1 July 1992. American copyright law emerges from Article 1, section 8, of the Constitution and is now governed in federal law by the Copyright Act of 1976.[7]

HOW THE LAW AWARDS COPYRIGHT PROTECTION

The role of artistic considerations in copyright law is ambiguous. Although the artistic is protected, legal criteria for defining what is artistic are rarely employed. The artistic is just one object of copy-

---

[4] "The prohibition of merit . . . implies seeking and funding a substitute criterion. Faced with this imperative, judges turned towards a concept less fluctuating a priori than that of merit: the originality of works" (*ibid.*, at 10). It will be seen that Carreau's observation of French law goes further in England where the originality requirement is much more highly de-subjectivised than its French equivalent, and therefore more certain, but not necessarily more appropriate, given the nature of the subject matter regulated.

[5] S. 305(3) of the 1988 Act. Part 1 (pertaining to copyright) came into force on 1 Aug. 1989 by SI 1989 No. 816 (9 May 1989).

[6] E.g., the law of 3 July 1985 on photographs which has not effectively removed the shadow of the difficulties inherent in the 1957 legislation. See Claude Colombet, *Propriété Littéraire et Artistique (et Droits Voisins)* (3rd edn., Paris, Dalloz, 1986), at 99. The 1957 statute, in art. 3, appertains to creative works in the very broadest sense, including literary and artistic works.

[7] Note, especially, the unexhaustive list of subject-matter eligible for copyright protection set out in s. 102, and s. 106 which may be said to identify the general nature of the rights which fall within the scope of American copyright. The 1976 Copyright Act dramatically reduced, without quite eliminating, the role of state copyright law (which does not contribute anything significant to the "definition of the artistic" bias of this monograph). S. 102(a)(8) of the 1976 Copyright Act, added by the Architectural Works Copyright Protection Act, includes "architectural works" as a category of copyrightable subject matter (Pub. L. No. 101–650, Tit. VII, 104 Stat. 5133 (1 Dec. 1990)). Literary works are included according to s. 102(a)(1) and pictorial, graphic and sculptural works by s. 102(a)(5).

right protection which exists to protect products of original labour. Because the original is broader than the artistic, because copyright's ambit is wider than the protection of the artistic, the dominant criterion for ascertaining the object of such protection is originality. This is itself an ambiguous term used in many different legal senses. In French and American law, it co-operates with a requirement, usually simply an assumption, of creativity. English law presumes no such co-operation of originality with creativity (no such implicit relationship). Notions of creativity are allied to notions of the artistic,[8] so in France and America, where creativity is linked to the test of originality, artistic considerations feature more markedly and overtly. Although definitionally creativity is the more obvious avenue by which artistic considerations are invoked as working criteria in determining the copyrightable, there are certain ways in which they also feature in the operation of the bare originality requirement.[9] Moreover, all three jurisdictions examined specify the artistic as one particular category of copyright protection[10] and give it attention as a unit notwithstanding that the provisions relating to that unit are somewhat unintegrated and therefore cause formal problems—for example, there is no clear-cut unity or division of treatment of the non-motion visual arts on the one hand and creative literature on the other[11]; if they are treated as distinct categories, classification problems are posed by phenomena such as algorithms which are not clearly artistic as opposed to literary in nature (or vice versa). One of

[8] Creative, as artistic, implies skill, and creativity denotes power of the imaginative faculty beyond mere construction, allying it to the artistic (as illustrated, for example, in the term "creative writing").

[9] In the exclusion of the trivial and the commonplace from copyright protection, for example.

[10] French judicial legal practice traditionally regroups "works of the spirit" (protected by art. 2 of the law of 11 Mar. 1957) into sub-categories including artistic works. The "plastic arts" are an aspect of the latter-mentioned category, and include paintings, sculpture, architecture and prints. Copyright law in France is classically termed "the law of literary and artistic property". In England, s. 3 of the Copyright Act 1956 is entitled "Copyright in artistic works"; s. 4 of the Copyright, Designs and Patents Act 1988 is entitled "Artistic Works". S. 102 of the 1976 American Copyright Act details pictorial, graphic and sculptural works as a category of "works of authorship" (to which copyright protection is given under s. 102); s. 101 defines pictorial, graphic and sculptural works as "two-dimensional and three-dimensional works of fine, graphic and applied art . . .".

[11] In English law, literary works were covered by s. 2 and artistic works by s. 3 (of the 1956 Copyright Act). However, here, as in France and America, the basic "originality" requirements that apply to one realm often also pertain to the other; text-books dealing with the originality requirement, e.g., may deal with it in the "literary works" chapter and cross-refer the reader of the "artistic works" chapter to the "literary works" one for the bulk of the explanation of the originality requirement.

Kandinsky's abstracts presenting his mathematical ideas could be said to be as much literary as artistic for, on one view, it is meaningful notation (which can be "read" though legibility is, in fact, not a requirement for something to qualify as literature in English copyright law[12]). US copyright law protects "writings"[13] but in a very extended sense, incorporating within the term many other art forms than the word literally connotes. American copyright law protects the "useful" arts[14] but, a little paradoxically, a predominance of utility in the artwork can preclude copyrightability.[15] French legislation's wider terms[16] avoid the issue of rigid classifications in the literary and artistic realm and facilitate the limiting of semantic and logical anomalies (without, of course, solving the basic difficulties of the ubiquitous art definition problem with which the *droit d'auteur*, no less than other copyright laws,[17] is faced).

There is a subtle relationship in copyright law between value[18] of a product and its copyrightability. English copyright law adopts the rough test that what is worth copying is worth protecting,[19] whereas the criteria for copyright protection are said to avoid any assessments of value.[20] In all three jurisdictions, there is a reluctance to adopt an explicit criterion of value in the legal test for copyrightability.[21] The test of originality is said to be value-free, and yet there is legal acceptance of a standard of value (albeit defused) that must be achieved before a work is copyrightable.[22] In the artistic realm the underlying

[12] In a similar way, a strip cartoon may enjoy literary copyright in addition to the artistic one.

[13] The constitutional term.

[14] The constitutional term again.

[15] Note difficult cases, such as *Poe* v. *Missing Persons*, 745 F 2d.1238 (9th Cir. 1984), in which the issue was whether "Aquatint No. 5" was a "swimsuit" or a "work of art which portayed an article of clothing". The 1976 copyright statute does not provide for the copyright of useful articles except to the extent that their designs incorporate artistic features that can be identified separately from the functional elements of the articles (see *Kieselstein-Cord* v. *Accessories By Pearl, Inc.*, 632 F 2d.989 (2nd Cir. 1980). The relationship between copyright and industrial design is awkward in many other systems than those I examine.

[16] Art. 3 of the law of 11 Mar. 1957, now codified.

[17] The general equation of *droit d'auteur* with copyright law is, of course, internationally accepted, not radical.

[18] Not, of course, price.

[19] Approved by Petersen J in the much-cited case of *University of London Press Ltd* [1916] 2 Ch. 601 at 608.

[20] A common statement about tests which are intended to be "objective" in application.

[21] For the obvious reason that value judgements are not considered congruent with the long-arm function of law which is not traditionally seen as having an explicit role as cultural adviser or dictator.

[22] See "A Further Look At Quality Tests", below.

operational value system is hard to identify but definitely exists (albeit indistinctly[23]) even if the criteria of value themselves are not strongly emphasised and are not *prima facie* artistic.[24]

In French law, originality is founded on creative origin[25] and in American law the requirements of creativity and originality are indistinguishable.[26] In divorcing its concept of originality from creation and creativity, English law avoids imposing in its criteria for copyrightability any suggestion of artistic prejudice that the other two jurisdictions fuse with originality. To equate creativity with originality is to adopt the Romantic conception of creativity as the unqualifiedly new; such a notion of creativity excludes copying, and there is consequently no accommodation of the older idea of creativity as imitation with enrichment.[27] In its working concepts, English copyright law does not promote one type of creativity over another because what it protects is simply what is original irrespective of creation or creativity: there is no nexus in the concept used to protect it between what is protected and a cultural phenomenon. In this way the legal test for copyrightability is not contaminated[28] by the uncertainty that notions of creation and creativity import. *A fortiori*, the legal test remains a legal test uncoloured by associations with artistic culture that creation and creativity imply.

Strict copyright law doctrine dictates that artistic merely describes the mode in which the work is brought into existence and is rarely an explicit criterion for copyright protection. On the rare occasions when it is so used, it reveals itself as ill-equipped for such a function, for what exactly does "artistic" connote?[29] This is perhaps one of the

[23] Presumably not covertly in conspiratorial fashion. Contrast Anthony Blunt's influential covert infusion of Soviet values into the British approach to the history of art—see D. Stephen Pepper, "Is Academic History Controlled by the KGB?", *The Journal of Art* (International Edition), Vol. 1, No. 5, May 1989, and John Costello's major book *The Mask Of Treachery* (Collins, London, 1988).

[24] See "A Further Look at Quality Tests", below.

[25] Derived from Roman law, Dig. Liv. XLI, tome 1,65, princ. Liv. XLVII, tomes 2, 14.

[26] Merged, e.g., by Miller J in *Burrow-Giles Lithographic Co.* v. *Sarony* 111 US 53,4 S Ct. 279 (1884). At the beginning of the general revision process, the 1961 Report of the Register of Copyrights recommended that in the new statute a copyrightable work "must represent an appreciable amount of creative authorship" (House Comm. on the Judiciary, 87th Cong., 1st Sess., 9 (1961)). This standard was abandoned but creativity is still fused with originality to the degree that the American originality test can still be termed a creative originality test.

[27] Richard A. Posner, *Law and Literature: A Misunderstood Relation* (Harvard University Press, New Haven, Conn., 1988), 349.

[28] In theory, understood.

[29] See, particularly, the general conclusions of this work.

most subjective and controversial issues in the definitional realm, causing general difficulty as well as specific problems in copyright law. "Artistic" does not possess a clear enough definitional core to be practical as a legal criterion. Its definition is nearly entirely penumbra, though, in terms of description, art has some recognised classes. There are traditional classifications of art—painting, drawing, sculpture . . .—but there is no definitive definition of the artistic *per se*. Art is a collective noun but we do not know the ambit of its collection. Artistic is an adjective connoting the quality of this collection but its metaphorical use is great and this expands its sense even further. Law requires clarity, of itself and of language, and law as an institution strives to make as its tests terms it can know as unambiguously as possible so that their legal application is as certain as possible.[30] The "fuzzy" term "artistic" is a definitional nightmare for the æsthetician as well as the lawmaker, and for the latter it is particularly dissatisfying because of the conclusive nature of the identifying function he requires of it to lead to a definitive legal result and consistent practice.

The term "artistic quality" is popular in common usage, but in copyright law differentiation is made between artistic character and artistic merit (which can both mean artistic quality) and artistic quality *per se* is removed from the language of the legal mechanism. To be copyrightable, purportedly artistic works require artistic character but those that do never require artistic merit.[31] The law excludes evaluation of artistic merit from its testing for copyright protection because the law is deemed not to be an arbiter of taste. Moreover, the law purports not to employ æsthetic considerations in discerning artistic character which seems at least quasi-paradoxical (but may be indirectly connected with rejection of the idealist theory of art based on beauty[32]). The question then remains: how is artistic character legally established? The apparent answer (seemingly simple) is "by the application of the adjective artistic to a work".[33] Artistic character is not really discerned because that implies the objective existence of

---

[30] Compare the situation in chemistry: if litmus is not first identified, it cannot be used as an acid test.

[31] See, further, "A Further Look At Quality Tests", below.

[32] Lord Simon of Glaisdale makes reference to this theory in the *Hensher* case [1976] AC at 93–4 (see below). This is a rare instance of serious treatment of art theory in the course of a copyright judgment.

[33] By either a judge or an expert witness (depending on the individual judge's reception to expert witnesses in this context: note the variety of judicial attitudes expressed on this matter in *Hensher* (below).

artistic character (there to be discerned); someone, rather, decides whether the work is artistic and says so.[31] It is difficult to believe that this decision is made without reference to æsthetic considerations or artistic merits: what else remains to denote artistic character?[35] Few judicial attempts are made to explain how the identification of artistic character is achieved.[36]

Cherpillod says that creation is the psychological act which gives birth to the new value i.e. is the mother/source of originality[37] (rather like an idea that precedes its material form). Consequent upon this interpretation, creation as well as idea are uncopyrightable, whereas the original and form are. I disagree with it. French law has as its focus creation as in the full act: idea and its material formation.[38] Although it is generally acknowledged that copyright protects forms, not ideas, only the US Copyright Act draws upon a firm distinction between form and idea to delimit the field of protection. Cherpillod says to be original is to be new[39] (and result from the activity of the author), but all three jurisdictions discussed here exclude "novelty" as a criterion for copyright protection.[40] Cherpillod rightly contrasts originality with banality; and if it is true that the law does not protect the commonplace, that implies a judgement of an artistic order. Emphasis in all three jurisdictions is on material produced, but in England alone is there no necessary legal cognizance of a creative step. Creation and creativity draw notions of the artistic in;[41] the English formulation of the "originality" test denies even that word its artistic association in the formulation's content-neutral *modus operandi*. English law gives a copyright based simply on the statute itself, whereas French law gives a right based on principle ("creation"), as does American law ("creative originality"). With the

[34] Carreau does not doubt a painstaking judicial "search" for artistic character: N. 3 above, at 14.

[35] Is the attraction of merit irresistible?: see *ibid*., at 82.

[36] None try to explain the complex psychological process involved when the viewer engages with the object before a decision on artistic character is produced. Do judges tacitly accept that this is a process of emotions, and avoid stating it, so that it is not formally registered that they make such judgement from their subjective "feeling" side (less that in this instance they have to)?

[37] Ivan Cherpillod, *L'objet du droit d'auteur* (CEDIDAC, Lausanne, 1985), 125.

[38] Hence the French emphasis on the author as well as the product. The French use of the term *"œuvres d'esprit"* (for copyright protection) also indicates the highly personal aspect of the French approach: "works of the mind or spirit" are protected, not merely results of industry (*"travaux"*).

[39] N. 37 above, at 142.

[40] See "A Further Look at Quality Tests", below.

[41] See n. 8 above.

common emphasis on the preserving of specific "forms" (neatly illustrated by the protection of the creative "pattern" of poetry), copyright law protects the artistic in the material sense in all three
jurisdictions.

The elimination of artistic merit in French law can be traced back
to nineteenth-century case law given statutory confirmation in the
1902 legislation. Article 2[42] of the law of 11 March 1957, which is
section L.112.1 of the new code, states the law explicitly, excluding
artistic merit as a criterion for *"droit d'auteur"* protection.[43] In English
and American copyright law, this exclusion is also judicially recognised (in *Hensher* as a "trend"[44]), arguably affirmed so consistently as
to be a rule[45] of common law. It is not always expressed as a proscription of artistic merit *per se*, for example section 3(1) of the 1956
Copyright Act (England) gave protection "irrespective of artistic
quality" to certain established categories of art, e.g. painting, but
retained a requirement of being artistic for "works of artistic craftsmanship" where "artistic" is interpreted to mean artistic in character.
In America, an abandonment of judgements of merit in ascertaining
the protectable in copyright arguably began with *Bleistein*,[46] but as in
England there is no specific legislative prohibition of artistic merit *per
se* as a copyright criterion, and it is a personal contention that matters
of merit coalesce with those of personal origin[47] in the common
English, French and American test of originality that as a legal term
of art gains an imprecise and extended meaning. More especially, the
American copyright concept of originality is inextricably fused with
that of creativity and the French emphasis is traditionally on the protection of "creation".[48]

---

[42] Art. 2 protects "authors' rights in all works of the spirit, whatever their type, form,
expression, merit or end".

[43] Pouillet, in *Traité de la Propriété Littéraire et Artistique* (Lucas, Litec, 1994), at 38 says that
the law protects blindly and weighs neither merit nor importance. This is an expression of
an ideal or a hope not a fact.

[44] But at 97 of *Hensher* [1976] AC, Lord Kilbrandon clearly sees judicial æsthetic appre-
ciations as permissible, but not required in this particular context. (Judgments in *Hensher*
deserve particularly close scrutiny not least because it is the leading case on the legal definition of "artistic" in English copyright law, without parallel in America and France.)

[45] Or a principle, depending on whether you adopt a Hartian or a Dworkinian standpoint.

[46] *Bleistein* v. *Donaldson Lithographing Co.*, 188 US 239, 23 S Ct. 298 (1903).

[47] In practice, despite what is formally held.

[48] A point repeated in my analysis because creation is so centrally congruent with the
artistic embracing person and process as much as product, hence *"droit d'auteur"*. Contrast
English law's more impersonal priorities relating to material rather than moral; witness
English copyright's tardiness in adopting any element of the *"droit moral"*.

A semantic consideration of some importance cannot be ignored. It is far from obvious that artistic is not a term of approbation *per se*, necessarily implying merit in the object to which it is applied because it definitely embraces skill.[49] It is tempting to conclude that applied to an object in a simple phrase of two words it always suggests credit, for example "artistic arrangement", "artistic child", "artistic chair".[50] However, were an object intended to be eminently practical, would the application of the epithet "artistic" to it demean rather than enhance it? If merit is implicitly involved when the word "artistic" is applied, can judges purport to avoiding evaluating merit (and finding it) in a given object when they attribute the adjective "artistic" to it?

Photographs physically exist as a result of a machine, a fact which set them apart legally from other artistic works, and caused much legal indecision as to their artistic character, especially in the early days of the camera. Law was accustomed to accepting only the results of direct manual creation as art, whether it be by pen, brush or chisel. The arrival of photography was, of course, a hurdle for art law in all jurisdictions, but it posed increased problems the more it became obvious that it was a technique with huge economic repercussions: even if photography had limited artistic character as far as art was traditionally recognised, art law had to embrace this new technique, and, if necessary, æstheticise it to enable new expanding and economically important industries based on film to gain the protection of copyright laws. Nineteenth-century copyright law, not renowned for approving of innovation, initially found it difficult to accept that photography was an art because of its peculiarly mechanical origin. The problem was particularly acute in France where creation on the part of an author gave rise to copyright protection—where was the author's creativity in merely operating a machine? In America, photography provided a problem of classification: was it a "writing"[51] in the extended constitutional sense? What was and was not within this legal term of art was a problem already familiar to American courts, so photography was eventually simply added to the list of objects so adjudged and included that had little or no relation to writing in the literal sense.

Despite the similar emphasis on creative authorship as in France, in America, then, photography posed no significant problem for

---

[49] See the *Oxford English Dictionary*'s definition of artistic.

[50] N. 35 above.

[51] "Writing" in its extended sense: compare the much more literal definition of writing in s. 178 of the UK Copyright Act of 1988.

copyright law that had not been tackled before: judges were used to accepting works literally unconnected with "writings" under that head (a similar phenomenon occurring with "speech" in the First Amendment). In France, with the emphasis on personal creation as the basic principle for copyright protection, photography had to undergo a more philosophical examination to satisfy the substantive demand for creation not *prima facie* evident in the photographic process. The course of this examination was arguably constantly underpinned by consideration of economic realities that demanded photography copyright protection as a matter of urgency for new industries based on it.[52] However, French *jurisprudence* initially opposed photography on the ground of its seeming dissociation with creation and personal creator alike (from *"esprit"*). As it began to change sentiment, it fluctuated in its techniques for accommodating technology's new "art" with a frequency and unpredictability that called into question the solidity of its authority. This sad history will be briefly traced.

At the beginning of the twentieth century, there were three co-existing French judicial attitudes to photography's entitlement to *"droit d'auteur"* protection, one excluding photographs altogether on account of the chemical and mechanical nature of the processes of their origin, one including all photographs because what were produced were pictures and therefore art, and a third protecting only those photographs with artistic character. In 1925, the Orléans Court of Appeal[53] introduced a selective criterion, deciding that photographs deserved protection when the photographer had adduced sufficient proof of taste, ability and discernment in his work.[54] The Court of Appeal noted that connection with sport did not exclude the artistic, reversing a Seine Correctional Tribunal judgment of 1932[55] that because the photographs in issue were taken in an aeroplane their quality was predominantly "sporting". The Orléans criterion clearly infringed the basic principle accepted in French *jurisprudence* that account should never be taken of merit, and it was substituted by the "imprint of personality"[56] test which involved the discerning of a photographer's personal stamp from, for example, choice of subject, lighting technique, angle of shot. . . . This approach

[52] For a more detailed account of the economic aspect, see Bernard Edelman, *Ownership of the Image* (trans. E. Kingdom, Routledge & Kegan Paul, London, 1979).

[53] Orléans, 4 Feb. 1925, D.H.1926.336.

[54] This had repercussions for interpretation in other cases (see the case at n. 53 above).

[55] Trib. corr. Seine, 16 Mar. 1932, D.H.1932.39.

[56] Trib. civ. Seine, 31 May 1944, D.1946.117.

had the disadvantage of potentially including all photographs indiscriminately. When the statute of 11 March 1957 was enacted, this provided protection for a special category of "photographs with artistic character", *inter alia*, which envisaged and expected no evaluation of merit.[57] Considerations of merit inevitably crept in. Although the law of 3 July 1985[58] set out to remove all ambiguity, photographs are still assimilated uncomfortably by the law relating to artistic property. Given the distinct conceptual difficulty they present (being arguably only quasi-artistic as a genus), they might be deserving of autonomous protection as is the case for fashion creations.[59] French law might then find its *"droit d'auteur"* provisions conceptually less compromised.

In England, photographs do not have to bear the stamp of creation but, rather, originality: a requirement easy to satisfy. The showing of sufficient relevant skill became English law's arguably artistic test in this realm (a mere photograph of a photograph, for example, is still not copyrightable). In contradistinction to French law's emphasis, English law's focus under the 1956 Act was on the material product's ownership: the owner of the film, not the photographer, held the copyright. Relevant skill had to be employed by the photographer but, strangely, this did not furnish copyright ownership. The protected was he who owned the film.[60] The "creator" (in French terms) or simply "photographer" (in English ones) was displaced by the owner who did not need to be skilful himself. The photographer's "art" provided the reason for another's right which took priority legally over that art. In not paying attention to art as a special factor for legal consideration, English law circumvented the problems French law unsuccessfully embraced.

[57] Although this was foreseeable. See Carreau, n. 3 above, at 110 and more generally, for an interesting and extensive review of French *jurisprudence* in this field that is without equal.

[58] Art. 11 of the First Title of the 3 July 1985 statute amends the law of 11 Mar. 1957, art. 3. The words "photographic works of artistic or documentary character and those of the same character obtained by a procedure analogous to photography" are replaced by the words "photographic works and those achieved with the aid of techniques analogous to photography". The latter have to accommodate a very broad field of technological and artistic innovation. For example, artist Tim Head's intention is not to paint but to imitate painting, so he has a fascination with technical experiment: photocopying printing designs on sheets of plastic with an ink-jet scanning system. It is arguable that such art-forms require new titles divorced from photography.

[59] By the law of 12 Mar. 1952 (but this is arguably inferior to the protective force of the law of 11 Mar. 1957 which also applies to fashion creations).

[60] A functionally efficient clear-cut scheme, but is it fair? Is it altered by s. 11(1) of the relatively new 1988 (UK) Copyright Act which gives copyright priority to authors? Presumably so.

Despite formally divorcing its criterion of originality from artistic or creative associations, English law uses artistic character as a litmus test for copyright protection for works of artistic craftsmanship. English law's wisdom (at least for the cause of efficiency) in trying to keep its criterion of originality free from contamination with subjective assessments is strangely abandoned in its adoption here of the test of artistic character, with all its obvious applicational difficulties, as a definitive test for copyright protection in a growingly important context. *Hensher* stands as a monument of the inherent inappropriateness of artistic analysis (if not evaluation) as the basis for a legal test, not just in the context of artistic craftsmanship but also more generally.

George Hensher Ltd produced a prototype of a suite of furniture comprising a settee and two chairs of a design described as "boat-shaped". They brought an action for infringement of copyright[61] in their prototype, alleging that their work was a work of artistic craftsmanship within the meaning of section 3(i)(c) of the Copyright Act 1956. The term "artistic craftsmanship" was judicially construed in many contrasting ways, the case proceeding through the hierarchy of levels, culminating in an illuminating array of different approaches in the House of Lords. Areas of common judicial agreement were few, but included the attitude that it is not the role of the judiciary to make æsthetic evaluations, the expertise of judges being in the realm of law, language and language construction, not art, æsthetics or any matter of taste. No *a priori* principle of English law to this effect was invoked to suggest that the judiciary in *Hensher* was bound to adopt this stance but, forced to definition in an area of taste, the difficulty from the judicial position was how to apply the word "artistic" to an object while at the same time avoiding the exercise of taste. It is arguable that the application of the adjective "artistic" to an object emerges from only the subjective side of man. This would confound any judicial attempt at objectivity in this realm.

The judges in *Hensher* allow themselves a defining role but, strangely, are unaware of, or choose not to elaborate on, the more crucial role they also perform, which is the application of that definition to a specific object, which, in the case of "artistic", involves the application of taste because the word tends to anticipate the exercise of taste in its application. Although judges strive for as much definitional certainty as possible, so that the law's language is as clear as possible and applied as consistently as possible, unfortunately for legal

---

[61] *George Hensher Ltd* v. *Restawile Upholstery (Lancs.) Ltd* AC at 64–99.

purposes at least, as will be seen, the word "artistic" cannot be confined exhaustively by other verbal formulae. Moreover, its application cannot be a matter of the application of language alone when it, possibly more than any other, is a term of taste, not only an adjective that has to be applied to a noun but a quality that has to be felt of a thing or exuded by a thing so as to be inferred by the subjective senses. The response begged is not primarily a verbal one; the word comes later. In the case of furniture (in this instance), vision comes first and an assessment based on the experience of the viewer that manifests itself in an æsthetic power he applies to the furniture that can evoke many possible words including, perhaps, artistic. The law ignores this complex human process intrinsic to discernment of the artistic, and prior to the application of the word "artistic", because its desire is understandably a clarity of terms *per se* for its own purposes i.e. an avoidance of anything that suggests unruled subjectivity of judgement. The law, for purposes of the appearance of "objective" justice, strives to eschew subjectivity or unlimited or boundless discretion in its tests divorced from the arbitrariness subjective judgement suggests and which society does not permit of law for very good reasons. In the legal criterion of artistic we have a contradiction of cultures.

In the course of *Hensher's* procedure through the courts, few judges had the inclination or temerity to try to define "artistic" *per se*; attempts in this area were understandably less ambitious and more circumspect than forthright definition. At first instance,[62] Graham J said of the furniture: "[it] possessed distinctive characteristics of shape, form and finish justifying the appellation 'artistic' and distinguishing it from purely utilitarian articles". In the Court of Appeal,[63] Russell LJ indicated that this approach was insufficiently exacting: "[m]ere originality in points of design aimed at appealing to the eye as commercial selling points will not, in our judgment, suffice". The House of Lords were in agreement that possessing "eye appeal" alone was inadequate qualification for an object to be considered artistic. It would appear that what is required is more like "merit", but the Lords denied that artistic merit was in any way assessed in determining artistic character for the purposes of the 1956 Act's section 3(i)(c).

The Court of Appeal in *Hensher* found itself floundering. Unlike in the Lords where each Lord had a different but coherent view on what artistic character was, the Court of Appeal juggled with one

[62] 31 Oct. 1972.
[63] 4 July 1973.

discernible test indecisively and imprecisely. Russell LJ stated, "[i]n our judgment, if it can be said of a work of craftsmanship that it is an object that would be expected to be acquired or retained rather for its functional appeal than for any appeal to æsthetic taste, it is not within the scope of the phrase 'other works of artistic craftsman-ship'". This begs the practical question "whose expectation?" as well as "whose taste?"; *ex cathedra*, it cannot be an appeal to the taste of a law court judge because by judicial consensus (a putative principle of common law), his is disallowed as an element of a legal test for artis-tic character. Later, Russell LJ expounded:

> "in order to qualify as a work of artistic craftsmanship, there must at least be expected in an object or work that its utilitarian or functional appeal should not be the primary inducement to its acquisition or retention."

This is a slightly different test from the other he propounded (above): his later formula holds that something is not a work of artis-tic craftsmanship if acquired or retained primarily for its functional use in contrast to the balance of competing claims of functional and æsthetic appeal in particular which operated in his first formula. However, the Court of Appeal unambiguously concurred with Noel J in *Cuisenaire* v. *South West Imports Ltd*[64] in rejecting the idea that because a work or object was partly functional or utilitarian it could not be an artistic work.

In the House of Lords, all five approaches differed. In Lord Reid's opinion a thing has an artistic character if "[a person] gets pleasure or satisfaction or it may be uplift from contemplating it".[65] The person he expressly envisages is of the general public not a specialist in art and he adopts the following test: "[i]f any substantial section of the public genuinely admires and values a thing for its appearance and gets pleasure or satisfaction, whether emotional or intellectual, from looking at it, I would accept that it is artistic although many others may think it meaningless or common or vulgar". Lord Reid went on to express the view that simply "looking nice" appeared to him to fall considerably short of having artistic appeal.

Lord Morris of Borth-y-Gest[66] unconvincingly and unhelpfully asserted that the word "artistic" stood "on and by its own strength" and did not require judicial definition. However, he nevertheless went on to make some interesting observations: the object in ques-

---

[64] [1968] 1 Ex. CR 493.
[65] N. 61 above, at 78.
[66] *Ibid.*, at 81.

tion should be viewed and judged in a detached and objective way; expert evidence is an aid to the court; expert witnesses should be heard to apply the precise legal formula "artistic character" to the object because satellite associative words alone do not suffice to indicate artistic character.[67] One may call Lord Morris' approach a very legalistic one, a procedural stance giving little attention to the material difficulties involved. Viscount Dilhorne expressed a similar stance more hesitatingly,[68] and Lord Kilbrandon joined him in holding that an artistic work must be a work of art.[69] Astonishingly, only Lords Reid and Simon of Glaisdale paid particular attention to the precise category for which section 3(i)(c) of the 1956 Act provided, i.e. artistic craftsmanship. Lord Reid observed that "the only idea of artistic craftsmanship is that you produce things which are both useful and artistic in the belief that being artistic does not make them any less useful", and he considered it "misleading" to equate artistic craftsmanship with a work of art. However, it was only Lord Simon who explored in detail this most relevant avenue.[70] Lord Simon explained in historical terms the Arts and Crafts Movement and the accommodation of it by copyright legislation in accordance with its arrival. It is precisely because artistic craftsmanship is not work of fine art that it was catered for separately in the 1956 Act, earlier Acts having equated works of art with works of fine art and provided for their protection only.[71] Lord Simon paid attention to what the composite phrase "artistic craftsmanship" means in real terms as an artistic genre co-extensive with showing considerable insight into the legal history of its acceptance by copyright law as worthy of copyright protection under the artistic category head.

The universal concept of what is art tends to augment as new schools and innovatory art forms are identified: Impressionism, Post-Impressionism, Cubism, Surrealism, Expressionism, Suprematism, Futurism, Abstraction, "Pop Art", Reductivism, Postmodernism all accrue, a host of collective nouns applied usually retrospectively to

[67] This last statement is the logical import of what the judge actually said.

[68] N. 61 above, at 86–7.

[69] *Ibid.*, at 96.

[70] *Ibid.*, at 87–95. David Booton, in his article "Legal Determinations of Artistic Merit under United Kingdom Copyright Law", in *Art, Antiquity and Law*, Vol. 1. Issue 2, May 1996, at 138, says: "[t]he legislation requires that it is the craftsmanship which must be artistic and not the work itself. It follows that whether or not the work itself is artistic will not be determinative of whether it is a 'work of artistic craftsmanship'. It is submitted therefore that any test which has as its basis the examination of the finished work itself is wrong in law."

[71] Notably the Fine Arts Copyright Act of 1862.

certain artistic genres embracing distinct artistic styles or ideas (some overlapping chronologically and/or thematically). For legal purposes, if criteria are used in a instrumental way to identify objects as artistic or not, the criteria are, of necessity, criteria acquired to that date. The general epithet "artistic" evolves from era to era and tends not to contract but ever expand (notwithstanding attempts under certain governments, notably totalitarian ones, to circumscribe the national concept of art for political purposes). To use "artistic" as a tool for identifying art is to demand of the object in question that it is within art's established definitions (as a legal tool that it is within legal aware-ness of art's established definitions). If it is not, it does not mean that it is not art (nor that in the future it will not be so recognised).[72]

FUTURE DEVELOPMENT

What follows here is a close critique of section 4(1) and (2) of the Copyright, Designs and Patents Act 1988[73] and how it compares with the equivalent provisions of the previous law contained in section 3 of the 1956 Copyright Act. It is hoped that it will provide some insight into legal accommodation of artistic developments in the field of postmodern art categorisation over the last 32 years (though in many ways the 1988 legislators had also to face the legacy of the nine-teenth century, and consider the prominence now of, for example, paintings and engravings in relation to newer forms of "graphics"). The reader might consider how useful is the providing for different forms of art,[74] a tradition that the 1988 Act perpetuates, when the basic legal difficulty of not knowing how to identify them continues to be largely ignored,[75] except in the 1988 definition of photographs and the general tightening up of legislative language from which the sections pertaining to art incidentally benefit.

[72] Scribbles, which would have once been regarded as too trivial or meritricious to be copyrightable, should not be under-estimated as art. On Tuesday, 17 Nov. 1992, an untitled abstact by Cy Twombly, the American master of scribbles, made US$2.14 million when sold at Sotheby's contemporary art sale in New York. In response to someone describing the pic-ture as little more than a series of doodles, Anthony Grant of Sotheby's said "Try and do it and you'll see how difficult it is" (*The Independent*, 19 Nov. 1992 at 2).

[73] Originally, the provisions of the Copyright, Designs and Patents Act were coming into force piecemeal, by statutory instruments, in accordance with its s. 305(3).

[74] The categories being left open are paralleled in s. 102 of the American Copyright Act of 1976 and in s. 3 of the French law of 11 Mar. 1957.

[75] The necessity for judicial interpretation of certain forms, e.g. paintings, has not yet appeared in practice.

Section 3(1) of the 1956 Act commenced with the statement that "[i]n this Act artistic work means a work of any of the following descriptions, that is to say . . ."; section 4(1) of the newer Act is much less vague and verbose with "artistic work means", a development symptomatic of the general plan to sharpen copyright's legislative language and to incline to definitions to improve clarity. The word "descriptions" of the 1956 section 3(1) invited expansive interpretations whereas section 4 of the 1988 Act attempts something approaching definitions of each category of artistic work—it indicates what each term, for example, "graphic work", includes, in an attempt to somewhat delimit the ambit of each more general term and clarify its contents. Although this latter approach moves towards assuaging the accusation of the lack of adequate definition of terms (aimed at the 1956 Act), the 1988 Act is still not substantively, and often not formally, truly definitive—it does not say "a building is", it says "building includes"; similarly, "graphic work includes . . .". This obviously leaves such categories open: "building", for example, includes what the legislation says it includes, but the legislation does not exclude other things. In substance, the position is much the same as under the 1956 Act where each type of work named was called a description.

Instead of the works "painting, sculptures, drawings, engravings and photographs" of section 3(1)(a) of the 1956 Act, section 4(1)(a) of the 1988 Act substitutes "graphic work, photograph, sculpture or collage" so only the categories of photographs and sculptures are kept. In the 1988 Act, drawings, engravings and paintings are subsumed under "graphic work" which is sub-defined in section 4's pursuant definition section (section 4(2)), an innovation of the 1988 Act. The enumeration of so many different art forms under the head "graphic work" displays awareness of currently popular forms, such as woodcuts, as well as cognizance of the multiplicity of types of work that exist in the realm of visual non-motion pictorial art. Less appropriately, section 4(2)(a) expressly accommodates what could be considered utility as opposed to art objects—"any diagram, map, chart or plan". Is this not a list of the primarily functional rather than artistic?

The retention of "irrespective of artistic quality" in the 1988 Act is disappointing from the standpoint of strict logic. How could an artistic object ever not be intrinsically connected with artistic quality? The phrase is, however, not a mistake or superfluous. It is intended to emphasise that a photograph or sculpture or other work listed here is *de jure* artistic, not requiring proof of such status. This legal assertion is, of course, useful, in that it obviates artistic analysis for at least one category of works; equally obviously, it is intellectually dissatisfying. It is somewhat ironic, too, that those works considered of their genus (self-evidently) artistic in the 1956 Act are not identical with those so deemed in the 1988 Act.

In section 4(1)(a) of the 1988 Act, "collage" is introduced as a new category of artistic work.[76] This accommodates non-motion visual art that may contain pre-created material by another but is so originally arranged as to gain its own copyright protection. It is one of the privileged class that does not have to engage with artistic quality, but it may then be difficult to identify. How is one to distinguish between a collage that is an artistic work and a random heap of old soup cans "originally" thrown together (simply owing its origin to an individual who possessed the relevant skill so haphazardly to amass them)? Are we sure enough about what a collage actually is and is not, in artistic terms, to be confident that something simply presented as a collage, without more, need not of itself demonstrate artistic quality to warrant copyright protection?

It would appear that "works of architecture" no longer need an artistic character or design to be so defined. There is no express stipulation in either the 1956 or 1988 Act that purports to perpetuate what was once required in the 1911 Copyright Act. This enables the law here to avoid the definitional problem of what is "artistic", a seemingly ineluctable analysis in connection, for example, with the phrase "works of artistic craftsmanship". However, an enterprising judge might resurrect the 1911 specification of artistic character or design, and include such a criterion in his own assessment of what a work of architecture is, on the grounds that a basic alteration of the law post-1911 was unintended and a subsequent statute or statutes

---

[76] The specific inclusion of the form "collage" has been long delayed. Collage played a pivotal role in the evolution of Cubism, and Cubism had, of course, a pivotal role in the evolution of modern painting and sculpture. In 1912 Picasso and Braque began to mix sand and other foreign substances with their paint, the granular surface thereby achieved calling direct attention to the tactile reality of the picture. Braque also glued a piece of imitation wood-grain paper to the surface of a drawing and introduced bits of green or grey marbleised surfaces into some of his pictures. His first collage "Fruit Bowl", was made by pasting three strips of imitation wood-grain wallpaper to a sheet of drawing paper on which he then charcoaled a rather simplified Cubist still-life and some *"trompe-l'œil"* letters. Picasso and Braque then began to use various pasted papers and cloth. Arp, Schwitters and Miró later developed collage, which arguably declined sometimes into (simply) montage. Gris restored the form with a strong emphasis on decorativeness. His collages lack the immediacy of presence of those of Braque and Picasso, and their monumental quality. It is safe to say that Cubism founded substantive collage.

would spell our clearly any change of position if Parliament intended to effect it.

There has also been legislative devolution in the context of "works of artistic craftsmanship". In the 1956 Act, the phrase "works of artistic craftsmanship" was followed by the phrase "not falling within either of the preceding paragraphs" (section 3(1)(c)) and this is omitted in section 4(1)(c) of the 1988 Act. The 1956 Act phrase suggested that the category "works of artistic craftsmanship" was a catch-all miscellaneous classification in which all art works that could not find a place in the other subsections might be accommodated.[77] Lord Simon of Glaisdale in *Hensher*, above, proves by reference to, *inter alia*, legal history, that "work of artistic craftsmanship" has, on the contrary, a specific meaning contingent on a very particular artistic movement and genre, embracing items identified with the Arts and Crafts Movement.[78]

Although the Whitford Committee was anxious to promote the specificity of terms and clarity of definitions in copyright law, in the 1988 Act's clarifying of terms in its section 4(2)[79] the only *bona fide*

[77] California led the way in a new movement to upgrade craft to the status of fine art. Whereas San Francisco played a key role in promoting ceramic sculpture, Santa Monica promoted hand-made home furnishings as art. At Santa Monica's Gallery of Functional Art, founded in 1988 by Lois Lambert, a former curator of the Chicago Art Institute, the "Chair as Art" show began in the last week of May 1992. Trent Hickman, for example, a self-defined "sculptor and furniture artist", worked on a series of rocking chairs, whose rockers were ingeniously derived from guitars. Other artistic chairs designed to indicate that art does not have to be useless, and made for sitting on, were made by Philadelphia artist Johanna Goodman. The exhibition also featured a Paul Colucci "Loveseat" that used recycled wood and paint: his work relies on strong geometric forms rather reminiscent of Henry Moore. Other striking works included a Jon Bok chair made from bits and pieces of car. See, further, "Chairs Designed to Upgrade Craft to the Status of Art" (Geraldine Norman, *The Independent*, 1 June 1992, at 7).

[78] See Lord Simon of Glaisdale's judgment, n. 61 above, at 87–95.

[79] S. 4 reads as follows:

"(1) In this Part 'artistic work' means—

(a) a graphic work, photograph, sculpture or collage, irrespective of artistic quality,
(b) a work of architecture being a building or a model for a building, or
(c) a work of artistic craftsmanship.

(2) In this Part—
'building' includes any fixed stucture, and a part of a building or fixed structure;
'graphic work' includes—

(a) any painting, drawing, diagram, map, chart or plan, and
(b) any engraving, etching, lithograph, woodcut or similar work;

'photograph' means a recording of light or other radiation on any medium on which an image is produced or from which an image may by any means be produced, and which is not part of a film;
'sculpture' includes a cast or model made for purposes of sculpture."

definition given is of what comprises a photograph. Viewed positively, at least one brand of artistic work is thus categorically legally
defined.[80] However, the others remain undefined. The eclectic col-
lectives, for example, "graphic work", remain ambiguous, and are
said to "include" certain works (examples of component members
whose own nature is insufficiently indicated for they themselves to
be clearly identifiable). For the most part, then, artistic labels in the
1988 Act still have to stand by themselves, and judges and experts will
be drawn on as interpreters to decide, for example, whether a tower
of baked bean cans welded together and covered in felt is a collage or
a sculpture or neither. Although the provisions relating to art in the
1988 Act indicate a greater awareness of types of artistic work than
their predecessors, they do little to help us identify members of each
mentioned type. The difficulty, we conclude, except in the case of
photographs, remains definition.

A FURTHER LOOK AT QUALITY TESTS

There is no direct relation between the generic concept "artistic
works" (the title of a head of copyright protection) and the criteria
used to confer copyright protection in the area: the operative criterion is only very rarely the quality of being artistic, and it is arguable
that the law eschews using the term "artistic" as its "litmus test"
except where this has proved ineluctable, for example, when the
word "artistic" appears in the name of a protected class of work (and
the import of it is subsequently questioned). Rather, criteria operate
that are directly linked to a requirement of quality and indirectly to
artistic quality. The law here is infused with certain "catch-words"
either accepted (as in the case of originality) or rejected (as in the case
of novelty). As much can be learnt of copyright law's quality requirements from the tests it rejects as from those it selects. Relevant "skill"
is sometimes used as a test in England to ensure that the over-
common or over-simplistic do not achieve protection,[81] and the
American and French reliance on the notions of creativity and creation, respectively, are a less explicit way of reaching these (and
other) distinctions. What occurs is the somewhat surreptitious
enforcement, beneath broad terms, of a quality standard that remains

---

[80] Note the legislative use of the verb "means" here instead of "includes".
[81] See, e.g., *Regent Publishing Co. Ltd* v. *Bamforth & Co. Ltd* [1923–28] MCC 150 and
G.A. Cramp & Sons Ltd v. *Frank Smythson Ltd* [1944] AC 329.

ambiguous because so diffusely and variously operated: its real terms are not stated and may, indeed, result from various unintegrated policies rather than a single but ramified one. If they result simply from individual (judicial) taste, they may combine as a policy of "upper-middle class" artistic preferences. Would it be better to have an explicit declaration on quality considerations in copyright law? The use of vague criteria transmuted by judicial discretion may not be entirely conducive to the consistency law requires. But the quality considerations would not be any better in this respect. Let us first examine the term "novelty", formally rejected as a test for copyright protection.

Novelty is the *sine qua non* for patent protection, and is required, for example, by the (English) Registered Designs Act of 1959, but is not a test for copyright protection in either England, France or the USA. However, against strict copyright doctrine, novelty and originality are sometimes, confusingly, embraced as synonyms, which is unsurprising given that they semantically overlap, a fact copyright law tends to ignore, by courtesy of forging legal tests that relate to "cultural" subject matter and yet have to operate with all the accuracy and consistency the function of law demands. The French use of the concept of relative originality[82] indicates that absolute novelty is definitely not a requirement there for copyright protection, and in all three jurisdictions novelty is restricted in meaning, excluding some of its ordinary dictionary senses, occasionally leading to paradox; for example, photographs have to be "fresh", not novel, to gain copyrightability, but one meaning of novel is fresh. The fact that novel can be used pejoratively to connote the unartistic and gimmicky is also ignored as the law, seemingly happily, continues to operate a novelty/originality distinction as if that distinction is obvious and unnuanced. The law is keen to avoid novelty as a requirement for copyrightability in order to protect those things that cannot be said to be entirely "new", such as compilations and anthologies of others' work, originally produced; but if novel means new, is it not true that all copyrightable objects are indeed novel?; is not a degree of "novel" newness required of all copyrightable works? In certain cases, novelty of an object is more obviously necessary: there are many plastic roses on sale which are substantially similar; for one plastic rose to have copyright protection from another demands that it has a certain novelty over the other, otherwise "a rose is a rose is a rose is a rose"[83] (all

---

[82] For derived works.
[83] An aphorism of Gertrude Stein, writer and arts critic, used by her to a different end.

undifferentiated). As broad principles are not copyrightable, so are non-novel common objects. In subtle ways, then, artistic considerations combine in the unclear legal use of "novelty" in unconvincing contradistinction to originality.

It is logical for a creative factor to feature as a dominant criterion in the protection of artistic property and somewhat perverse of English law to de-emphasise it as it does. Whereas France and America adopt the mother and daughter notions of creation and creativity as basic frames of reference against which to test a given object, France in its tradition of protecting the created "œuvre", and America in allying creativity and originality, indistinguishably, in one relatively fluid method, England maintains its highly impersonal test of originality. However, in certain contexts, reference is made in English law to a requirement of creative, as opposed to imaginative, labour[84] and to creative "input".[85] A personal view is that English copyright law is more concerned about the presentation simply of "effort" in a work than in any artistic colour of such labour. Interestingly, though, English law justifies protecting compilations, for example, by emphasising that they arise from independent effort, as if that, anomalously, makes up for a missing creative element English law purports not to require.

Skill, of the artistic variety, is not of major concern to English copyright law. On the rare occasions when skill is in issue, it is a low requirement, as established in *Kenrick*.[86] In one extreme case, moreover, skill is not rewarded in England when it is in America: the copier who exactly copies a work gains copyright in the USA but not in England. Extreme simplicity goes unprotected in all three jurisdictions. England does not protect the titles of works; in certain circumstances America does, and France does.[87] The slightness of titles is perhaps equated with simplicity in English law; too quantitatively insubstantial to warrant protection, titles are, of course, not regarded in English copyright law in an artistic light.

If utility is set in opposition to artistic, the law encounters complications as reflected in, for example, the difficulty of establishing borderlines between protection by copyright and protection by register of design and the necessity for establishing tortuous tests such as the

---

[84] See *Walter* v. *Lane* [1900] AC 539—while Lord Rosebery's skill was in composing actual words and thoughts, the reporter's comprised recording them for posterity.

[85] As in the case of compilation (creative assembly).

[86] *Kenrick & Co.* v. *Lawrence & Co.* (1890) 25 QBD 99.

[87] Titles are specifically protected by art. 5 of the French law of 11 Mar. 1957.

American physical and conceptual separability test to ensure the protection of only a certain artistic range of works,[88] excluding items that are not considered copyrightable on account of artistic deficit. In the postmodern age of high technology culture,[89] can we retain a priority for the artistic in copyright law without admitting items whose character is essentially technological and useful rather than artistic as conventionally conceived, or can distinctions still be drawn between the purely "commercial" and the partially commercial and partially artistic and purely artistic so as to retain artistic categories in copyright law, as we do literary and musical ones (terms whose ambit is narrower than "artistic" which renders them more practical as legal terms of reference and tools)?

CONCLUSIONS

If the criterion for copyright protection in England is originality divorced from creativity[90] (as on the face of it it is), that suggests, prima facie, that English copyright law's raison d'être is extra-artistic (which is not so[91]). By way of contrast, France and America protect creation and creativity, which terms and the artistic process are inextricably linked in concept and in practice. In all three jurisdictions, a practical distinction is made between the protection of the originality of the industrial (by registration) and the "intellectual" (by copyright) and there is a correct general assumption that the hypostasis of copyright is artistic terrain. As the current English law operates, qualifications for admission into that terrain are minimal. Should they be? Can I realistically claim that mere juxtaposition of pre-made commercial objects, like soup cans or bricks, is art[92] (in contradistinction to, for example, the picture-making of a collage from such materials)?

[88] Can a picture, for example, ever be physically separate from the tray's utilitarian aspects? Should the overall shape or configuration of a utilitarian article be per se copyrightable?

[89] Gianni Vattimo, The End of Modernity: Nihilism and Hermeneutics in Post-Modern Culture (Policy Press, Oxford, 1989). Because of the difficulty of this notion of the "postmodern" age, I have attempted a personal definition of it within the context of the arts to assist the reader: see Appendix, Essay A, below.

[90] For evidence of the minimal nature of the originality requirement see Graves' Case (1869) LR 4 QB 715 at 723; British Northrop Ltd v. Texteam Blackburn Ltd [1974] RPC 68; Solar Thomson Engineering Co. Ltd v. Barton [1977] RPC 537 (CA).

[91] See n. 98, below.

[92] In the most general sense. Andy Warhol's Campbell's soup-can arrangements and Carl André's "Equivalent VIII" are considered art by the art world.

There used to be bounds to what was art; now that the boundaries are gone, and we have only the self-labelling artist rather than a standard for art, the law finds it difficult to justify imposing quality standards on what is now a culture independent of standard. This causes copyright law particular problems because it is not intended to protect the worthless. Law finds itself having to impose its own criterion of cultural worth, and it does this by more subtle means than declaration of an artistic policy outlining criteria for what is, and what is not, of sufficient quality to warrant protection. Any imposition of a legal definition of art would outrage the art world, which has no rules itself about what is art. However much it may be denied, the law is obliged in copyright law to regulate a definitionally vague culture and, because of the very nature of its role, impose at least minimum standards for the identification of art that art itself now lacks. There has not always been such lack. Once there was the standard of beauty.[93]

Art remained comparable to law when, like law, it was a means to create the "good"[94]; as law was an instrument which was to produce justice, art was a skill which was to produce beauty (the *techne* of the Greeks, the *ars* of the Romans, the *Kunst* of the Germans). Art and law both served traditions, the former of beauty, the latter justice. The romanticism of the nineteenth century shifted attention from art to the artist. Instead of being for the most part dutiful artisans, artists came to be recognised and accepted as extra-, sometimes anti-, social beings. The artist is no longer expected to respond to his fellow man's sense of beauty and it is said that there is no longer such as thing as art; there are only artists. Copyright law has to accept this position whilst trying to attend to its legal aim of concrete, conscious and coherent order which the contemporary fluid concept of art impedes. Contrary to the trend of non-exhaustive definitional approaches[95] to art by artists and art philosophers, copyright law, in its function of protecting original art, has to decide what "art" is that is worthy of legal protection in this sphere. The arguably élitist criterion of beauty is avoided by contemporary art and copyright law alike, but the law nevertheless has to make sure it protects only what

[93] It almost goes without saying that beauty is not a criterion for copyright protection in contemporary copyright law. See Cherpillod, n. 37 above, at 71–2. Is it part of "artistic" character?

[94] Albert A. Ehrenzweig, *Psychoanalytic Jurisprudence* (Oceana, New York, 1971), 169–70.

[95] This is not to say that plenty of evocative descriptions of art and the artistic process are not forthcoming today or that distinct art philosophies are not now produced. There is simply a marked reluctance to set limits to what is art.

it is worthwhile to protect, otherwise the copyright protection of artistic works, and therefore art itself, is trivialised. However, despite the assumption of the English rough practical test that what is worth copying is worthy of protection, what is not worth copying is also in theory protectable as a result of the lack of formal admission of a criterion of quality or worthwhileness in operation. Reasons for this could include that the law fears the accusation that a protection of quality would merely be a disguise for the imposition of conservative taste. However, there is also a danger that in the purported protection of the artistic, the artistic is demeaned by law's appearing to include the qualityless. Should not the artistic incorporate only the quality associations the adjective suggests? As has been seen, "artistic" *simpliciter* is an inadequate criterion for copyright protection.[96] Instead, should the law tell us explicitly what art it intends to protect, and why, within its artistic category? For practical legal purposes, is the law entitled to employ its own definitions of art so as to facilitate the consistency and clarity of its operation? Would that go at least some way to ensuring that copyright law avoids inhibiting freedom of expression[97] (by the meticulous but needless protection of items that do not deserve the advantage and kudos of being legally considered artistic and, yet, so legally considered, potentially inhibit true artistic expression by the wielding of their copyright)? Can we justify saying that a main aspect of copyright law is the protection of original art when the criteria for copyright protectability do not usually relate to art, or do so only very loosely? Is the situation not really that something only achieves copyright when it is used by another to the originator's annoyance to the degree of his bringing an action,[98] rather than because it is an original work worthy of protection *per se* (resultant from some discernible quality in itself)? Is it not judicially determined infringement of copyright that effectively indicates copyrightable (as well as copyrighted) artistic status?

[96] Is artistic also an inappropriate (misplaced) criterion in law?

[97] On the potential difficulties in attempting to balance the two constitutional values of the (copyright) protection of original work and freedom of expression see Bruno De Witte, "Cultural Policy Limits to Fundamental Rights", in Arthur Kaufmann *et al.* (eds.), *Rechtsstaat und Menschenwürde: Festschrift für Werner Maihofer zum 70-Geburtstag* (Klostermann, Frankfurt am Main, 1988) 652–60.

[98] "Copyright law is, in essence, concerned with the negative right of preventing the copying of physical material existing in the field of literature and the arts. Its object is to protect the writer and artist from the unlawful reproduction of his material" (*Copinger and Skone James on Copyright* (12th edn., Sweet & Maxwell, London, 1980), 1st para.). This statement was approved by Lord Kilbrandon at the end of his judgment in *Hensher* [1976] AC at 98. (referring to the learned text's 11th edn.).

4

The Concept of Art in Defamation Law

INTRODUCTION

In England, France and the United States of America, the law of defamation is basically designed to protect the reputation of individuals. In France, this protection extends to the dead. In America, the Supreme Court has altered defamation law by the development of a constitutional standard, and the availability of legal protection in all three countries against being defamed moderates any general right of freedom of expression. Defamation law is underdeveloped in its operation on the specific freedom of artistic expression, though in America a doctrine known as defamation by fiction is now recognised. However, defamation law distinguishes between potentially defamatory statements of fact and (mere) statements of opinion without attention to the unique position of art as non-fact, and non-opinion.[1] Neither is art "comment" in the (legal) sense of "fair comment", on which a defence to a charge of defamation can be based in Anglo-American law. This chapter reveals problems involved for law and art in lacking a particular legal apparatus for the treatment of art within the existing internal structure of defamation law, focusing primarily on the possibility of art as an agent of defamation.

Prior to independence, the American courts applied the common law rule that any published attack, whether on an individual or an organ of government, is punishable as a criminal offence irrespective of its truth, because it is a threat to the stability of society. In the eighteenth century, as in England, juries began to rebel against this authoritarian doctrine, and in due course the law was changed to make the truth a defence to a libel prosecution, provided the statement was published in the public interest—a development which

---

[1] More generally, on the contrasting legal and literary possibilities for definitions of character, see J. Boyd White, *The Legal Imagination* (abridged edn., University of Chicago Press, Chicago, Ill., 1973, 1985), ch. 3: "How The Law Talks About People—'Who Is This Man'?".

began in America towards the end of the eighteenth century and which was copied (without attribution) in England only as late as the Libel Act of 1843. In the course of the nineteenth century, as in England, and unlike in France, Americans who considered themselves defamed began instead to use civil libel actions to suppress their critics.[2] The French law of defamation still remains firmly centred in the *"droit pénal spécial"*[3] and civil action is subsidiary (the opposite of the current position in England and America).

In French law, article 29 of the 29 July 1881 statute states that defamation comprises "every allegation or imputation of a fact which casts a slur on the honour or esteem of the personality or body to which the fact is imputed". This law is still current and confirmed in the new penal code. The defamation refers to a fact (true or false). As a matter of common law in England and America, it is similarly a statement of *fact*, rather than the honest expression of *opinion* (on matters of public interest) that is targeted by defamation law. Since one of the facets of the law of defamation is its operation on a fact/opinion distinction, and art is neither fact nor opinion, its position in defamation law is inadequately catered for. This chapter considers the consequential concomitant difficulties involved for both art and law.

In English law, the standard of proof of justification is the normal civil one of balance of probabilities, but as in other civil cases the seriousness of the defendant's allegation may be taken into account in determining whether he has discharged that burden.[4] To what degree alleged defamation in works of art (notably fiction) is diminished by the transmutation of fact into art has not been considered in English law; in the context of the defence of justification, a case has not arisen about, for example, the novel *à clef*, where real life facts are only very thinly disguised as fiction. Where art is in issue, it is usually the defence of fair comment that is raised. It is a defence to an action for defamation that the statement is a fair comment on a matter of public interest, and it is a question for the judge, not the jury, whether the matter is of public interest.[5] Such matter has not been confined within narrow limits, and matters of public interest clearly include the publication of a book or the exhibition of a picture. However, the statement must be an expression of opinion and not an assertion

[2] For a thesis that aims to destroy the simplicity of this traditional story, see Norman L. Rosenberg, *Protecting the Best Men: An Interpretive History of the Law of Libel* (University of North Carolina Press, Chapel Hill, NC, 1986).

[3] Art. 29 of the statute of 29 July 1881 is the central art. still in force.

[4] *Laurence* v. *Chester Chronicle*, The Times, 8 Feb. 1986.

[5] *South Hetton Coal Co. Ltd* v. *N.E. News Association* [1894] 1 QB 133, 141, *per* Lopes LJ.

of fact, and what is contained in art is neither fact nor opinion, as previously mentioned, but a collation of artistic ideas,[6] a distinctive circumstance surprisingly unacknowledged in English law as exceptional and meriting separate treatment.

In US law, the defence of "truth" (justification) exists in an altered and much stronger form under *New York Times* v. *Sullivan*, some of the effects of which are stated here. The burden of proof has been shifted to the plaintiff, who must prove that an allegedly defamatory statement is a false assertion of fact. Respecting public-figure plaintiffs, a defamation is not actionable unless it is false, and the plaintiff must allege that the publisher knew it was false or acted in reckless disregard for the truth. A lower standard of proof of fault is established for private individuals: as a minimum, private plaintiffs must prove[7] that "media" defendants were negligent.[8] The defence of fair comment has acceded to an absolute protection afforded opinion: once the courts have decided as a matter of law that putatively defamatory matter is an expression of opinion, it has absolute protection under the First Amendment. The traditional common law defence of fair comment has thus been superseded by a defence that protects even unfair comment from libel actions.

THE PROBLEMS

This sometimes impassioned excursus questions the suitability of the law of defamation's application to artistic material and highlights the law's dilemmas when faced with a category called "art" whose independent cultural identity before the law tends to be ignored. This may reveal defamation law's more generalised scheme as ill fitting this particular medium: with the lack of a unitary body of rules to deal specifically with art, the art-related aspects of defamation law are inappropriately dispersed, and it is only in America that a notion of defamation by art has eventually been recognised as a category warranting special attention, notably under the head "defamation by

---

[6] There is an assumption here that the art is cognitive, it being impossible to attempt to discern identities in a non-cognitive art-work.

[7] In *Philadelphia Newspapers* v. *Hepps*, 106 S Ct 1558 (1986), the Court, by a 5–4 majority, reaffirmed the rule that it is for the plaintiff to prove the falsity of the libel. The narrow majority could indicate the possibility of change.

[8] As Burger CJ predicted in his dissent in *Gertz* v. *Robert Welch, Inc.*, 418 US 323, 41 L.Ed.2d. 789, 94 S Ct 2997 (1974), the great majority of states require private plaintiffs to prove negligence.

fiction", which is the paradigm instance treated here of defamation by art.

The concept of art has no special place in English defamation law. As in American law,[9] art is protectable by a fact/opinion distinction[10] which mischaracterises art as opinion. Arts critics are furnished with the defence of "fair comment" (better described as honest comment) which restrains arts criticism to limited emotiveness and the character of the art while disallowing excessively vituperative comment and comment which goes to the professional probity and character of the artist (English law here missing or avoiding the point that the integrity of art and artistic integrity of the artist are somewhat more combined than in most professions courtesy of the highly subjective nature of the product). Art is therefore accommodated in rules of general application inattentive to the subtlety of art's *modus operandi* as a culture and the confusion its distinct nature can infuse into law when its difference from other facts on which the law operates manifests itself on a case-by-case basis, raising conceptual problems the law has chosen not to cater for at a legislative level. Treating art as a separate category from other facts, acknowledging it is different, would remove a number of conceptual complexities the art law case precedents currently inflict on the rest of defamation law. It is bemusingly unenlightened and self-defeating of the framers of defamation law to shut their eyes to the distinctiveness of art and the artistic tradition when other disciplines and cultures, such as philosophy, not to mention the general public, recognise it as a distinct area of human concern to which the rest of society habitually applies different and distinctive rules (ranging from accepting eccentric conduct from an artist as typical of his vocation to accepting that vocation as of peculiar intrinsic worth).

Defamation law is unnecessarily complex *per se* and in need of radical reform. Separating art from other "fact" categories on which it operates paves the way to its more general improvement (not just to the advantages of art and legal clarity). A general lesson to be learnt from the problems law has incurred by inattention to the particularly distinct mechanics of the artistic process is that law cannot treat facets of civilisation on which it operates as unrealistically simplistically as it tends to do, for example, by imposing general rules on complex and

---

[9] Below.
[10] Ultimately the classification of any statement as fact as opposed to opinion seems to turn on an assessment of the likelihood that a reasonable reader would understand that the statement should not be taken as an assertion of literal fact.

singular phenomena. Law must respect the objects of its operation and find out the nature of these objects so as to be able better to regulate them justly and efficiently in accord with what they necessarily and really are according to their endemic cultural ontologies. Law is there for us, not us for law.[11]

Too many subjective-view-reliant tests inhabit the English law of defamation: the ordinary reader, the reasonable man, the right-thinking man, the public,[12] all have their place in determining various elements of the tort. Overwhelmed by what could be called (these) "composite" subjective tests, the law is at the sacrifice of the jury, who embody all of these tests at once and practically shape the law by what they decide rather than the law guiding them to a decision. Being so protean, it is unsurprising that defamation law has no consistent attitude to the problem of art. It is generally ill-conceived in theory and in form. This is widely recognised by legal academics and practitioners alike but, despite reports such as that of the Faulks Committee, it has not undergone basic reformulation.

Defamation law encounters many of the general problems of the art–law relation. Whenever we look for foundations, there are paradoxes everywhere. The law calls upon reason, whereas art calls upon taste, a parallel concept of self-authentification, and yet in defamation law they co-habit the same arena. With taste in the arena, the autonomy of the task of reason (on which the law relies) is suddenly jeopardised unless taste is integrated into the system by playing the role of a type of reason whose operation within law the law can then justify/accept. Art becomes a pal, a fellow-worker, but for law's purposes: at once an ally and a threat, for art has its own operations beyond any constraints law would put on its criteria for self-identification. Two cultures elide, one assimilated partially into the other, but only ever partially. Art has an autonomy beyond law that can resist it—one area of the amœba art is consumed; the other, where the nucleus is, can still struggle to be free of law's grasp, is still independent. Independence yet assimilation: another paradox. Abandoning notions of a cultural hierarchy, it is difficult to convey

[11] The autonomy of law is contingent on society needs and interests. Art is one large culturally distinctive unit of civilisation the idea of law was created to serve and enhance.

[12] These single or corporate figures are, disjunctively, common tools in different areas of the established English common law of defamation. For a favourable view of the integrity of the ordinary reader, see *Lewis* v. *Daily Telegraph* [1964] AC 234: the House of Lords decided that "the ordinary man, not avid for scandal" would not infer guilt if an enquiry were under way. It is beyond the ambit of this text to penetrate all the ramifications of these well-known legal tests.

the art–law relation within law except by such an image: one finds oneself relying on art itself (a picture) to serve one's legal purposes. Before abstracting further, let us pin down our butterflies, defamation law's inner flutterings, much as law itself seeks to contain free flight of art.

Let us take caricature. Where the plaintiff complains of a caricature, no general rule can be laid down defining absolutely what particular variety of publication of this nature will be defamatory. The limits of what is permissible in the way of cartoons and satire are undefined. Words "obviously"[13] intended only as a joke are not actionable, whereas serious imputation of fact lying behind the superficially jocular may well be. But effective humour (and effective art) often relies on fact (hence *"Schadenfreude"*). Another paradox. Strangely, too, even if the cartoon is defamatory the limits of permissible criticism in political life are wide.[14] The donning of a political life, it would seem, makes you more (implicitly) accepting of being defamed, the argument being that you have set yourself up for public exposure.[15] The seventh edition of *Gatley* makes the point without any hint at the absurdity of the implication: "where the person portrayed is not . . . a person who seeks notoriety . . . different considerations apply".[16] There is something of a difference between becoming a public figure and inviting "notoriety", the use of which word implies you almost deserve to be defamed. In all this, not one syllable rests in law that caricature is art, and as such should be immune from the same considerations as non-art, no rule that art is free.

Statues, pictures and other physical representations of a man may convey an imputation defamatory of him, either by their content or their context or by the circumstances in which they were published. There is a failure in defamation law to recognise that art may be from life (and its best examples arguably are) but is not presenting life: it presents merely itself and only certain viewers'/readers' associations make a real-life parallel that transform (by what magic?) art to reality. All of a sudden, it is the plaintiff in the novel and not the fictional character its author conceived. Law is the mechanism which permits

[13] See *Russell* v. *Pressdram*, *The Times*, 4 Feb. 1966. Note the difficulty of ascertaining what is obvious to whom.

[14] See *Massey* v. *New Zealand Times* (1911) 30 NZLR, 929.

[15] But surely not ridicule (unless we accept that politics and farce are closely aligned, which is not, in fact, a wholly untenable position).

[16] Sir Robert McEwen and Philip Lewis, *Gatley on Libel and Slander* (7th edn., Sweet & Maxwell Ltd, London, 1974), 15.

such absurd "retransmutation". If art is thereby forced to divorce itself from life as inspiration, and therefore from its strength, what concept of legitimate art ensues? Art based solely on fantasy (insipid as that could be)? Any art theory thereby espoused and perpetuated by law radically attenuates art's force.

The law is strangely inconsistent in its approach to artistic distinctions. It is sometimes convenient for the law to use them as its own and to use language in an uncharacteristically imaginative way far from the dictionary sense. By the Theatres Act 1968, the publication of "words" in the course of a performance of a play is treated as publication in permanent form i.e. libel. As in the Defamation Act 1952, "words" includes pictures, visual images, gestures and other methods of signifying meaning. Using "words" thus is interesting, not only because of its use to signify even art which is not cognitive but more generally because it is a deliberately artistic use of the word "words". The literal meaning is happily abandoned to serve legal art. There seems a certain irony in the legal use of "terms of art", in which contexts the law not only permits but invents and embraces artistic techniques of transmutation it refuses to allow even standard art forms. It denies for art a thing of art that it itself unreflectively employs as if of its own mechanism's peculiar right. It takes on a not insignificant artistic dimension when it suits itself, and defamation law, at least, points to the conclusion that law is a somewhat selfish cultural monolith. If law can change the meaning of words, why cannot art change the meaning of life? Why is only legal fiction legitimate here as a modification of fact? What of the basic genre of artistic fiction for which such modification is essential?

Of course, defamation law does accommodate art very indirectly and within certain boundaries, and when law employs terms of art there is little potential for defamatory harm arising from them, though they can have destructive consequences (such as the confusion of those to whom they are addressed but who do not understand them). The defence of fair comment is a sop to free speech but not to art *per se*, which, if here protected, is done so as a sub-category within the protection of "opinion". Art, a collation of interwoven artistic ideas, lacks the didactic/political motive the word "opinion" suggests.

The law distinguishes between misstatements of fact and fair comment.[17] This is difficult to do except in the most obvious cases of

---

[17] See *Merivale* v. *Carson* (1887) 20 QBD 275.

positive misdescription. Only honest comment is protected, but the limits of criticism are exceedingly wide. It must be such as to be fairly called "criticism" (an ambiguous word); it cannot be used as a cloak for mere invective.[18] There is much material written on this, as there is on the latitude of the fair comment defence. Room is even made here for emotive as well as reasonable criticism which rests uncomfortably with the reasonable and right-thinking man tests.[19] Feelings are here allowed an airing detached from reason (within limits): a sort of artistic licence for the critic to become impassioned without going too far. Going too far is when there is not only malice but where criticism "passes out of the domain of criticism itself".[20] This provides for somewhat inefficient circularity of argument.

The principle underlying the plea of fair comment is that a man who appeals to the public must be content to be judged by the public. Only a public disclosure of art invites such defence. The creator, it would seem, dictates the purview of public interest. The public, accordingly, has no general right to comment on a book printed for private circulation only or on a picture privately exhibited.[21] Defamation law here, probably inadvertently, upholds a certain moral right of an artist only to be judged (adversely) publicly if a public audience was what he intended. The concept of art here is therefore of art being tied to the creator, not leaving it free for public consumption: art is not free on mere production of critics' (unfettered) appraisal, whereas every kind of literary production placed before the public is the subject of fair comment, whether it be a book[22] or other form of art. It is not actionable fairly and honestly to criticise a picture, or statue, publicly exhibited. This is a long-established principle of English common law: any man has a right to express his opinion on the merits or demerits of artistic works. However, the private life of author or artist is not a matter of public interest. Art and artist are here divorced, personal privacy being the concept that shapes the law not the social nature, public or otherwise, *per se*, of art.

A critic's right to criticise in the public domain is far from unconditional, and the law is forced into adopting what it would probably not acknowledge as artistic distinctions to see whether or not the conditions for the fair comment defence apply. However severe or

---

[18] *Per* Collins MR in *McQuire* v. *Western Morning News* [1903] 2 KB 109.
[19] Which tests aim at a sort of certainty the law likes to consider a form of objectivity.
[20] See [1903] 2 KB 109.
[21] See *Gathercole* v. *Miall* (1846) 15 M &W 334.
[22] *Carr* v. *Hood* (1808) 1 Camp. 355n.

unjust his criticism may be, the critic will not be liable provided (a) he does not misrepresent the contents of the book, (b) he does not go out of his way to attack the character of the author, (c) his criticism may be fairly termed criticism, and (d) his criticism is the honest expression of his real opinion.[23] Legal application of these conditions suggests the necessity on the part of the judge and jury of a degree of artistic awareness. For condition (a), the book has to be comprehended with artistic insight into its meaning. For condition (b), the ascertainment of what constitutes a literary attack (permissible) and a personal attack (not permissible) demands discernment on the part of judge and jury of what is strictly artistic appraisal. Regarding condition (c), the question what is criticism and what is not demands acute artistic awareness, the like of which few have. This is why the condition includes the phrase "may be fairly termed" criticism: it allows an approximation. The law permits a compromise in the absence of expertise. Artistic criticism is being judged by law, and the law employs its own practical methods to overcome the difficulties an academic debate on what is criticism and what is not would invite and which would postpone (*ad infinitum?*) a decision. Within the legal structure, ends compete: here the intellectual is sacrificed for the legal. Condition (d) demands psychological more than artistic powers on the part of the judge and jury.

There is something disturbingly factional at large in the law of defamation, its tests often over-reliant on subjective opinions, not just of individuals but of groups "in the know". Where the plaintiff has pleaded an innuendo, he may, in addition to calling evidence of the extrinsic facts on which he relies, call witnesses to state the meaning in which they understood the words. Where a libel is contained in a picture or cartoon, witnesses may be asked what they understood its meaning to be[24]; where a libel is contained partly in a picture or cartoon, and partly in words, witnesses may be asked their understanding of the entire libel.[25] These rules apply whether the words are foreign or slang expressions, or local/provincial, or technical terms not in universal use but familiarly known by certain people who form a group. It is disturbing to think that the plaintiff can call witnesses to read an art-work according to what they know as a particular informed group i.e. esoteric information that is not universally known and not known to the artist (who can quite feasibly unknow-

[23] *McQuire* v. *Western Morning News* [1903] 2 KB 100 (CA).
[24] N. 14 above.
[25] *Cassidy* v. *Daily Mirror* [1929] 2 KB 331 (CA).

ingly incorporate signs or phrases a particular minority interprets vastly differently from himself and everyone else). It is unjust to the defendant to have the painting interpreted by a group of witnesses simply looking for their own terms of reference in it. The picture can only justly be presented as itself, artistically interpretable only by its creator and experts, all of whom (especially the former) best know what it presents. Art should not be reducible to the interpretation of a group unqualified and unwilling to judge it on its own terms as an entirety: as witnesses for the plaintiff, they look at it for innuendo and not for itself. These narrow visions with a minority backcloth of idiosyncratic knowledge (presumably non-artistic) should not be empowered to reduce an art form to their own particular perspective. Art is then being treated politically and unfairly and not as art. Defamation law's provision for art to be read for a few esoteric preconceptions, for "innuendo", demonstrates how artificially law can treat art for legal purposes.

As frequently repeated, the law is almost uniquely ill-equipped to deal with art-related problems, the facts of which are often conceptually insusceptible of legal synthesis by the existing type and structure of rules (too general and unspecialised to be applicable efficiently to a specialist culture like art). Consider the following hypothetical but not unrepresentative situations in the specific context of defamation.

(a) *Situation 1*

You are a poet from a provincial town you love dearly. You are published, and famous. A newspaper writes of your gay life in the city. It is not true but pertains to one or two of your poems which critics agree are gay in theme. However, they are your artistic voice, part of your persona, but being gay is not intrinsic to you; in fact, you are bisexual, or simply heterosexual. Although your city friends are unaffected by the article, back in your home-town you are shunned.

Questions:

(1) Was it fact or opinion in the newspaper? If fact, not true enough for justification to succeed as a defence? If opinion, does the defence of fair comment apply? If the allegedly defamatory article also elucidates some of the poems, does this "review" make the rest fair comment? Or does the article hit too firmly at your private life and private issues rather than at your work?

(2) To what degree is a poet a public person? Is his work not privacy made public? Even though he does not occupy a socially-recognised professional category, he is known. How well-known does a figure have to be to be "public"? What is the nature of the societal role he has to fulfil to be classified as a public plaintiff? Is this consideration as relevant in English law as in American law? If not, why not?

(3) Consider the article as fact. What has it said? If it says that he is merely intrigued by or likes gay culture, it is factually accurate. Could any reasonable man consider this defamatory? Would it not be unremarkable for any young poet (or any young person)? Should the law conform in any way to the opinions of a (local) community that cannot comprehend such nuances? Should the "average reasonable man" test be as locally contingent as it is? Would not the "intelligent civilised man" be a better test (at least in certain circumstances, such as when art is in issue)?

(4) What are the implications for the gay community if it is legally accepted that it can be defamatory to say that someone is gay? Is the law permitted to consolidate prejudice like this?

(5) The poet and the reviewer may both know that sexual orientation is of no moral consequence. But the poet has been shunned. He is obliged to bring an action for defamation so as to be treated humanely in his home environment. Ironically, if the article had said his poetry was bad, he himself would have been more upset, but such comment would clearly have been protected by the fair comment defence (and his local community would probably not have shunned him on account of it!).

(b) *Situation 2*

X writes Y a beautiful platonic love letter. Y amends the letter considerably and incorporates it in a novel. X is not named as a protagonist in the novel but a certain group infer it is him: like the protagonist, he once boasted of his virginity and is black. The novelist refers to his being a "lilac" which the group knows to signify a lack of sexual potency (a true innuendo exists). The novel is considered of great literary merit but X's girlfriend is furious about the suggestions that her boyfriend is impotent and sexually uninterested in her. She cannot differentiate art from life. She sees it as simply a defamatory description of her boyfriend that reflects badly on her. Reluctantly, he brings an action for defamation and there is adequate

proof of shunning by (alleged) friends who have ridiculed then
shunned him.

Questions:

(1) If X is held identifiable in the novel, how could a court determine if what was said of him was true or not?

(2) If the defence of justification were to fail (for example, on the
girlfriend's evidence), could a novel be appropriately protected by a
defence of fair comment? Y has not presented opinion but creation:
X has been transformed into a created persona X2. Should a special
category of defence exist for the protection of art works which are
neither fact (what the law calls and equates with "truth") nor opinion, but simply created "art" (a category acknowledged as a distinct
form of human activity by most other societal cultures except certain
branches of law)?

(3) If X accused Y of plagiarism, could Y succeed in an action for
defamation? Is it not more defamatory to say that Y is (professionally)
dishonest than that X is chaste? There is better reason to protect
someone against a charge of dishonesty than sexual incompetence
because society values (or should value) honesty higher than sexual
capacity. Does the law of defamation tend to reinforce bad values e.g.
over-concern for ego and status, over-reverence for gossip and its
effects, lack of respect for art and creativity . . .?

In the USA, the Supreme Court first constitutionalised defamation
actions to protect the media's ability to publish politically relevant
information.[26] It subsequently purported to extend First Amendment
protection of defamatory speech beyond the realm of purely political
debate to protect all "speech that matters".[27] However, whatever the
implications for freedom of political speech and expression, the *New
York Times* case[28] and its subsequent modification in *Gertz* v. *Robert
Welch, Inc.*[29] offer no First Amendment protection to one significant
form of expression, *viz.* artistic works which, because of their creative artistic as opposed to factual representative character, are insusceptible of examination by the constitutional actual malice test
established in *New York Times* which rests exclusively on the concepts
of factual truth and falsehood, i.e. was the alleged defamatory statement made with knowledge of its falsity or in reckless disregard for

---

[26] *New York Times Co.* v. *Sullivan*, 376 US 254 (1964).
[27] *Gertz* v. *Robert Welch, Inc.*, 418 US 323, 341 (1974).
[28] N. 26 above.
[29] N. 27 above.

whether it was true or false? This demonstrates forcefully, once again, in a very important field, the ineptitude of the legal mechanism in refusing to address itself to acknowledging the peculiar nature of one of the areas on which it operates, an essential preliminary to accommodating it within its scheme of working which in practice has it as a central object of its operation: artistic expression is every bit as central a human activity as political expression (and, arguably, a much more intrinsically valuable commodity). In addition to the inevitable injustice done to art by law's hamfisted indifference to attempting to understand its character before operating on it, the inner integrity of law also suffers by its own subsequent inefficiency (not to mention the harm done to its already philistine[30] reputation). It is bemusing that judges and legislators have not previously registered (in this and other legal contexts) that the basic source of legal difficulty when art comes before the courts is the lack of concerted legal attempt to systematise how to treat it. Ignoring addressing the potentially messy problem of art and art definition at a general level, and doubtless inhibited by the worry of failure but also of the possibility of being seen somehow unfairly to privilege art with special attention by treating it as a distinct cultural category (that other disciplines recognise it is, a recognition increasingly important in plural postmodern society) only compounds the frustration of the smooth working of the law when frequently incidentally faced with it.

Many conceptual problems law encounters by not taking account of the nature of art are encapsulated by the legally-created phenomenon of defamation by fiction, definitionally and practically an impossibility but instituted (somewhat ironically) as a creative legal "term of art" to emblemise a sad series of unjustified lawsuits and concomitant legal misconceptions.

It is only in a superficial sense that fiction can be considered false. Creation rather than representation is not equivalent to either calculated or inadvertent falsehood. Neither does it purport to express literal truth. It is meaningless to enquire (in the vein of the *New York Times* case) "[d]id the writer know he was falsifying?" with reference to a fictional character identified by someone as an unflattering portrayal of himself. First, except, presumably, in the case of an obviously undilutedly favourable portrayal as the plaintiff sees it (for who is to say "objectively" what the content of truly favourable portrayal is?), the creative writer always risks the charge that one of his creations

---

[30] The Philistines were in fact a highly cultured race.

tends to defame. The availability of a lawsuit symbolises legal supporting of the notion that the subjective view of the plaintiff as he sees himself is an object worthy of protection. The lawsuit is allowed to begin on a sort of ultra-vain hunch which is, I contend, morally indefensible. The creative artist is immediately put in a position where he has to explain his creation against a background of only alleged fact i.e. the alleged identification of the plaintiff in the work and his alleged reputation (a tautology really, for a reputation is always alleged and never a fact). Secondly, unless it is accepted that the work is a creative work and never purports to be factual (unlike a report which, ironically, can be more easily defended), fiction is denied the legitimacy of its form, which denial goes against a whole moral and cultural tradition. To ask a novelist if he knew he was falsifying is completely to ignore the creative nature of the genre and enquire of "falsifying" intent that is alien to the already proven creative vocation (as instanced by the work itself). It is rather like asking a law judge if he is blaspheming by acting in his capacity as a law judge. He would reply he is only doing his job, and this is socially accepted as an explanation. However, according to an arguably higher religious rule, he is flagrantly going against a Christian commandment and judging his fellow men.[31] The analogy reveals to us that the law will facilitate doubting the integrity of some vocations with impunity but that we will fail if we doubt certain others. The judge is judging, the novelist creating: even if we doubt the judge's judgment, we are not doubting judging; when we ask the novelist if he is falsifying, we are doing worse than miscasting creativity, we are denying it its method.[32] Legal disrespect for art is here at its height.

Life is often the source of the fiction writer's material, but it is very seldom that life provides the writer with a ready-made story. However, if the main features of a contemporary novelist's work correspond too closely to the plaintiff's life and too little to what he and his "witnesses" consider the exemplary aspects of that life, it is only

---

[31] See Appendix, Essay 3, "Art and Defamation: A Comparative Moral Perspective", below.

[32] Art is an expression of, and stimulus for, imaginative life, which is divorced from actual life by, *inter alia*, the necessary absence of non-contemplative responsive "action" on the part of the receiver. Art's responsibility can include the presentation of æstheticised moralities; it is freed from the binding necessities of extra-artistic morality by courtesy of its inherent operation as art. ". . . [t]ruth is a property of symbolisations of reality, not reality itself" (Robert Motherwell, Exhibition Catalogue, Städtische Kunsthalle, Düsseldorf, 1976). Art speaks to the world in a language of its own, and that requires the reader or viewer to enter art's world in order to hear it properly.

too easy for a court to conclude that the plaintiff has been identified and defamed. The coincidence of some people's real-life character reference and artistic portrayal has been identified without sufficient attention to the highly subjective-opinion-contingent nature of reputation and the intrinsic and necessary functioning of art. If we now impose the traditional US legal tests, the plaintiff who is a public figure will have little difficulty in showing that the writer harboured constitutional actual malice, in the sense that he knew what he was doing, and the plaintiff who is a private figure will likewise prevail, i.e. the defendant will be seen to have acted in negligent disregard for the factual truth of the matter.

The plaintiff has to show clear and convincing proof. The present author is not sure it is possible to prove reputation, for reputation is only a rumour a few choose to share, but the whole *raison d'être* of defamation law is that this rumour, albeit unfactual, large and nebulous (in the case of public plaintiffs) and unfactual, small and nebulous (in the case of private plaintiffs), is worthy and capable of legal protection.

Because of the lack of an agreed method of dealing with defamation by fiction, decisions are, predictably, inconsistent, reasoning for such decisions widely diverse. This does not conform to what is required of a legal order (which is here, in method and effect, patently disorder[33]).

It is undeniably difficult to establish a workable standard to eradicate all the difficulties that arise from defamation by fiction. The situation is not improved by state courts confusing what this author has termed "constitutional actual malice" with "classical malice" i.e. "spite" or "ill will" *simpliciter* by calling them both simply "actual malice". Having resort to classical malice is arguably more profitable in this area than utilisation of the constitutional actual malice doctrine defined in *New York Times* v. *Sullivan* because the latter inappropriately focuses on the creative writer's knowledge of the truth or falsity of his statement, i.e. it ignores the fact that fiction is intrinsically founded on a type of falsehood of which the creative writer is perfectly well aware and consciously unashamedly employs as an habitual part of an artist's *modus operandi*. False "speech", *per se*, is not afforded constitutional protection, and it is self-evident that fiction should not be artifically slotted imprecisely into this category, as was

---

[33] Defamation law's internal disorder is the subject of perennial criticism and too broad a field to be discussed here in general terms.

the unfortunate case in *Bindrim* v. *Mitchell*,[34] for example, where the defendant, an author of a novel, met the *New York Times* standard. Of necessity fiction writers often draw on their real-life experiences to produce effective art, and works of art are not conceived with the intention of their exponent to convey literal truth but often a "higher truth".

A classical malice standard has been advanced by Mary Frances Prechtel.[35] What is to be considered is whether the artist bore ill will or spiteful motivations in what he created around a plaintiff who has allegedly been defamed in the fiction concerned. Classical malice is better than the *New York Times* approach because it applies as a universal test i.e. it is not restricted to public officials or public figures; in addition, *New York Times* furnishes absolutely no specialised protection of the artist, whereas such protection is assured under classical malice because the latter centres on the intention of the author, which comprehends the artistic intention mechanism. Classical malice also has the virtue, oxymoronically, of being applicable to all kinds of fiction, i.e. the standard can embrace pure fiction and the *roman à clef*, and even faction and related media. Under classical malice, if there appeared an instance of coincidental use of someone's real name, when there was no spite or ill will on the part of the artist, the plaintiff would fail to meet the burden of clear and convincing evidence of fault. You cannot intend to harm a plaintiff you do not know of, as illustrated in *Clare* v. *Farrell*,[36] where the court decided the plaintiff had no cause of action for this very reason. However, conversely, a once-close relation between the plaintiff and the defendant artist might prove a very useful factor in establishing classical malice. The classical malice standard, then, does not afford absolute protection even for the "pure" fiction writer in such circumstances. Nevertheless, the latter should not be required, in Prechtel's words, "to scour his memory to eviscerate all possible resemblances between his fictional characters and real persons". In the instance of a *roman à clef*, an author bases his characters on real people but conceals their identities by the use of fictitious names. The classical malice test is particularly useful in the context of this medium because the effort to transmute and conceal the real person is evidence that no ill will towards the real-life individual was intended. Where "faction" is

[34] 155 Cal. Rptr. 29 (Cal Ct. App.).
[35] "Classical Malice: A New Fault Standard for Defamation in Fiction" (1994) 55 *Ohio State Law Journal*, 187.
[36] 70F Supp. 276 (D Minn. 1947).

created, in which the plaintiff's real name is used, there is no concealment as in the *roman à clef*, but the author's creativity is safeguarded against successful prosecution because he intended no harm to the plaintiff as required by the classical malice doctrine. Although the motion arts are beyond the ambit of this book, the reader may be interested to note that even "docudrama" is protectable when it adds fictional dialogue to a biographical account of a famous person's life: although the creative exponent is attempting to recreate real-life events, he is doing so in the context of an artistic medium, and lack of intended harm to the real-life person should insulate the creator from any liability.

Greatest certainty in the law is probably achieved by the "absolute protection" approach, courtesy of its unconditional character. Black J posited this approach when dissenting in *Communist Party* v. *Subversive Activities Control Board*[37]: ". . . the Founders . . . gave the Government the fullest power to prosecute overt action in violation of valid laws but withheld any power to punish people for nothing more than advocacy of their views". Concurring in *Garrison* v. *Louisiana*,[38] Douglas Dayler J opined: "the only line drawn by the Constitution is between 'speech' on the one side and conduct or overt acts on the other". Professor Alexander Meiklejohn writes that "[l]iterature and the arts must be protected by the First Amendment. They lead the way toward sensitive and informed appreciation and response to the values out of which the riches of the general welfare are created."[39] In addition, absolute protection has been fostered in practice by some courts which seem to have almost intuitively granted such immunity in accordance with the principle that being simply "invention", fiction cannot defame.[40]

The common law defence of fair comment is instrumental in protecting artistic as well as political criticism, and in this regard champions, albeit indirectly, the arts in general. It is not directly suited to the defence of artistic expression *per se* and has its origins in political concern; these origins subsist in the approaches of scholars such as Professor Silver,[41] who urge the application of the fair comment doc-

---

[37] 367 US 1, 168 (1961).

[38] 379 US 64, 82 (1964).

[39] A. Meiklejohn, "The First Amendment is an Absolute" [1961] *Sup. Ct. Rev.* 245 (Black and Douglas JJ, and Professor Emerson, are also known as absolutists).

[40] See, e.g., *Clare* v. *Farrell*, 70 F Supp. 276 (D Minn. 1947) and *Lyons* v. *New American Library, Inc.*, 78 AD 2d 723, 432 NYS 2d 536 (1980).

[41] R. Silver, "Libel, the 'Higher Truths' of Art, and the First Amendment", 126 *UPa. LRev.* 1065 (1978).

trine to protect that class of literature in which public figures inhabit the fictional world. Though consent is always a defence to a defamation charge, it has no *particular* relevance for artistic works, though it may have in appropriate circumstances. Truth is another available defence, but in practice so strict a test is not a suitable defence for a creative work, infused as it is with other than literal truth, which addition is seen as diluting the literal truth and in effect the defence (based as it is on literal truth). The type of truth that arises from the moral consciousness of the writer is not the type which a court will consider a defence: when it comes to justification, the law restricts itself to the hardest facts. Art is again a no-man's-land in a sea of rules unsuited to it.[42] Law unaccommodated for treatment of one of its prime objects is particularly remarkable in a country where the constitutional dynamic purports to ensure promotion of all things good and worthwhile.

French defamation law is based on a dual interest, in the protection not just of reputation but of honour. This is embodied in article 29 of the statute of 29 July 1881, confirmed, as stated earlier in the new penal code. There is no crime without the element of public exposure, and this is deemed possible via a number of written and visual artistic works: drawings, prints, painting, emblems and images. As is common in French law, such a list is not exhaustive, albeit comprehensive and highly illustrative of what the legislators had in mind, and categories such as "images" are deliberately chosen for their semantic breadth open to flexible interpretation. The list in article 28 is not interpretable as finite and, although it is true that the decree-law of 29 July 1939 abrogated article 28 respecting obscenity ("outrage of good morals"), article 28 retains its legal value for specifying certain means of fulfilling the publicity requirement in defamation.[43]

In preserving reputation and honour, the law purports to protect essentially moral values. I am of the firm belief that this is morally, if not practically and socially, misguided.[44] French law in this respect

---

[42] For a similar conclusion, see Vivian Deborah Wilson, "The Law of Libel and the Art of Fiction" (1981) 44(4), *Law and Contemporary Problems*, 27 at 49. For a less sympathetic stance towards creative writers, see Frederick Schauer, "Liars, Novelists, and the Law of Defamation," 51 *Brooklyn Law Review*, 233, 1985.

[43] Cass, 23 Jan. 1950, D. 51–217, note Mimin. Art. 29 states that defamation comprises "every allegation or imputation of a fact which casts a slur on the honour or esteem of the personality or body to which the fact is imputed". Art. 28 states that publicity can result from drawings, prints, paintings, emblems or images put up for sale, distributed or exposed to the public.

[44] N. 31 above.

adopts a traditional stance comparable to English law (and American law, based as it is on English law), its root in societal mores long since demoded. Oddly, these old mores are not based on the Christian morality one might expect for Christ does not uphold reputation as a value but, rather, scorns it. How bizarre it seems that "honour" and "reputation" should have been perpetuated as of moral value by law independent of the prevailing religious ethic. This is something of an anomaly. The author's contention is that it would have been, and is, more consistent with morality (and Christian morality) to promote creativity (art) without attention to whether art harmed reputation, the latter being of negligible or no intrinsic moral worth. The crux of Christian morality, and life, is creation. To promote reputation at the expense of creation and creativity, for which defamation law sometimes, if not always, arguably stands, is to establish a legal morality at odds with a more basic human and spiritual value system. In the healthy creative liberality of postmodernism the latter system is happily gaining prominence once again, and defamation law should be reformed in the light of eclectic postmodern ethics, anti status-awareness and pro artistic creativity.

Particularly anomalous is the case of defamation by fiction. In France, the regulation is of direct and clearly personal attacks, as in England and America. It seems improbable that fiction could be either a direct or a personal attack on anybody, not least when the artistic context of the communication is clear. However, defamation law has strained to accommodate defamation suits/prosecutions against novelists, particularly in America where libel actions against fiction are altogether more prolific in a society which, it is fair to say, is more "libel-happy". In England and France, there are very few defamation actions against fiction, less to do with the structure of the law than a reluctance so to utilise and thereby develop it.

In France, as in England and America, there is a presumption of bad faith on the part of the accused that the proof of absence of personal animosity does not remove. Art is not free to express simply because the artist's conscience is free: French defamation law punishes defamatory results of expression irrespective of the artist's lack of *mens rea*.[45] This situation requires the artist to be very vigilant before making his œuvres public: he must check the range of the law to try to ensure he does not infringe it (a difficult task, given the legal scope for victims unknown as well as known to him). When he

---

[45] As in England and America.

knows the breadth of his potential liability, this undoubtedly affects the unfettered nature of his future creativity and, arguably, harms the purity of the creative process, blocking the channels of creativity with intruding lumps of law that his mind must consider and his imagination not overwhelm. Somewhat inequitably, whereas imposition of the presumption of bad faith on the artist is a set burden, the presumption elides in the context of "objective" literary or artistic criticism devoid of polemic.[46] Although this gives a degree of protection to the arts critic (as opposed to the artist), it nevertheless begs the question how emotive artistic/literary criticism is allowed to be; it would seem that French law only guarantees protection for the sober review and, consistent with this, in practice favours protection of scientific criticism, more devoid as it is of emotion-based content.

Merle and Vitu assert,[47] without giving authority, that an action for defamation cannot arise from artistic critiques of an arts critic so long as he restricts his criticism to the insufficiency of talent of the given artist without criticising his professional probity. The critic finds the demand for such a balancing act difficult to meet, since an artist's job and talent merge so completely. Indeed, it is arguable that it is impossible to criticise the integrity of an art-work without simultaneously/co-extensively criticising the professional integrity of the artist. Compare distinguishing the dancer and her dance.

Unsurprisingly perhaps, given its close relation to political concern, the Cour de Cassation is relatively tolerant of political polemic,[48] and it will be seen to be a feature of defamation law in all three jurisdictions that comment on politics is considered more valuable than comment on the arts, so is better insulated by the law against defamation charges. The dubious justification for this preference is that society has a greater "real" interest in the political. If this is the case, society needs its sense of values revamped; more likely though is that the law is not up-to-date in its notions of what society really wants: plural late postmodern society places great emphasis on the organic and spiritual side of Man[49] (after an early postmodern somewhat passive cultural eclecticism[50]) and is deeply concerned

[46] Aix, 28 July 1947, JCP, 1948.II.4031, note Colombini; Paris, 12 Dec. 1956, JCP, 1957.II.9702, RSC, 1957, 378, with observations by Hugueney; Trib. Corr., Paris, 24 Nov. 1969, JCP, 1970.II.16217, note PMB, RSC, 1970, 395, with observations by Levasseur.

[47] Roger Merle and André Vitu, *Traité de droit criminel; droit pénal spécial (par André Vitu)* (Editions Cujas, Paris, 1982), ch. II at 1578.

[48] Cass. Crim., 23 Mar. 1978, "B.", 115, RSC, 1979, 332, with observations by Levasseur.

[49] Hence New-Ageism, for example.

[50] See Appendix, Essay 1, below, for further information on postmodernism.

with the promotion of creativity, the creative arts and concomitant criticism.[51] Here, as elsewhere, defamation law can be blamed for not being sufficiently activist. A dynamist approach would be to eradicate the concept of defamation by art (in law) and thus help create a society of more robust individuals who could not resort to law to protect their ignoble fears of social rejection (and economic disadvantage) indirectly resultant not from art but the evil of status-consciousness or convention-consciousness that presently dominates so many lives, making them less free, less creative and more petty. Eradicating the possibility of defamation by art would also encourage public understanding of art as something independent of life, offering not attacking, but, if characterisable as "attacking", only so in a very oblique way and insufficiently to harm in other than a thought-provoking and ultimately positive way. Art improves[52] and is provided for contemplation, inner digestion unintended to spur outer negative impacts. There is something morally repulsive about legally protecting a rich plaintiff who claims to have had merely his image tarnished, and more so for him to receive vaster sums of money than, for example, victims of mindless physical aggression.

In French law, there are some surprising policy preferences evident in the case law regarding the legal power to appreciate an allegedly defamatory statement in context. One might think art a medium (context) incapable of defamation because its form alerts us to the fact that it is not fact, not opinion, just art. However, the law makes no such assumption. Instead, consideration of context unqualifiedly protects a different area, namely, off-the-cuff insults which are undoubtedly meritless and the most obviously directly offensive things! A sober response to this appalling example of the law's moral inversion of society's morality would be the following plea, that as well as accepting the nature of "spur of the moment" abuse in a heated argument, and the nature of a joke, the law should accept the nature of art and that the artistic context is as much a defamation-exempt environment as these others, which have decidedly less noble aims to justify their utterance and insulation from prosecution. To its credit, French law does put a strong general emphasis on the need not to isolate any putatively defamatory comment from its complete context.

---

[51] The increasingly leisure-based nature of Western society also invites an increase in creative activity.

[52] Art can reform as well as inform thinking. At the very least, it is a beneficial cultural experience, usually pleasurable.

Successful actions for defamation by fiction, for example, are facilitated by the rule that the victim does not have to be indicated by name[53]: it is enough that he can be identified by quite a wide circle of recipients of the writing. This "test" is deliberately vague; the number of people who are needed to identify the victim successfully varies according to the precise circumstances of each action.[54] To identify the victim by the uncomplimentary portrayal in a novel, his "circle" must, of necessity, identify him with the image he finds so unflattering. In effect, the portrayal must be substantially true. This, sadly, does not protect the novelist despite the established legal defence of truth which in other circumstances obliterates the defamation charge. In all circumstances, truth has to be "completely" evinced for the defence to be successful[55]—an impossible task for creative fiction where the real-life model is usually not "truly" presented, i.e. in the sense of literally and strictly according to life. Strangely, whereas the ordinance of 6 May 1944 widened the ambit of the *exceptio veritatis* by declaring that proof of truth can always be established, it does not apply in cases where, *inter alia*, the defamation strikes at the private life of the victim (in which area a novelist often finds inspiration). The divide between public and private life is rather indistinct; similarly, which image of his life is a person entitled to protect, the arguably false one he projects in society which he argues should be preserved because this image is the one his "reputation" relies on or the private one we are led to presume is his real side? Should a victim only be allowed to protect his "true" self-image, if at all? When are we really ourselves? In private, or in public, or, perhaps, as presented in fiction by another (of arguably quite some percipience)?

Protection of the reputation of the dead by law is a function of criminal law and amounts to no more than a protection of heirs and other people closely associated with the defamed dead person. Article 34 of the 1881 statute in effect protects living people via the reputation of the dead person. If it is conceded that honour is a value to be protected by law, would it not be appropriate to protect the very people who cannot possibly exercise any right of reply to their critics i.e. the dead? There is surely nothing so dishonourable as to defame someone totally incapable of putting forward his own view in his defence. It is likely that the law does not protect the reputation

---

[53] Art. 29, L.1881.
[54] Cass. Crim., 17 Mar. 1932.
[55] Paris (1st ch.), 23 Dec. 1981, Gaz.Pal., 1981, I.128.

of the dead because it is simply inexpedient to do so: their inert position means they are no longer power-units in the game of real life (cannot assert any rights), so the law feels no corresponding compulsion to protect their honour or reputation even if severely damaged.[56] A personal contention is that this indicates that the law only protects hurt feelings and economic interests, not honour. It is a charade to dignify defamation law with having honour as its object; and in the course of purporting to protect honour, it makes it dependent on life.

The creative artist is again one of the peculiar victims of this approach. It is often the case that artists find recognition after their life-time. Not only does defamation law inhibit their using of real people as models for art but denies them an ultimate right to their own "honour", precisely when it becomes of any or particular note. I have often been offended for deceased artists when critics have seemingly unjustly "defamed" them with a significant degree of insensitivity.[57] Fortunately, appropriately appreciative critics often prove their champion. This is no thanks to law, but to the integrity of respectful sensitive individuals who comprehend the value of art and the difficulties and high-mindedness inherent in the will to create.

CONCLUSIONS

From the available sources it seems that if in a work of art the plaintiff is not named and the portrait is such as to be defamatory, it must be so dissimilar to the plaintiff as not to be truly identifiable as him; naming is therefore necessary, but not sufficient, for purposes of identification, and anything else is not.

In providing for fiction to be defamatory, the law runs the risk of preventing the dissemination in society of real moral messages based on bad as well as good experience of life. Novelists will be afraid to

---

[56] It is a lamentable habit of society to debunk deceased heroes and heroines on a whim: we eventually hear of sexual "kinkiness", for example, on the parts of nearly all of them—war heroes such as T.E. Lawrence, a great number of artists and writers including, recently, John Betjeman, social reformers and humanitarians such as Albert Schweitzer and Gandhi. It is to be hoped that Mother Teresa, for example, will never be subject to such misconceived and destructive prurience, but the likelihood of her being spared is, shamefully, remote.

[57] Consider certain critical treatment of Boris Pasternak (*Times Literary Supplement*, 9–15 Feb. 1990 at 135–6). Did the weight of concrete evidence explain the negative slant of the article? Can it be argued that Pasternak, author of, *inter alia, Doctor Zhivago* and Nobel Prizewinner, was not (at least) a "very good" artist?

transmute their bad experience with the degree of realism it demands if they are made vulnerable (again) to lawsuits from the bad. Moreover, is not the novelist as much at liberty to penetrate and present a personality independent of rumour as the plaintiff is at liberty self-satisfiedly to enjoy the pretence of an image he considers more favourable (which may be just a facade)? Is it the law protecting reputation that in fact promotes a "falsehood" to the detriment of higher truth? In addition, from an artist's standpoint, an artistic product may be improved (be created more intensely) if the artist has an "axe to grind" from real experience. The opposite can also be true.

It is impossible to construct an argument that the defendant has negligently defamed in an art work because harm from an art work is only possible contingently, i.e. via harm inflicted by the interpreting audience who have misinterpreted art as fact. Causation is too remote, not least because created art is a passive medium, and meant to be interpreted as food for the mind and senses, not to instill retribution of someone i.e. shunning on the part of the audience.

It is sometimes suggested that a fiction writer use a disclaimer, the function of which includes evidence of the author's intent not to harm anyone, thereby undermining a counter-contention of classical malice. But such disclaimers are based on the assumption that a universal level of ignorance exists about how to approach an art-work. Moreover, an artist, in whatever medium, should not have to encumber his creations with such legalese. Imposing liability on an artist for using an ineffective disguise of a real-life character or for his inadvertent coincidental use of a name someone has in real life is a very primitive abrogation of basic art appreciation.

Anyway, standard disclaimer language cannot be enough to guide an audience to the conclusion that what they are presented with is art. What it would be sufficient to say is that the material aspired to being art, and as such was not meant to be interpreted or acted upon as fact.

If one examines the type of plaintiffs who bring libel actions (who in Britain have to be rich because there is no legal aid to bring action for defamation), can it not be observed that the real *raison d'être* for the preserving of defamation law is the preserving of bourgeois snobbery and status-consciousness?[58] In contrast to the *avant-garde* attitudes of the artistic, is not the law also imposing the lawyers' and

---

[58] Consider the case of Jeffrey Archer, who "ran for Oxford", and other irrelevant considerations such as his having, according to Caulfield J, a "fragrant" wife. See, further, "Libel Trial of the Century", *The Observer*, 14 Nov. 1989.

politicians' traditional sense of public decency, which is notoriously conservative, hence why are one's private affairs, including those in the sexual realm, often the object of protection? Why is Anglo-American society, in particular, so antagonistic to sexual openness?

Why should there be legal concern for the factually contentless notion of reputation? What other rumour gains legal protection? In the context of defamation by the novel, what place is there for the consideration that the philosophical education/advancement of the public is a public good? Does this deserve more credit for being of worth than the perpetuation of obsession with "reputation" (others' opinions of you)? If the First Amendment accommodates the gossip-monger, why not the sophisticated reader of novels?[59] Moreover, if the individual's sensitivities are sacrificed for the purposes of politics or medicine,[60] why not for art?

In the US, distinguishing between public and private plaintiffs, is the law being fair? The argument is that public plaintiffs have less right to reputational privacy because they have consciously exposed their lives to public scrutiny. But is it just that men who have had the vigour, ambition and success to become public figures should be so penalised (while "shrinking violets" are coddled into being ever weaker)?

Why does the First Amendment protect the dissemination of bla-tantly cruel, destructive and negative ideas without more, but permit the censorship (by defamation law) of some art (creative and enjoy-able medium that it is)? Contrast the moral merits of tort law's pro-tection of a rich public figure such as American evangelist Jerry Falwell for having been parodied with the inappropriate lack of legal protection of a community against stark racist antagonism in which the American Nazi Party was granted permission to march through the predominantly Jewish community of Stokie, Illinois, even though the court acknowledged that the march would cause serious psychological harm to some community residents, many of whom were survivors of Nazi concentration camps.[61] Can the First Amendment be used to justify the protection of such vicious politi-cal ideas, and at the same time allow the restriction of artistic ones?

---

[59] My concern here is moral rather than practical. The law protects people from the evil effects of a rumour because an adverse rumour can in certain circumstances socially, eco-nomically or politically disadvantage them. Art presents artistic portraits that are ontologi-cally incapable of these effects: art is *only* art, and should be received as such.

[60] See "Scare over Reagan's Health", *U.S. New & World Rep.*, 22 July 1985, at 9–10.

[61] See, *inter alia*, cert. denied, 439 US 916 (1978).

Which is more seriously-intended real harm, that to rich successful public figures by parody or the Jewish Community by the Nazi marchers?

Authors of fiction aim at realism rather than literal descriptive accuracy. Fiction is about life without purporting to be factual. Fiction-writers aspire to truth-statement uncommitted to what many consider facts, because they know that these perceptions of fact are not necessarily true; fiction-writers look round and through and over things, create from experience. What defamation law terms the defence of "truth" or "justification" is fact-based, not truth-based in the artistic or philosophical sense. Writers of fiction that presents truth from experience of, *inter alia*, facts, cannot employ the legal defence which requires that their text, to be "true", presents true not creatively transmuted facts the law can then evaluate against those stated by the plaintiffs. The legal defence of truth or justification is unaccommodating of the higher truth beyond the world of literal fact. Only special rules will give effect to the fact that artistic fiction causes no harm when treated as art.

Some commentators maintain that fiction should be classed as opinion, and thereby in the USA protected under the First Amendment. While this would protect pure fiction, an art form based on both fact and opinion might be jeopardised: "faction", as this is sometimes called, is a medium increasingly finding favour with creative writers. In this instance, the ascertained facts in the work might be sufficient to defeat the defendant author under the *New York Times* standard. In *Pring* v. *Penthouse*,[62] it was found that an article that ridiculed the Miss America competition could not be taken as true, focusing on the reader's perception for the author's defence. But this form of protecting free speech is inadequate because the test is too subjective and therefore precarious: what one reader thinks will differ from what another thinks. Focusing on the intent of the creative writer is a more effective method of insulating his work from being outlawed.

We cannot defame the dead *per se*, except Christ, the defaming of whose reputation we call blasphemy.[63] Ignoring the theological contentious point that He transcends death to be ever-living, so cannot after all be considered dead, the law of blasphemy is *ex facie* evidence that only the very special dead are entitled to reputation preservation. The law of blasphemy is little-used but could usefully be supplemented

---

[62] 695 F 2d 438 (10th Cir. 1983).

[63] Legal measures against blasphemy are arguably against the First Amendment. They are enforced in England.

by a law of defamation of the dead to help prove (or even suggest) that reputation/honour, as opposed to something more expedient, is indeed the central justification for having a law of defamation. The author maintains that contemporary defamation law is a (false) image-preserving device designed for the perpetuation of a status-consciousness[64] and "social front"-based culture, the bastion of the touchy, *pro hubris*, anti–truth and openness in effect and, as such, anti normal healthy organic inter-human communication.

Consider the benefits to a plaintiff mean-spirited and pompous enough to bring a defamation action against an art work he finds unflattering. A hypercritical portrayal may do him a service if he reflects on it (presuming he has a self-critical dimension). Consider how defamation law devalues the roles of truth, art, humour and humility and consider what it does value. Is what it upholds really of value? To either individuals or society? Would a state without defamation law but with the right of reply produce a more creative, wholesome and refreshing society?

Qualified privilege as operated in English law protects the maker of an untrue defamatory statement, but only does so if the maker of the statement acted honestly and without malice. If the plaintiff can prove "express malice", the privilege is displaced and he may recover damages, but it is for him to prove malice, once the privilege has been made out, not for the defendant to disprove it. It is for the jury to decide whether malice has been proved, but it is for the judge to rule whether or not the occasion is a privileged one. Malice in this connection may mean either (a) a lack of belief in the truth of the statement or (b) use of the privileged occasion for an improper purpose. As a matter of legal reform, qualified privilege could be used to protect art, with an appropriate modification of the concept of malice in rebuttal. Malice here could comprise the disingenuous use of an art-form for defamatory purposes.

Factual statements must be justified but honest opinions or comments which refer only implicitly to facts can be successfully defended if in the public interest. Though art is of public interest as an important sphere of cultural activity, art necessarily constitutes neither facts nor honest opinion nor comment on facts. It might alternatively be described as "value".[65] This makes it a difficult cate-

---

[64] N. 58 above.

[65] On constitutional development from this standpoint, see Michele Ainis, "Per una Storia Costituzionale dell'Arte", *Politica Del Diritto* a.XXIII, no. 3, Sept. 1992, Sect. 1.1. at 475: "L'arte costituisce, da sempre, un valore . . .".

gory for existing defamation law, of only opinion/fact distinctions, to regulate. The situation is not helped by art's non-recognition in defamation law as a distinct category with its non-factual non-opinion peculiar characteristics of cultural value and public interest. It is arguable in these circumstances that the law should operate on art as a category in addition to fact and opinion. Though defining art causes difficulty for its isolation for legal treatment, the ignoring of the problem of art means law's existing mechanisms are confused by it. Isolating art as a special category of defamation law would at least disinfect the operation of the fact/opinion distinction from art's contamination of legal clarity when artificially forced into one or other inappropriate category. This can be achieved by recognition of art as a cultural category without need for its definition but, rather, with recognition of the elusiveness of its definition, which is part of its ontology. Art, like obscenity, can be singled out in the general and legal interest without defining it.

5

The Public Funding of Art

INTRODUCTION

Apart from adumbrating the basic purposes of public funding bodies and the bureaucratic hierarchies of decision-making, law plays a very marginal role in the actual exercise of arts policy, and decisions on grant allocation in particular cases, which shape the concept of art fostered in this context. An exception is when legal adjustment to policy is required by other public policy considerations such as the proscription of obscenity. Law then helps ensure the social respectability of sponsored art in accordance with public majority sentiment. In other respects, artistic ideas and trends espoused by personnel in the public funding of the arts remain variable and fluid, particularised and topical, in accordance with active specialist involvement including consideration, in their discretion and judgement, of artistic quality, but also of prospective public sympathy or interest as factors in the approval of individual art projects. The intended result is populist and consumerist as well as meritocratic. This does not preclude positive discrimination in favour of "minority" art if that is deemed to be considered politically correct by the majority. The public funding of the arts thus presents a context wherein factors extraneous to artistic merit are employed to determine officially-approved art of the funding body in accordance with the criteria of perceived public support and for consumption as well as artistic quality. Their precise formulation, and relative weight, go unpublished publicly; and law does not prescribe otherwise. This means that popular art is privately determined with the use of public funds.

The public funding of the arts is an area that is constantly changing in policy as well as detail. For this reason, this chapter lays emphasis on some historical trends and airs particularly pressing current problems. A recurrent feature is the importance of government in dictating arts policy. This is an obvious facet in France where there is a well-established Ministry of Culture. The newly-established Ministry of Culture, Media and Sport in England has yet to develop fully its relationship with the allegedly "independent" Arts Council (previously held at "arm's length" from government), and the American National Endowment for the Arts has come under increasing pressure from government, as evidenced by the recent Congress interference in the allocation of public funding to "indecent" and "obscene" art.

The concept of art in public funding is institutionalised. The arrangement of departments within a ministry or quasi-independent body in itself defines artistic categories. The confidentiality of funding decisions also insulates the process. Because of the acceptance of discretionary decisions in arts funding, the onlooker can only infer artistic strategies, which tend to be politically shaped (unless they are explicitly stated, and even then they can conceal more indirect goals than simply the advancement of the arts, such as the advancement of the existing government).

To avoid prejudgement of artistic goals and policies in the realm of the public funding of the arts, a somewhat descriptive approach has been necessitated, and also some political evaluation, prior to the more incisive drawing of conclusions. Interest in this area does not centre on substantive law but on the operation of arts policy and artistic judgements against a very basic legal background which gives the simplest of frameworks by which the relevant institutions have been constituted.

No arts policy, as a major public policy, had existed in France before the creation of a specific ministry, in 1959, by Charles de Gaulle and André Malraux. From 1959 to 1969, Malraux installed a considerable policy which aimed at conservation as much as art promotion and creation. This policy was modified by nine ministers from 1969 to 1981. The Arts Council of Great Britain was formed in August 1946 to continue in peacetime the work begun with government support by the Council for the Encouragement of Music and the Arts. The Arts Council operated under a revised Royal Charter granted in 1967 in which its objects are stated as:

(a) to develop and improve the knowledge, understanding and practice of the arts;
(b) to increase the accessibility of the arts to the public throughout Great Britain;

(c) to advise and co-operate with departments of government, local authorities and other bodies.

In 1965, in America, the first statute supporting the arts since the Depression was passed. The National Foundation for the Arts and the Humanities Act of 1965 established the National Foundation for the Arts and the Humanities.[1] The Act was unique in creating an agency specifically for the arts and humanities and established the National Endowment for the Arts (NEA) and the National Endowment for the Humanities.

PUBLIC FUNDING POLICY

(a) *England*

In Britain, the funding of the arts has rested unhappily on two discordant principles without ever finding a successful method of harmonising them. Although arts policies after the Second World War have altered radically from government to government,[2] two basic central preoccupations are constant:

(1) The need to be seen to be socially fair in approach to grant allocation.
(2) The need to promote artistic quality.

These objectives reside together very challengingly because quality implies excellence and excellence implies elitism.

In 1946, the Arts Council of Great Britain was established to continue the guiding principle "the Best for the Most". From the start, there was better catering for the performing arts than for the static arts, notably in favour of the National Theatre, the Royal Opera, ballet and classical music. The source of this preference is obscure, but probably rests in the theory that most people prefer to watch than to paint or to write: it was a consumptive view of art, to give satisfaction to the most. Much smaller grants were given to authors. Despite this disproportion, the Arts Council was generally received as a welcome constitutional invention. Politically, it was a hybrid. The money was given by government to an independent body which

[1] Pub.L. No. 89–209, 79 Stat. 845 (1965) (codified as amended at 20 USCA 5.951–968 (West 1974 and Supp. 1983)).
[2] See, more generally, Boris Ford (ed.), *The Cambridge Guide to the Arts In Britain* (Cambridge University Press, Cambridge, 1988) vol. 9.

was posed between politicians and artists, and so grant-making decisions were made at "arm's length" from government (by volunteers experienced in different art forms and not by bureaucrats). Conceptually, it seemed fair and efficient but by the mid-1980s (after six years under a Tory government) the Arts Council was thought by many to have become "a creature of government".

The Arts Council annual reports reveal the fluctuations in the success of arts funding from the standpoint of the arts. In the 1950s, the prevailing economic austerity was reflected in the titles of the Council's reports: "Art In The Red" and "The Struggle For Survival". In the 1960s, the arts fared better, but by the early 1970s the world oil crisis had hit the economy and arts spending was adversely affected. It is significant that the Labour government which was turned out in 1979 had voted a sum for the Arts Council which the in-coming Tory government reduced by over a million pounds. The new government shifted the balance from public funding to business sponsorship (reflecting, *inter alia*, increased modelling of US policies?). Charitable giving was gradually displaced by business dealing, publicity and advertising for the sponsor. Thatcherism heralded the inauguration of the commercial approach to all aspects of organic and artistic life, arguably sterilising the "feel" of living in favour of a depersonalising economic emphasis. This attack on emotional and creative subjectivity penetrated not just arts funding but the basic focus of the British mentality. In short, it was damaging for culture in the broadest sense: "economising" life visions.

A certain leftist political cynicism has also arguably harmed the development of the arts. This entailed the mistaken equation of the promotion of artistic excellence with political elitism. This will probably sadly reappear in reaction to the Thatcher–Major régimes (promoting as they did the flourishing of the well-footed ambitious and successful). In the realm of the arts, any reaction should really be focused against depersonalising influence. Government should promote creativity and organic inter-enriching on all levels of human life—a personable society. This can co-reside with a theory of excellence in the arts very happily if artistic standards are not (very naïvely) confused with politics. All that is needed is ensured meritocratic evaluation of art irrespective of the socio-political origin of its creator. The arm's-length principle should operate to the exclusion of any hint of political preference in the shaping of the nation's artistic growth. Art should be allowed its own wings with more adequate funding from a beneficent but undemanding source: indulgent, loving and altruistic patronage for the good of the nation's creative life and ultimate richness. Ironically, fostering free and unharnessed creativity would probably generate greater national economic benefits than deliberately consumer-conscious art created in a strait-jacket. Resultant art would be better, and the best art encouraged by grants awarded by experts in accordance with the criterion of intrinsic artistic quality. Any eye to posterity will ensure that the struggling painter or poet with his more durable product will gain priority for grant receipt over the audience-oriented performing art preference currently exercised. Heritage will then accrue.

In the 1950s, a noble attempt was made to restore the artistic standard of excellence, but the poor economic climate precluded success of what was easily (if mistakenly) caricatured as an elitist policy. "Few but roses" is the maxim of the promotion of beauty, not of a pernicious clitism; it is in everyone's interest that the state fosters only good, as opposed to shoddy, art. In the 1960s and 1970s, there was a strange and negative phobia prevalent, a fear of saying that anything was better than anything else. Thatcherism exploited the flavour of this uncertainty and led the disillusioned to more selfish economic goals. Culture was shifted aside like a tree by a great wind; economics pressed art against the wall. What then evolved was more culture-free than cultural, and a community greyness resultant from artistic inertia and creative emphasis deficit (a governmental lacuna).

Making excellence accessible is far from bourgeois cultural imperialism. It is the offering of the best to the most. It is not simply condescending to assume that the general public has no eye for, or no interest in, the best. It is also untrue. It is the sort of lie a branch of the political left like to promote to provoke "the people" into feeling dissatisfied (in order to fulfil their own selfish, mediocre and political purpose). They do not want what is best for people and country and world.

The linking of the concept of education to the arts in the mid-1970s (arts organisations with educational programmes) was a genuinely positive sensible attempt to overcome both elitist accusation and leftist fears, and is still succeeding in helping enrich people's lives, despite inadequate funding.

The 1970s and 1980s also saw the rise of attention to arts in the regions. This is the source of great current friction. The basic idea was to ensure that the metropolis did not have a monopoly of funding. This suffers from the assumption that geography should be a factor in grant allocation over, perhaps, superior artistic merit conse-

quently disfavourably geographically placed because in the metropolis, and therefore implicitly prejudiced against in favour of the
more "equitable" distribution of funds in accord with a geographical
rather than artistic concept of equity. A personal opinion is that
excellence should always prevail over geographical or "ethnic" considerations in the allocation of grants, which considerations can be
accommodated independently so that evaluation of artistic merit and
positive discrimination are not applied together in what should be an
exclusively meritocratic test.

The present short outline of the funding of the arts in Britain ends
on a sombre note. Britain spends less on the arts per head of popula-
tion than any of its European neighbours. The USA alone has a worse
record. For the nation's artistic welfare, the Thatcher–Reagan, then
Thatcher–Bush, political intimacy was less than fortunate. One has
only to witness the dominance of consumer culture in America to
appreciate the need in Britain for greater cultural affinity with older,
less shallow cultures. Old does not necessarily mean good, but it suggests greater cultural richness. Age has a depth youth cannot possibly
have, and the benefits for Britain in Europe should be fully espoused.

United we stand, divided we fall?: the arm's length principle was
arguably jeopardised by intended devolution of Arts Council powers
to the regions. It is for the Arts Council to determine, under its Royal
Charter, any reorganisation of arts funding, not the government.[3] It
is for the Council, and not the minister, to decide whether, and, if so,
to what extent, it should have a strategic rather than a hands-on operational role; and it is for the Council, not arts bureaucrats and local
politicians, to evaluate the effectiveness and efficiency of such
regional arts bodies the Council may consider appropriate to receive
devolved funding or functions. Certain policies expounded by Arts
Minister Richard Luce suggested to some the endangering of gov-
ernment-manipulation-free arts funding autonomy.

The Minister himself had no such fears.[4] Mr Luce said that Britain
was on the threshold of a flowering of artistic endeavour and that his
changes, in which most funding would be devolved from the Arts
Council to smaller regional bodies, would increase accountability.
Suspiciously, this was part of a "wider" governmental perspective and
the Thatcher government had a poor record for arts promotion

---

[3] See *The Independent*, 30 Mar. 1990, at 18, "Letters", "Resignation of the Arts Council's
secretary-general", letter of Henry Lydiate.

[4] See, *ibid.*, 9 Apr. 1990, at 3, "Luce Attempts to Quell Fears over the 'Devolution' of
Arts Funding".

initiative (demonstrable not least in its inadequate funding of the arts[5]). The new Ministry of Culture, Media and Sport, under the charge of Chris Smith, suggests positive change.

The Luce reforms themselves were hardly overtly pernicious. They constituted the Regional Arts Associations (that became boards) as a set of consistently organised institutions for the first time. The new boards have not only more responsibility and money, but a place on the Arts Council as well. In theory, this could mean that, for the first time in many years, the Arts Council is able and strong enough to speak for all the nation's artists and organisations. More dangerously, if the Arts Council is left with only half a dozen bodies to fund, and some hazy think-tank functions, it will be in effect just another small arts board.[6] This would leave a serious vacuum at the national level, with no organisation strong enough to stand up to either an interventionist government or the collective parochialism of local authorities. The British scene would mirror the Swedish situation: impressive local facilities but little national or international significance. A personal view is that the consumptive superficial immediate-enjoyment-based cultural priority of the Thatcher government impoverished the nation's wealth in the long term by the blatant devaluing of the excellent in favour of the populist and provincial. The "reform" move was merely a sop to what that malingering government considered would please an impulsive public appetite (a public they envisaged wanting lots of cheap thrills on their doorstep). Regionalisation in this form helps dissolve attempts to encourage artistic heritage of enduring worth and to facilitate government control of what is allowed to be art (if art is of sufficient interest to it, which itself is doubtful).

Robert Hewison has observed[7] that "[t]he British system is pure muddle". He states that:

> "on the one hand, the government funds our national art galleries and museums directly; on the other, local authorities are allowed to support local museums and arts activities, but are not legally obliged to do so, and get no financial help from the government if they do. Between these two rather shaky pillars of central and local government direct-funding lies the Keynenian quango, the Arts Council of Great Britain (now divided into

---

[5] A report on arts spending published on 10 Apr. 1990 put the UK second only to the USA at the bottom of a league table of 7 countries' direct expenditure per head by central and local government in 1987: see *Cultural Trends*, Issue 5 from the Policy Studies Institute, 100 Park Village East, London NW1, and the summary "British Arts Spending Lags Behind" in *The Independent* of 10 Apr. 1992.

[6] See n. 3 above, letter of Simon Mundy.

[7] *The Sunday Times*, 9 June 1996, Sect. 10, at 8–10.

English, Scottish and Welsh Councils) and the ACGB's offspring, the regional arts boards. Their money still comes from the taxpayer, but it is filtered by this peculiarly British form of intermediary body, which is supposed to be accountable both to the artistic community at large and to their public, but which, in practice, is accountable to nobody. Overall, our record on funding the arts is poor. The last European-wide survey showed that while direct public expenditure on arts and museums in Britain was £9.80 per head, in France it was £17.40, the then West Germany £24 and Sweden £27.50.

The ruling idea governing institutions such as the Arts Council is 'the arm's-length principle', which is a truly British manifestation of British culture in that it combines pragmatism and hypocrisy in equal measure. The government controls the arm, determines its length and financial strength—but someone else gets the hand dirty with the difficult business of deciding who should receive the shillings being handed out.

The lack of institutional clarity is then very much 'part of our culture', and has its virtues. It is gradualist, it is pragmatic, it is empirical, it is founded on tradition and precedent, above all, it is pluralist . . ."

John Major's decision to create the Department of National Heritage in 1992 was supposed to bring a new coherence. The responsibilities of the DNH—arts, sports, the heritage, museums and galleries, royal palaces, libraries, film, broadcasting and the press—did add up to a workable definition of "culture"; a former secretary of state Peter Brooke once described it as "what we do when we are not working".

In theory the strength of the Art Council's decision-making process is that it is based on peer-group assessment, and the council is fortunate to be able to call on the advice of leading arts practitioners who give of their time for no material reward. Inevitably those practitioners are connected with leading arts organisations which may receive funding from the Arts Council or may be seeking lottery money. The question of conflict of interest is met by the operation of a strict ethical and procedural code, approved by the parliamentary ombudsman and even more rigorous than the code required by the Treasury.[8] However, in practice, it suffers from a criticism of insularity implying favouritism and even nepotism in its awards. David Lee, editor of "Art Review", has written[9]: "knowledge of [the] guaranteed avoidance of government interference has been exploited by the [Arts] Council, which knows that its policies, however unfair and unrepresentative they become, are inviolate".

[8] Mary Allen, Secretary-General of the Arts Council, Letter to *The Independent*, 25 July 1996.
[9] Letter to *The Daily Telegraph*, 17 Oct. 1998.

The Ministry of Cultural Heritage was proclaimed by its first Minister, David Mellor, as "the Ministry of Fun" and its art-emphasis was minor. The regulation's dilution of Arts Council central power was parallelled by the over-broad ambit of the new Ministry. Both arguably indicated a weakening of control of artistic standards. In "A Creative Future", the Arts Council "national arts and media strategy" submitted in October 1992 to the then Minister for National Heritage, Peter Brooke, the Arts Council promised to be more effective, more open, to delegate decision-making more closely to the people most concerned, to seek advice more widely, to institute "contracts" between the funders and the funded, to co-operate with local authorities and, significantly, to deliver "value for money". For funding, "quality" would be the pre-eminent criterion, though definable *only in relative terms*. This ensured that the currently-considered "evil" word "quality" did not lead to the dissatisfaction of the hopes of even the most low-brow consumer. Such an approach was not in the interests of art and was woefully inattentive to the dubious standard of the "heritage" the state would accumulate.

In the introduction to a consultative document entitled "New Lottery Programmes (1996)" Lord Gowrie, the then Arts Council's chairman, described the move to funding creative activity from the National Lottery as "probably the most significant change in the funding of the arts in Britain since the Arts Council was founded 50 years ago". In 1996, the then Heritage Secretary, Virginia Bottomley, and the Arts Council agreed to widen the remit for lottery spending on the arts to include people, education projects and accessibility, as well as buildings. It is certainly the case that arts funding from the lottery reduces the financial pressures experienced by prior funding sources, and is to be welcomed, despite puritanical fears that England is thereby promoting a nation of morally-deficient gamblers. This positive initiative was complemented by New Labour's "Road to the Manifesto (1996)" which identified the economic significance of the arts as well as their "enormous impact on education, leisure and the quality of life", which augured well for them. Prior to the Labour election victory, David Lister reported[10] that the Department of National Heritage was due to change its name to the Department of Culture and Communications, but under Chris Smith the title of Department for Culture, Media and Sport has been conferred on it. The arts may well be entering a more dynamic phase under the

---

[10] *The Independent Long Weekend*, 7 Dec. 1996.

Labour government, under which a broader variety of activities are liberalised as art, such as Amanda Moss and Marissa Carr's bizarre body show in a Soho strip club, funded by the Arts Council in 1998. On a more conservative note, Andrew Motion, chairman of the Arts Council Literature Panel, has given assurance[11] that he is working hard on schemes to help finance not just poetry but also individual poets. In a general context, the arts are likely to thrive under a Labour government, not least because of their critical-moral encouragement of artistic initiatives from sexual minority quarters and the under-privileged.

(a) *France*

Unlike in England, there has been a striking growth in the quantity of French government funding of the arts. Jumps in the budget stem from important capital investment programmes not decided by minister or parliament but by the president and his minister for the arts acting as a couple. A cultural monarchy, rather than a cultural ministry, therefore rules the French cultural policy system: de Gaulle and Malraux launched the Maisons de la Culture; Mitterand and Jack Lang co-operated closely.[12]

This system does not make for democracy. This is unsurprising since there is a well-known enmity between the arts and democracy (minority tastes have to be financed by a majority of non-practitioners). Although the arts budget has to be approved in detail by Parliament, debates on it are poorly attended by members ill-informed on the subject and since there is a consensus among all parties in favour of a growth in the arts budget, the ministry's proposals are adopted in 99.9 per cent of cases. There is no real democratic debate. Moreover, the ministry does not have panels composed largely of arts representatives to advise it; civil servants predominate in its consultative panels. Artists are effectively excluded from the decision-taking process. This is *prima facie* bad.

However, the ministry clearly supports the arts and does not seek to influence them. National and local authorities provide protection and

---

[11] Letter of Adrian Mitchell (poet) to *The Independent*, 16 Jan. 1997.
[12] It remains to be seen to what degree comparatively recent personality changes will affect arts policy in the long term. Jacques Toubon replaced Jack Lang in Mar. 1993. In Apr. 1994, in England, the Earl of Gowrie took over the chairmanship of the Arts Council from Lord Palumbo, retiring from the post in 1998.

money but do not presume to impose contents. Instead, the art world (or, rather, world of artists) presents a catalogue of proposals to the government or local governments on which the latter act, in conformity with existing (past) policy. This is co-operative, if unenterprising.

The French Ministry of Culture is not monolithic but built of many forces. There are eight departments, corresponding to particular art forms, each with its own clients and lobbies more powerful than the minister and his staff. The departments compete for finance. There is no coherence. Neither is there an "evaluation body". However, cultural policies are publicly visible, notably at one stage under the charismatic *"au courant"* Jack Lang, who, *inter alia*, supported graffiti as a popular art form. There is organic interaction of minister and public; the arts are much publicised by their minister; and policy is malleable by public feedback. The direct relation between state and art thereby avoids the creation of an official art without avoiding an official view.

Although the system may appear dangerously undemocratic, it does not seem so in effect. The French happily embrace this irony. The decision to create a Pompidou Centre was fought by nearly everyone except the Communists and the Gaullists. It was thought undemocratic to concentrate so much money on one such project. But the result was that access to art in Paris was hugely increased and there was almost universal stimulus and praise subsequently.

There is no guarantee, though, that good artistic judgements are made. The response to this is that only time can tell whether the right decisions are made for the right artists, and Brigitte Mayer, General Administrator of the *"Ensemble Intercontemporain"*, maintains that the French prefer to work with the government than boards and better trust people with a strong expertise in funding than fellow artists.

Since the beginning of the 1980s, culture in France has been wielded as a political instrument, and a vast structure has been put into place to uphold and define contemporary art. In 1982, the *"Délégation Aux Arts Plastiques"* (one of the departments of the Ministry of Culture), and the 22 regional purchasing funds, were created. Their dual mission was to discover young artists and introduce international arts into all the regions of France. Thus, new arts centres soon sprang up all over the nation and modern art museums opened in the most unexpected places (Villeurbanne in 1982, St. Etienne in 1987), and many adventures were launched in new spirit. In contrast to in Britain, the proposed invigoration of the regions was to promote internationalisation and existing talent where found. It was not a step merely to parochialise the production of art for local satisfaction.

The French system suffers from having too big a bureaucratic identity. All 20,000 or so civil servants in the area are protected by the statute of the civil service, which is rigid. Whereas legal rules are useful for control in a ministry of finance, for example, they do not fit a very mobile activity like that of cultural affairs which changes (and should change) regularly, being alert and responsive to new ideas. If the minister has a new idea, it will take two years in the present budgetary system to launch this activity. Consequently, the minister is constantly bypassing the rules. Pompidou established a special account in the prime minister's budget for the building of the Pompidou Centre, and Lang multiplied special funds subsequently managed by quangos.

In the French ministry model, there is a lack of rationality in the decision-making process. The case of the Opéra Bastille is a good example. All who knew the management of opera and all the Socialist members of Parliament were against it (because they fought for no new investments in Paris and investments in the provinces). Nevertheless, Jack Lang approached them and explained that the President was really very keen on the idea as part of his long-term vision of popular access to culture. So they voted for it, and in a sense were obliged to.

The tendency in France towards the institutionalisation of contemporary art brings with it the danger of over-academisation. However, decentralisation contributes to the strengthening of such new and vigorous enterprises as the CAPC (*"Centre d'Art Plastique Contemporain"*) in Bordeaux, the Magasin in Grenoble, the Rochechouart Museum, the Municipal Cultural Centre in St. Etienne and the Villa Arson, homes of the Nîmes Contemporary Art Museum. The exhibition programmes are quick to include what is happening abroad: CAPC, for example, has privileged relationships with the Spanish Ministry of Culture. However, there is a circularity in the French art scene that is perhaps ineluctable: galleries have begun to show more and more works liable to be bought by the *Fonds Régional d'Art Contemporain*, and hence shown in a museum. The confusion of functions between gallery and museum has left its mark on French æsthetics. The French public finds itself somewhat locked into looking at only established artists and acquiring a rather *retardataire* view of art (so that an experimental artist, such as Vercruysse, completely escapes notice[13]).

[13] See n. 8 above, Vol. 1, No. 5, May 1989 at 12: "Letter from Paris—'In French they say *"déjà-vu"* ' ", by Oscarine Bosquet.

Fortunately, the tendency to enthrone an academy is avoided at events such as at the *Centre National d'Art Plastique* where Alfred Pacquement and Catherine Bompuis piloted the institution into a singular role. For three hours, space was made for 40 paintings by Bruno Carbonnet, a young painter unestablished in the gallery world. Making such occurrences more frequent would encourage escape from the trap of the *déjà-vu* and contribute to a sense of continually living artistic process. This is healthy and necessary for the organic artistic life of a nation.

(c) *America*

American reliance on voluntarism and private initiative to discharge many public responsibilities coupled with a scepticism and mistrust of government and the centralisation of government power are characteristic of American society in a variety of different public policy areas, not least in the arts. The major government contribution to the arts is in foregone taxes, amounting to at least four or five times more than direct contributions from the National Endowment for Arts (NEA)[14] and state and local agencies. Despite the various sources of philanthropic support, the US system is principally market-driven, with all the disadvantages to the quality of art that that implies.

Nevertheless, the specific fields rest on radically different sources. Folk art is one of the rare areas in which the government plays a leading role, and the arts of minority and tribal communities have been chiefly supported by federal, state and local governments.

An arguable strength of the American system is its diversity, energy and resiliency. An arguable disadvantage is its consumptive emphasis.

The NEA's legislation clearly recognises the essential contribution of private support for the arts. Many support the arts as a means of enhancing their business' corporate image in the community or to write off the cost as a tax deductible charitable contribution.

Critics of the NEA suggest that there is a tendency to reward those artists who are already recognised. Experimentation is thus discouraged. It is undeniably true that the professionalism of the applicant, as

---

[14] Government aid to the arts is not confined to NEA funds. However, the NEA is the centrepiece of funding and the most obvious exemplar of the state approach to it. Various fragmented art-assisting legislation reflects the same underlying policies but not as demonstrably.

well as the worth of his project, is considered important when a project is evaluated.

Applications to the NEA are reviewed by the NEA's professional panelists and outside consultants. All applications are then referred to the National Council on the Arts, comprised of presidential appointees and the NEA chairperson. The National Council only rarely rejects an application that has been recommended by the NEA panelists who are private citizen experts. In 1989, President Reagan earmarked funds for educational purposes reflecting a number of changes in federal arts programmes. In 1981, his administration's budget had moved in the direction of eliminating entirely the Endowment's appropriations.[15] The administration claimed that the proposed 50 per cent cut in the budget would encourage individuals and corporations to make up the difference. Congress resisted all such reductions. As Edward M. Block stated before the House Appropriations Subcommittee on the Interior, "[i]f the Federal Government gives authority to the notion that the arts are merely frivolous diversions to be indulged in good times but abandoned in bad times, I strongly suspect that the private sector will not be disposed toward heroic efforts to pick up the shortfall".[16] The tendency in America to leave promotion of art in the hands of volunteer and business-minded sponsors in accordance with some rather naïve self-sufficiency ideal of nationhood endangers not only the progress of the unself-publicising artist but also the quality of art, encouraged by a good degree of only amateur interest or dictated by the requirements of a business brain. So strongly controlled by government, the NEA is not the type of autonomous body needed to secure what is best for art independently of political pressure.

In 1989, Jesse Helms, Republican of North Carolina, made a proposal to prohibit federal financing of art that violates broadly defined "moral" standards. Relatively mild restrictions for the NEA were unanimously agreed upon. The NEA had angered Congress by its support of an exhibition by the photographer Robert Mapplethorpe. In contrast, Luke Rittner, the General Secretary of the Arts Council who resigned in 1990 because of the Arts Minister's proposed "reforms", monitored the effect of the government's legislation outlawing the promotion of homosexuality (section 28 of the Local Government Act 1988) to see if artists were being affected, and

---

[15] *The Journal of Art* (International Edition), Vol. 1, No. 4, Apr. 1989, at 1 (article entitled "Back to School").

[16] *New York Times*, 26 Mar. 1981, para. C., at 15, col. 1.

declared he would make his views known.[17] In the world of arts funding, personalities are crucial.

In America, conservative forces, fundamentalist and organised, are engaged in creating harassment of minorities, especially homosexuals, and, perhaps most importantly, attempting the imposition of special "moral" interest claims to dictate to the majority.[18] It may prove appealing to the weaker-minded to espouse a narrow spirit self-disguised as "moral", and such influences have always been antipathetic to the large-spiritedness of the arts. The NEA is notably weak in succumbing to such antagonism to freedom of expression, which freedom is crucial for the continued unhindered expressivity of artists whom the NEA is intended to assist, and whose causes promote. It is an ineluctable conclusion that the NEA is more politically than art influenced when political forces oppose a direction artistic endeavour happens to be taking. This is to abdicate one of its most potentially useful as well as expected roles as protector of artistic interest beyond all else.

The early Endowment administrators developed a panel system for grant-making that marked the triumph of professional judgement over political patronage. The Peer Advisory Panels evolved, staffed with experts in various fields. "Professional standards" and "professional excellence" were emphasised and encouraged. A number of pressures reshaped this politically non-interventionist professional orientation, including the assertion by historically-marginalised groups of their identity whereby deference to established professionals was attacked for perpetuating a "majority culture" domination.

Ironically, the demise of professionalism has led to the censoring of minority art such as homoerotic art. Content-based standards now threaten artistic quality criteria. The guidelines comparatively recently passed by Congress, however, represent the first substantive limits on what the Endowment may fund. In passing the guidelines, Congress responded to outrage over two Endowment-sponsored productions: "Piss Christ", a photograph by Andres Serrano of a crucifix immersed in a jar of urine, and "The Perfect Moment", an exhibition of photographs by the late Robert Mapplethorpe that contained a selection of his works on homoerotic themes. Although it rejected the broad language proposed by Senator Jesse Helms, the

---

[17] See "Arts Council Monitors Effects of Clause 28", *The Independent*, 21 Dec., 1986, at 6.

[18] See n. 8 above, Vol. 2, no. 3, Dec. 1989 at 1, 5: "Artists Space vs. N.E.A." by Andrea M. Couture.

Congress did bar Endowment funds from being used to create or present allegedly "obscene" materials:

> None of the funds authorised to be appropriated for [the Endowment] may be used to promote, disseminate, or produce materials which in the judgment of the National Endowment for the Arts . . . may be considered obscene, including but not limited to, depictions of sadomasochism, homoeroticism, the sexual exploitation of children, or individuals engaged in sex acts and which, when taken as a whole, do not have serious literary, artistic, political, or scientific value.

The NEA cannot impose whatever content restrictions it chooses; it must deal only with matters of "art". It is clearly arguable that "decency clauses" are so vaguely worded that they tend to impinge on the First Amendment's guaranteed right to freedom of speech. It is unconstitutionally restrictive to require that a person evaluate art by taking into consideration general standards of decency.

In one skirmish, the recent NEA chairman John E. Frohnmayer suspended a $10,000 federal grant for an AIDS exhibition and requested that the Endowment not be listed as a sponsor of the show, "Witnesses: Against Our Vanishing". Somewhat paradoxically, Frohnmayer explained that politics must be removed from grants "if the Endowment is to remain credible to the American people and to Congress". While Frohnmayer found some of the work in the show of "questionable taste", his main quarrel was with the catalogue containing criticism of pubic figures. These included Cardinal O'Conor, the Roman Catholic Archbishop of New York and Senator Jesse Helms. For his part, Cardinal O'Conor expressed surprise at the action, adding, "I do not consider myself exempt from or above criticism by anyone" and, if consulted, "would have urged very strongly that the NEA not withdraw its sponsorship". This contrasted with Jesse Helms' pleasure at the NEA action. It is very doubtful that the NEA's action coincided with the view of the more truly moral man.

Unquestionably, a precedent has been set in which the particular sensitivities (or prejudices) of a special interest group are dictating public policy for the majority of Americans of both religious and non-religious persuasions. "Personally, I think the Helms Amendment is part of years and years of a growing political movement that's very well organised", said Timothy S. McClimon. This opinion is shared by many and is the cause of considerable anxiety. New York University's Grey Art Gallery and the others of the 15-member committee that organised a national AIDS Awareness Day on 1 December, in which over 500 arts institutions participated, received a letter from Bob Jones III, president of Bob Jones University in South Carolina, with this announcement: "the world-renowned gallery of art at Bob Jones University will open additional hours on December 1st to protest your misplacement of sympathy", amongst other comments. Setting aside whether such a inhuman stand could ever be called moral, in Christian as well as other popular senses, art should not be inhibited from developing in its own sphere because of such external interest pressures.

President Bill Clinton has refreshingly declared in his cultural policy that he and his vice-president will defend freedom of speech and artistic expression by opposing censorship or "content restrictions" on grants made by the NEA. This contrasts with the conservative non-confrontational course articulated by Republican Anne-Imelda Radice, John Frohnmayer's successor as NEA Chairman, in the face of pressure from Congress and "the American public" to fund things of appeal only to the widest possible audience.

CONCLUSIONS

Art is not a democratic process, but operates in democracies which impose principles of democracy on its funding. The best art has excellence (quality), and this is what public bodies are morally obliged to promote so that public money is seen to be used to best effect. It is unrealistic to think that the community wants other than the best for its culture. Any prevailing superficial consumptive emphasis is only a government expedient (notably under the former Conservative government in Britain); the popular trend to espouse it is only the inevitable result of disingenuous government policy aimed at achieving its own political rather than artistically worthwhile goals.

In all three states considered, the performing arts are more highly valued if the extent of public subsidy is our criterion. This is in accordance with what can be called the "greatest audience satisfaction" principle, which is often at odds with the promotion of the truly worthwhile and antagonistic to emphasis on the permanent arts, notably literature. The comparative lack of government interest in promoting literature is shocking; it is totally disproportionate to the value great literature is known to provide and inattentive to the durability of the cultural product, intended as much for posterity as the present.

These flaws stem from government interest in satisfying "popular" taste to the detriment of achieving real cultural wealth. Emphasis is on consumption rather than creation, but public funding of the arts is for the arts and only incidentally for the audience. There is no contradiction in using public money to promote something known to be of public good, whether utilised as such immediately or not.

Funding individuals (artists and writers) is a very low priority in public funding policy, notably in England, and less so in France. And yet individual talent is the very source of artistic production. Again, the consumptive preference of current state practice in England and America insists that most public money is spent on bigger bodies providing for bigger audiences: a quantitative emphasis going hand-in-hand with the preferred promotion of "immediate" culture. The emphasis is on the dissemination of cultural gratification, and not on the building of artistic wealth *per se*.

We find in all three states an interest in promoting ethnic minority culture from public funds as something of a key priority. This is sensible in the sense that culture that appeals to a majority is more readily funded by that majority and consequently less dependent on the support of a public body. However, in another (artistic) sense, there is greater difficulty in justifying such preferential treatment. Uncomfortable with the elitist association of promoting only the best artists (unfounded and irrational though it is), the state finds itself promoting the best of a range of art in accordance with social group diversity rather than artistic diversity *per se*. Achievement of the promotion of the best art is diluted by attention to extrinsic sociological phenomena. This emphasis goes hand in hand with the consumptive approach to culture currently favoured by America and England and, more nobly, the expansive eclectic plan for culture of the French régime.

Difficulties arise when innovative art or art that challenges government ideals presents itself.[19] It is arguable that the best art always

[19] In the public funding of the arts, we see an arm's-length principle of a very precise kind operating: in delegating choice of art to be funded to extra-legal (and extra-political) assessors, the law, like government, relinquishes in this area control of the produced concept of art *except* when that concept threatens to contravene the law, and the American experience is that government intervenes in funding not only if such art contravenes the law but also if such art is reacted against by a strong or large enough public element. This threatens to make theoretically independent bodies making decisions on art only quasi-independent and the art promoted pre-censored. This in turn contracts the heuristic capacity of funded art to what is deemed publicly acceptable, and, in turn, the healthy capacity of the public to question its values by exposure to art which confronts them. It forecloses funding for much stimulating as well as "revolutionary" art.

challenges accepted assumptions of the established socio-political *status quo*. The British and American stance against homosexual art is a deplorable example of indifference to art and attention to votes. It is common knowledge (though not common enough) that homosexuals have a significant tradition of producing great art. Antagonism to gay art illustrates emphatically that the (government) funding priority is not the promotion of art but concealed ulterior ends. To maintain this charade of merely purporting to promote the arts is to deceive the public as well as the art world. Public bodies to promote the arts are precisely for that end and for no other purpose.

Paradoxically, the limited attention paid to the present creation of permanent arts (such as poetry) is complemented by great attention to "heritage" arts. We admire and preserve the fruits of arts we are no longer willing adequately to encourage. A cynic might say that it is more convenient for government that people watch a play than write a book: consuming takes less time and government wants men as economic tools, not creative souls. Creativity is energy-consuming and antagonistic to work-force efficiency an economics-based leadership favours.

Crucial to the way art develops pursuant to the public funding policy are the personalities behind such policy. In so subjective a realm, what the leading voice or voices desire in effect shapes an arts policy that implicitly shapes the policy-contingent art.[20]

Cultural relativism and egalitarianism have not only democratised culture but have also, inevitably, reduced the absolute quality of what is produced as, and accepted as, "art", and what is subsequently considered art by experts. There is no rule of recognition of art based on a criterion of (at least minimum) skill, and there is no guarantee of quality except the accepted opinion of grant-allocators. The recent preference for subsidising "amateur" art suggests the toleration sometimes of a very moderate artistic standard, and, more than in any other era, begs the question "is popular culture a contradiction in terms?".

---

[20] President Reagan's switch from anti to pro NEA funding, though welcome, indicated his lack of basic personal commitment to the arts. Richard Luce, the British Arts Minister, was hardly a connoisseur of the arts before he was appointed, which is worrying despite his "conversion" AFTER obtaining the post—see "Enthusiastic Convert Wins High Praise from the Arts World" (*The Independent*, 4 JAN. 1990, at 4.). Jack Lang is charismatic as well as profoundly personally interested in the arts, which was fortunate for the French: in this way the arts gain a greater public profile in an increasingly commercial and sterile world. Of the three states studied, I am confident in only the French as having a genuine passion for arts promotion at government level.

Assessment of relative artistic merit cannot be regulated except to provide equity and meritocracy of process. Confidence has to be placed in the integrity of assessors. Their comparative consideration of artistic skill in the works before them should rest as far as possible on objective criteria rather than personal taste. It is ineluctable though that certain art forms should find favour at different times according to current artistic trends: in 1993, for example, installations and site-specific works were particularly popular. Law could not begin to dictate precise criteria of assessment to accommodate fluctuations in artistic fashion because it lacks the power of prophecy, and artistic trends are quickly revolutionised in contradistinction to the durability of legal provision demanded by the need for legal certainty. This is why the public funding of the arts offers itself to politico-artistic critique to ascertain prevailing art-evaluation method, and the non-definition of art, as opposed to its attempted conceptual fixity by law. The compromises that take place in the realm of the public funding of the arts are based on political factors that the law is called upon occasionally to reinforce, such as the optimal reconciliation of the highly emotive notions of obscenity and art (and concomitant "moral" and artistic freedoms).

6

The Concept of Art in the
Anglo-American Law of Trusts

INTRODUCTION

A peculiarly English phenomenon, that has spread to kindred legal systems, a trust is a relationship, recognised by equity,[1] initiated by the settlor or testator, which arises when property is vested by him or her in persons called trustees, who are obliged to hold such property for the benefit of other persons called beneficiaries. The interest of the beneficiaries will usually be laid down in the instrument creating the trust, but may be implied or imposed by law. The subject matter of the trust must be some form of property. The beneficiaries' interests are proprietary in the sense that they can be bought and sold, given away or disposed of by will, but they will cease to exist if the legal estate in the property comes into the hands of a *bona fide* purchaser for value without notice of the beneficial interest. For the purposes of this chapter, such a description of a trust is adequate, the precise definition of a trust being generally considered by all experts to be elusive.[2]

Trusts can be classified in a plethora of ways. On one analysis, there can be simple and special trusts, statutory trusts, implied and resulting trusts, constructive trusts and express trusts. Within the category of

---

[1] Equity is a branch of the English law which, before the Judicature Act 1873 came into force, was applied and administered by the Court of Chancery: the field of equity is delineated by a series of historical events, and not by *a priori* plan or theory. The division between law and equity is less marked than it was over a century ago, but it is still necessary for various reasons to know whether a rule originates at law or in equity. There is not space to deal with those here. See, further, Pettit, *Equity and the Law of Trusts* (8th edn., Butterworths, London, 1997), chs. 1 and 2.

[2] Many attempts have been made to define a trust but none is completely satisfactory. See, further, *Halsbury's Law of England* (3rd edn., Butterworths, London, 1962), vol. 38, at 809–10; also Sir A. Underhill, *Law of Trusts and Trustees* (with D.J. Hayton, 13th edn., Butterworths, London, 1997), 1, and G.W. Williams and L.A. Sheridan, *Law of Trusts* (12th edn., Barry Rose, Chichester, 1994), 2–6.

express trusts are executed and executory trusts, completely and incompletely constituted trusts, private and public trusts, discretionary and fixed trusts, protective trusts, secret trusts and, the most important trusts regarding art definition, non-charitable purpose trusts and charitable trusts.

For a trust to be valid, three certainties must be present: certainty of words, certainty of subject and certainty of object. First, with regard to certainty of words, since "equity looks to the intent rather than the form", it is unnecessary to use specific technical expressions to constitute a trust. All that needs to be conclusively ascertained is an intention to set up a trust. Respecting certainty of subject, only if the property subject to the trust is clearly identified can the trust be valid; and, finally, regarding certainty of object, for the trust to be valid it must be for the benefit of individuals, except if it is a particular brand of non-charitable purpose trust or a charitable trust, which happen to be two of the most usual situations in which we find art featuring. When a settlor declares a trust he must also comply with any formalities as well as satisfy "the three certainties" and, unless he has declared himself trustee, he must do everything he can to ensure that the trust property is transferred to the trustees. If no steps are taken to transfer the property, or further action is required by the settlor to effect such a transfer, the trust will be deemed incompletely constituted.

THE LAW OF CHARITABLE TRUSTS[3]

Charitable trusts are an important but rarely noted source of arts funding, and enjoy generous tax advantages due to their charitable status.[4] The concept of "trust" is not used in French law, but is a distinctive feature of Anglo-American law: arguably the most important creation of equity. A strength of the trust in facilitating institutional philanthropy is that it fulfils the philanthropist's desire to have property applied in the manner specified in the trust instrument. Moreover, the trust is useful for settlors who are artists because markedly individualistic ideas can be stamped on the manner in

---

[3] A variation on this section appeared as P. Kearns, "Art in the Law of Charitable Trusts", in *Art, Antiquity and Law*, Vol., No. 1, Feb. 1996, at 5–10 inclusive.

[4] It is not the purpose of this ch. to detail the fiscal implictions of charitable status. For these, see G. Moffat and M. Chesterman, with J. Dewar, *Trusts Law Text and Materials* (Weidenfield and Nicolson, London, 1988), 643–7.

which property is applied. In broad terms, a "settlor" provides that property is administered by one or more "trustees" for the benefit of "beneficiaries". The trust, to continental lawyers, may appear an application of a principle of representation, but the trustee, for historical reasons, becomes very much the owner, rather than the agent, of the property placed in trust. The restriction placed on his right of ownership is of a moral rather than of a legal nature, and the law intervenes in cases of abuse of the confidence placed in him. The trust in Anglo-American law is a legal application of the internationally recognised moral concept of trust. Charity morally complements this idea, combining with the trust mechanism to ensure additional benefit to both public and art that charitable status entails.

The trust mechanism does not exist in France, so this sub-chapter is restricted to an English law orientation (the US law on charitable trusts being based on the same antique English source[5] and drawing heavily on English case law even today[6]). In France, *"fondations"* present an equivalent to "charities", but reliance in France on an institute-centred mechanism without a partner trust function means that to aid charitable purposes in certain contemporary contexts extra legislation has to be implemented to supplement the basic legal design, which legislation marks a conceptual divergence from the original scheme. For example, the once Minister of Culture, Jack Lang, presented a bill to the French Council of Ministers concerning foundations for the arts which modified the 23 July 1987 sponsoring law. Prior to this, businesses not specifically recognised as working in the public's interest which sponsored the arts were forbidden to label themselves *"fondations"*. The 1987 law had failed to create a legal framework which would welcome sponsoring activities undertaken by the business community. A charitable trust mechanism would have neatly accommodated the problem.

The English Statute of Charitable Uses of 1601 provided machinery for the enforcement of charitable trusts. The Preamble to the Statute contains an enumeration of charitable purposes to which both English and US courts have subsequently habitually had recourse as showing the kind of purpose that is charitable. In *Commissioners for Special Purposes of Income Tax* v. *Pemsel,*[7] Lord MacNaghten summarised and unwittingly contracted the scope of charity:

---

[5] The Preamble to the Charitable Uses Act 1601.
[6] The reverse does not occur.
[7] [1891] AC 531 at 583.

" '[c]harity' in its legal sense comprises four principal divisions: trusts for the relief of poverty; trusts for the advancement of education; trusts for the advancement of religion; and trusts for other purposes beneficial to the community, not falling under any of the preceding heads."

These four heads may be referred to as heads one, two, three and four in accordance with their order here. In effect, the ambit of charity was thereafter reduced, as courts chose to rely on the summary as their guide. Even the 1976 Goodman Committee,[8] reporting on "Charity Law and Voluntary Organisations", suggested an updated version of the Preamble based upon the *Pemsel* classification; courts have in the meantime adhered to MacNaghten's four principal heads as the exclusive touchstones for charitability. Such emphasis perpetuates a monopoly of charity by the four McNaghten-isolated areas of purpose, the fourth head being in practice a much more limited category than is suggested by its residual catch-all description. The arts benefit only if they happen to fall within the ambit of "MacNaghten's four" (heads two or four, or two and four, proving the most frequently judicially employed avenues for charitable relief in specific instances). The system is cumulative in the sense that a purpose which is more or less analogous to one or more of the purposes already established as charitable may then itself be deemed charitable. The process is not unlike the attributing of a painting to a school of art: a judge dictates if object X is sufficiently like object Y to be deemed in the same category.

Art appears in various forms in the case law in an uncollective way.[9] In *Royal Choral Society* v. *Inland Revenue Commissioners*,[10] the court had to decide whether the appellants were a society "established for charitable purposes only" and thus entitled to exemption from income tax. The society's objectives were "to form and maintain a choir in order to promote the practice and performance of choral works, whether by way of concerts or choral pageants in the Royal Albert Hall or as otherwise decided from time to time".[11] The Court of Appeal held that the society was charitable as being established for the purpose of the advancement of what was termed "æsthetic education".[12] Lord Greene said that a body of persons

---

[8] *Report of the Goodman Committee: Charity Law and Voluntary Organisations* (HMSO, London, 1976), paras. 16–32.

[9] There is no provision in the current law for the category of art as a distinct unit.

[10] [1947] 2 All ER 101 (CA).

[11] *Ibid.*

[12] *Ibid.*, at 104.

established for the purpose of raising the artistic taste of the country comprises an educational purpose because the education of artistic taste "is one of the most important things in the development of a civilised human being". "Education" was held to be broader than merely teaching.

Similarly, in *Re Shaw's Will Trusts*,[13] Vaisey J, upholding the gift of grants, contributions and payments to any foundation having for its objects the bringing of the masterpieces of fine art within the reach of the people of Ireland, said: "education includes . . . not only teaching, but the promotion or encouragement of arts and graces of life which are . . . perhaps the finest and best part of the human character.[14] The advancement of 'good' art, at least, is therefore a perceivable charitable purpose, but the courts prefer to phrase the purpose in terms of education in the established tradition following *Pemsel*.[15]

From such cases, under the advancement of education head, a subclass of the advancement of æsthetic education has thus evolved. The case law in this area also focuses on museums, where the reputation of the subject receiving the gift is very influential in determining charitability. It appears, for example, that a gift to an "established" museum is clearly charitable following the authority of *British Museum Trustees* v. *White*[16]; and in *Re Holbourne*[17] a gift to trustees of *objets d'art* to form an art museum was held to be a valid charitable gift. In the later case of *Re Pinion*,[18] a case concerning trusts to form a small art museum, merit in the *Re Holbourne*[19] collection of objects was "assumed"[20] by Harman LJ (rather than explicitly judicially evaluated). Such "assumption" in this context nevertheless presupposes some interest in quality. Harman LJ went on to say, *tout court*, that "a gift to found a public museum may be assumed to be charitable as of public utility if no-one questions it".[21] Such questioning would inevitably necessitate a quality test. The reluctance on the part of elements of the judiciary to voice even the possibility of a deliberated judicial assessment of artistic quality is explained by the fact that a judge in the legal sense ought never to be an *arbiter elegantiarum*.[22]

---

13 [1952] Ch. 163.
14 *Ibid*., at 172.
15 N. 7 above.
16 (1826) 2 Sim. & St. 594.
17 (1885) 53 LT 212.
18 [1965] Ch. 85.
19 (1885) 53 LT 212.
20 [1965] Ch. 85 at 105.
21 *Ibid*.
22 A judge of taste.

Instead, in practice, an implicit exercise of taste by the judiciary sometimes takes place. Any formal judicial acknowledgement of a matter of taste being judicially assessed threatens legal certainty because such an exercise is on principle outlawed by the common law. Complicating matters further, judicial reference to expert opinion is sometimes evinced to indicate a purported substitution of an external expert artistic standard for any formally illicit judicial one.

In *Re Pinion*,[23] what is remarkable is Harman LJ's clear and vitriolic expression of taste that so contrasts with his formal meeting of the phenomenon: he can conceive of no useful object to be served in "foisting upon the public this mass of junk".[24] He decides that the testator's object was simply to perpetuate his own name and the repute of his family. As for the works collected, he draws on the authority of "competent persons" as to their almost entire worthlessness, but it is self-evident that his own remarks are not a merely vicarious exposition of taste: he voices his own value judgement that the "haphazard assembly" does not merit the name collection "for no purpose emerges, no time nor style is illustrated".[25] It is a normal judicial convention in such cases to purport to defer to "an accepted canon of taste on which the court must rely"[26] but that taste is affective not objective. Judges tend to prefer to make it seem objective because the judicial object is to be definitive, whereas in reality matters of artistic taste are too indeterminable to be convincingly reduced to incisive final proclamations demanded by litigation.

In *Re Pinion*,[27] Harman LJ and the Court of Appeal reversed the decision of Wilberforce J (as he then was) who had concluded that there was "that scintilla of merit which was sufficient to save the rest".[28] The question appears then, very directly, how much or little merit a collection needs to succeed as a charitable purpose. Unfortunately, there are few intermediate cases which present illuminating expert opinion battles: the purposes usually either succeed because they involve "greats" such as Shakespeare,[29] or fail as virtually entirely meritless rubbish.[30] Two cases, however, do not quite

---

[23] [1965] Ch. 85.
[24] *Ibid.* at 107.
[25] *Ibid.*
[26] *Ibid.*
[27] [1965] Ch. 85.
[28] *Ibid.*, at 97.
[29] See *Re Shakespeare Memorial Trust* [1923] 2 Ch. 398.
[30] As in *Re Pinion* [1965] Ch. 85.

conform to this pattern of extremes, namely *Re Delius*[31] and *Re Shaw*.[32] In *Re Delius*,[33] concerning trusts for the advancement of the musical works of Delius, Roxburgh J doubted the composer Delius's artistic stature, as compared to that, for example, of Beethoven,[34] but it is significant that Delius was here judicially acknowledged as having the approval of Sir Thomas Beecham, which illustrious connection helped secure charitable status for the trust. In *Re Shaw*,[35] Harman J held that the gift in issue, to ascertain the utility of a new British alphabet, was not educational under the second head of charitable purpose because it merely tended to the increase of knowledge, and did not qualify under the fourth head because it was not itself a beneficial purpose but, rather, for the purpose of persuading the public by propaganda that it was beneficial.[36] What is unusual here is that the connection with the very distinguished George Bernard Shaw was not influential enough to secure a decision favourable to the attribution of charitable status to the trust concerned. In art trust cases, the judiciary is more commonly prone to deference to the intentions of renowned public figures in the arts.

Two American cases demonstrate more typical negative results for the charitability of trusts for art of little acclaim. In *Hanson Estate*,[37] a testatrix declared that a novel written by her should be sent to a designated publisher and the royalties given for a certain charitable purpose. The publisher offered to publish it on payment of a certain sum. On the basis of a negative artistic appraisal by witnesses, the court reached a pragmatic decision: since it was clear that there would be no royalties because the novel was worthless, it ordered that the amount offered be paid directly to the charity. Although a financial intention was thus satisfied, an artistic one failed. In *Medical Society of South Carolina* v. *South Carolina National Bank*,[38] a trust to establish an art museum in which to exhibit objects acquired by the testatrix which were of little or no artistic value was held not to be valid as a charitable trust. The testatrix's intention was the conferment of artistic benefit. As in the later English case of *Re Pinion*,[39] this was over-

---

[31] [1957] Ch. 299.
[32] [1957] 1 WLR 729.
[33] [1957] Ch. 299.
[34] *Ibid.*
[35] [1957] 1 WLR 729.
[36] *Ibid.*
[37] 8 D & C 2d 620 (Pa. 1956).
[38] 197 SC 96, 14 SE 2d 577 (1941).
[39] [1965] Ch. 85.

ridden on consideration of the very limited artistic value of the museum's intended contents. The underlying rationale of the courts is essentially economic: to give charitable status to worthless objects is simply a waste of public money. There is no suggestion that "bad art" collections could foster more relevant harm in the sense of adversely affecting the public's judgement of what is really art or "good art". In the context of charitable trusts, "bad art" is simply economically disadvantaged by judgments against its charitability: charitable status is won only by art sufficiently outweighing in importance economic advantage to the taxpayer. Art is vulnerable in such analyses because it is a well-known fact that contemporary judgements on what is art and, concomitantly, what is "good art", are notoriously wrong and unvisionary when examined retrospectively.

At present, the system of charitable art trusts operates as follows: to be adjudged a charitable purpose in the law of charitable trusts, art and art-related projects have to be assessed, according to contemporary criteria, as either educational in a direct sense (because in some way pedagogic or didactic) or educational in an indirect sense (communicable, such as art research, but not yet communicated) or for the state heritage. In the last case, considered mainly randomly under the fourth head of Lord MacNaghten's summary of charitable purposes, the intrinsic value of the art rather than its communication to others is the most relevant factor for charitability. In evidence, therefore, is a tacit differentiation between brands of art which can be deemed educational and therefore charitable and brands of art which are deemed charitable though not educational. It would be better to avoid making such an artificial non-artistic distinction that happens to suit a current antiquated legal structure based on the four heads of charitability and, instead, to state all art to be one new undifferentiated charitable category. "Bad art" according to contemporary standards could be saved as charitable, thus allowing for the event of current criteria for "good art" being later deemed incorrect; the indirect subsidising of all art by endowing it with charitable status would not herald a great economic problem, not least because cases of art ventures seeking charitable status are comparatively rare; in postmodern theory, all self-legitimating art should be covered by the single art categorisation now advocated for this charitable trusts context in accordance with the legal equivalence attributed in this era to unitary legal subjects. If adherence to the idea of Lord MacNaghten's main charitable heads in *Pemsel*[40] is judicially entrenched, art could

[40] [1891] AC 531.

be suggested as a new fifth head to add to the formula, but it is doubt-ful whether the law currently favours the creation of new heads rather than simply charitability of specific trusts by analogy with existing charities. The step needed is one of innovative judicial cre-ativity or amendment of existing law by statute.

Although the worthiness of art as a charitable cause may be doubted by some, for a majority it goes almost without saying that it is highly beneficial for a society to produce artists and art, and, to this end, to foster optimal circumstances for their achievement. In addi-tion, it is beneficial for a society to have a living cultural conscious-ness beyond a more functional routine. In determining charitability, the law should make allowance for the possibility of initial talent coming to genuine or grand fruition and, in this light, adopt a vision-ary rather than conservative stance, funding provenly serious artists yet to achieve celebrity; even if not synchronous, a worthwhile cause and public benefit clearly exist.

The aim of charity is to assist worthy causes, and artistic endeav-our is a worthy cause in need of fiscal relief in more than one respect. The nature of the artistic vocation is such that it often precludes wage-earning in an organised nine-to-five form; assisting artists is assisting an element of the public who are often in practice poor. In *Thompson* v. *Thompson*,[41] unsuccessful literary men, for example, were deemed to come under the description "poor". Regrettably, though, the law of charitable trusts is generally averse to exempting from tax the careers of individuals as opposed to institutions. This policy bias means that the collection of art, literature or music by museums, for example, is better assisted by the law of charitable trusts than the process of artistic creativity itself, and the contingent welfare of certain impecunious artists. The relief of poverty head of charity is therefore of only limited use to needy artists.

There is also some convergence of art and the advancement of reli-gion charitable head. Some art critics, including Sister Wendy Beckett, a Catholic nun, consider art to be spiritual, and sometimes sacred, even when not explicity religious or iconic.[42] Art, including abstract art, from the subliminal aspect of man where God and man arguably meet, can then be viewed as an element of the advancement of religion, if religion is construed broadly. Such a contention is not as esoteric as it may at first seem; even very traditional religious posi-tions, such as that of Saint Augustine, affirm that in certain more

---

[41] (1844) 1 Coll. 381, 395.
[42] See Sister Wendy Beckett, *Art and the Sacred* (Rider, London, 1992).

limited circumstances art may foster religion, namely when the beautiful is an avenue to God.[43] Even more secular personalities, such as the poet Charles Baudelaire, have recognised art's spiritual qualities as an element of the eternal.[44]

However, any treatment of artistic purposes under the relief of poverty or advancement of religion or education heads inappropriately delimits the independent value of art *per se*, and the general fourth head is used only arbitrarily for artistic advancement. The purpose in producing art is rarely purely religious or pedagogical, and the advancement of religion or education is only ever an incidental consequence of artistic endeavour. One recalls Oscar Wilde's contention that all art is essentially useless, yet admirable.[45] Moreover, current implicit judgment in the law of charitable trusts that art is usually of public benefit only if educational demeans the intrinsic cultural worth society frequently imputes to art in its own right. It is also worth remembering that even if the public were not to benefit directly from the work of certain artists, it is always life-enhancing to know that such people paint, have deep thoughts they write down or compose or perform music.

In conclusion, while the judicial scheme of following Lord MacNaghten's four heads[46] of charitability in *Pemsel* persists, art is done a disservice. In essence, it is not analogous to poverty, religion or education, though it may have aspects in common with all three. Charitable priorities shift with time, and retention of analogy with Lord MacNaghten's guide on the test of charitable status ignores more current community concerns in an increasingly leisure-based society. Art as creation and recreation should not be fitted inappropriately under the existing *Pemsel*[47] heads but should, instead, be deemed of charitable worth in its own right and within its own category of legal consideration. Only this approach satisfies a rational view, and the postmodern demand for legal equivalence of all society's self-classifying units, including the autopoietic sphere of art.

When a charitable trust fails, the cy-près doctrine, derived from Anglo-French, may be applicable. Under this doctrine, the courts will, where appropriate, apply the property of a failed charitable trust

---

[43] For a contemporary vindication of æsthetic experience as a basic value see Professor John Finnis *Natural Law and Natural Rights* (Clarendon Press, Oxford, 1980).

[44] See J. Mayne, *The Salon of 1846: Art In Paris* (Phaidon, London, 1965).

[45] See Oscar Wilde, *The Portrait of Dorian Gray* in *The Works Of Oscar Wilde* (Galley, London/Portland, Ore, 1987).

[46] [1891] AC 531.

[47] *Ibid.*

as nearly as possible to the original object for which it was given. Before 1960, when the Charities Act 1960 came into force, it was only possible to apply the cy-près principle where the object of a trust had become impossible or impractical. It was not permitted to apply the cy-près rules in a case where the trust was deemed a financially wasteful way of affecting the charitable object or where it was considered that, in view of the changing needs of society, the charitable object was no longer appropriate. To eradicate the problem section 13 of the Charities Act 1960 was enacted. It provides that in a certain set of circumstances the original purposes of a charitable gift can be modified so the property can be applied cy-près; for example, where the original purposes, in whole or in part, have been as far as may be fulfilled or cannot be carried out, or, at least, cannot be effected according to the directions or spirit of the gift. In theory the cy-près doctrine can accommodate trusts pertaining to art, but to date there are few practical examples that have come before the courts.

To be charitable, the purpose of a trust must be exclusively charitable and not merely include purposes which are charitable. Where a trust's purposes are deemed beyond the limits of legal charity the court may reach one of a few solutions. It can decide that the non-charitable purposes are only incidental so the trust remains valid. Conversely, it can decide that the trust is void because it could, for example, wholly serve non-charitable purposes. Finally, the trust fund could be separated into parts, some being applicable to charity and some not. However, this particular step can only be taken where the terms of the trust instrument can be interpreted as directing such a division. For a settlor attempting to create a charitable trust involving art, it would be relatively easy to satisfy the "exclusively charitable" requirement for a valid charitable trust by focusing the trust clearly only on its (supposed) charitable subject, linking it only with what are already established charitable purposes, for example, and keeping keen attention on its public benefit.

In *Dingle* v. *Turner*,[48] Lord Cross stated: "[c]harities automatically enjoy fiscal privileges which with the increased burden of taxation have become more and more important and in deciding that such and such a trust is a charitable trust the court is endowing it with a substantial annual subsidy at the expense of the taxpayer . . .". In England, the income of a charity applied for the charitable objects of

---

[48] [1972] AC 601.

that charity is exempt from income tax,[49] corporation tax,[50] national insurance surcharge[51] and capital gains tax,[52] and a charity has the advantages of lower stamp duties and remission from VAT in certain circumstances. There is also a 50 per cent remission of rates on hereditaments occupied by the charity wholly or mainly for its charitable purposes, and a further remission from rates at the discretion of the local authority. More specifically, no charge is made to Inheritance Tax in respect of transfers to the National Gallery, British Museum, National Trust, local authorities, government departments, universities and various other museums and galleries. A court is naturally cautious to grant charitable status to trusts when the significant tax advantage motive underpins the plea for charitability. In the context of charitable trusts pertaining to art, the removal of such financial burdens is undeniably attractive, but it is obviously wise as well as candid to ensure the (supposed) charitable purpose and (alleged) public benefit are the central and unambiguous kernel of the trust, and reason for the trust, when aspiring to charitable status.

THE LAW OF NON-CHARITABLE PURPOSE TRUSTS[53]

Whereas a private trust is essentially a (valid) trust in favour of ascertainable individuals and a charitable trust is a (valid) trust for public purposes, which are treated in law as charitable, a question for consideration is whether or not it is possible to establish a (valid) trust for non-charitable purposes. These are sometimes referred to as trusts of imperfect obligation, and as a general rule they are void. However, there are a number of exceptions to the general rule which have arisen including trusts for building or maintaining monuments and sites, tombs and graves.

In *Re Hooper*,[54] a testator left trustees £1,000 to provide, "so far as they can do so and . . . for as long as may be practicable", for the care of: (a) a grave and monument in Torquay cemetery, England; (b) the care and upkeep of a vault containing the remains of the testator's

[49] Income and Corporation Taxes Act 1970 s. 360.
[50] *Ibid.*, s. 250 (4).
[51] Finance Act 1977 s. 55.
[52] Capital Gains Tax Act 1979 s. 145.
[53] A variation on this section was presented by the author at an international seminar on legal structures of private sponsorship and participation in the protection and maintenance of monuments arranged by ICOMOS, Weimar, Germany, 17–19 Apr. 1997.
[54] [1932] 1 Ch. 38.

wife and daughter; (c) the care and upkeep of a grave and monument in Ipswich, England; (d) the care and upkeep of a tablet and window in a church, to the memory of various members of the testator's family. Maugham J held that the first three aforementioned gifts for the care and upkeep of the graves were non-charitable but were nevertheless valid purpose trusts which had also been limited in perpetuity.[55] As the trustees were willing to carry out the purposes, it was held that they should be permitted to do so. The fourth arguably more artistic gift was held to be charitable. In *Trimmer* v. *Danby*,[56] the testator here also gave £1,000 to his executors but directed them "to lay out and expend the same to erect a monument to my memory in St. Paul's Cathedral, among those of my brothers in art". The bequest was upheld by Kindersley V-C who commented thus:

> "I do not suppose that there would be anyone who could compel the executors to carry out this bequest and raise the monument; but if the residuary legatees or the trustees insist upon the trust being executed, my opinion is that this Court is bound to see it carried out. I think, therefore, that as the trustees insist upon the sum of £1000 being laid out according to the direction in the will, that sum must be set apart for the purpose."

Significantly, the rule against purpose trusts in general is directed mainly in this monuments category against bequests and gifts which involve the maintenance of a monument, tomb or grave, as this would go on indefinitely, as emphasised in *Mussett* v. *Bingle*.[57] Here, the testator gave £300 to be applied for the erection of a monument to his wife's first husband, and £200, the interest of which was to be applied in keeping up the monument. It was held that the latter direction was void for perpetuity.[58]

In *McCaig* v. *University of Glasgow*[59] the testator left all of his substantial estate to be used to build statues of himself, together with towers in conspicuous places on his estates; and Lord Kyllachy said in judgment:

> "I suppose it would be hardly contended . . . if the purposes . . . were to be slightly varied, and the trustees were, for instance, directed to lay the truster's estate waste, and keep it so; or to turn the income of the estate into money, and throw the money yearly into the sea; or to expend income in annual or monthly funeral services in the testator's memory . . ."

[55] The "perpetuity rule" is one of the ways in which the English law has insisted on the observance of a practical policy against the tying up of property for an undue length of time. Its details need not be considered here.

[56] (1856) 25 LJ Ch. 424.

[57] [1876] WN 170.

[58] See n. 55 above.

[59] 1907 SC 231.

No such purpose, he opined, would be consistent with public policy. Similarly, in another Scottish case, *McCaig's Trustees* v. *Kirk-Session Etc.*,[60] the testatrix directed that 11 bronze statues costing not less than £1,000 each should be erected in Scotland to various members of her family. This form of artistic memorial was also refused validity because it was considered wasteful and of benefit to nobody.

The Court of Appeal case of *Re Endacott*[61] involved a trust the purpose of which was held "of far too wide and uncertain a nature" to qualify within the class of monument cases cited because it was a gift of about £20,000 to the North Tawton Devon Parish Council for the purpose of providing some useful memorial to the testator. As also suggested by the Scottish cases discussed, it would seem that there is a particular reluctance on the part of the courts to uphold grandiose schemes as opposed to reasonable ones, a policy actually articulated in *Re Astor*,[62] though not in the context of monuments. The Law Reform Committee endorsed this approach and recommended that it should be permissible to use the income of "a limited sum of money" for the maintenance of a grave, tomb or monument (in perpetuity). The Parish Councils and Burial Authorities (Miscellaneous Provisions) Act 1970 now provides that a burial authority or a local authority may agree with any person, in consideration of the payment of a sum by him, to maintain (a) a grave, vault, tombstone, or other memorial in a burial ground or crematorium provided or maintained by the authority and (b) a monument or other memorial to any person situated in any place within the area of the authority to which the authority has a right of access but with the caveat that no agreement may impose on the authority an obligation with respect to maintenance for a period exceeding 99 years from the date of that agreement.

CONCLUSIONS

The law of trusts presents a novel paradigm for continental lawyers unfamiliar with its somewhat idiosyncratic frames of reference. In the specific context of art we are to be grateful that the English law often sees fit to privilege trusts for movable and immovable cultural heritage as either valid non-charitable purpose trusts or charitable trusts.

[60] 1915 SC 426.
[61] [1960] Ch. 232.
[62] [1952] Ch. 534.

It is to be hoped that the criteria discerned from the trusts case law for the creation of both valid, arguably artistic purpose trusts and art-related charitable trusts are sufficiently comprehensible to an international audience to be practically useful should the occasion of the use of the trust mechanism arise. In the course of the continued contemporary private sponsorship of art within the jurisdictions of the Anglo-American legal family, the equitable framework for favourable and efficient handling of art issues is now more predictable in practice than some of the older seemingly *ad hoc* case law decisions may appear to indicate. The trust is a benefit for the genuine, not a snare for the unwary.

7

The Conceptualisation of Art in its International Movement

THE INTERNATIONAL MOVEMENT OF ART

In international art trade, interested professionals of different disciplines differ on what should be called a work of art and what an artefact. In his seminal article, Paul M. Bator used the term "work of art" or "art treasure" loosely, to cover all items that are prized and collected, whether or not they are initially designed to be useful, and whether or not they have scientific as well as æsthetic value. Rules governing the legality of exports and imports in fact infrequently differentiate between archæological material and conventionally-termed works of art. Some states simply proscribe the export of all or some classes of art treasures and many require that a licence is obtained before some or all works of art are exported. The problem of ascertaining title to many art antiquities and lack of public concern have contributed to the comparatively rare prosecution of an importer or possessor of looted antiquities, notably primitive and ethnographic art. Similarly, the illegal export of "high" art of the USA and Western Europe seldom constitutes a serious problem. Ownership claims to antiquities have to accommodate dual values: the appreciation of beauty and the search for knowledge. Æsthetic qualities alone are seldom relied on as the sole basis to a claim. However, in the case of monumental and architectural art, the interest of preservation clearly justifies a strong presumption against its movement. In this way the æsthetic integrity of a work can be preserved. Likewise, works of art in a series should not be "dismembered", but the creation of new art can be invigorated by the possibility of comparison and juxtaposition resulting from the acquisition of foreign art. From a practical point of view, the category of art whose import is prohibited must also be reasonably narrow, so that interdiction does not promote the appearance of a huge and intrusive customs apparatus. To accommodate changes, specific import restrictions should be readily repealable and amendable and not set in the stone of stereotypical statutory law.[1]

EXPORT AND IMPORT REGULATIONS ON ART IN ENGLAND, FRANCE AND AMERICA

(a) England

The operation of the export control regime for cultural goods is the responsibility of the Export Licensing Unit within the Department for Culture, Media and Sport.[2] The purpose of the export control is to provide an occasion for the retention in the United Kingdom of cultural goods considered to be of outstanding national importance. The system is intended to balance the various interests involved in an application for an export licence including, *inter alia*, the following: the protection of the national heritage, the rights of the owner selling the goods, the exporter or overseas purchaser and the position and repute of the United Kingdom as an international art market. An "expert adviser" may object to the granting of a licence to export where he or she believes that an object satisfies one or more the Waverly criteria (see below), which can include an object by a living producer; "expert advisers" are entitled to view an object before reaching a decision. If no objection is lodged, the export licence will normally be granted. The 1997 position was that the Department of National Heritage's "expert advisers" collectively objected to few licence applications: between 25 and 50 objects annually out of a total of 3,000 to 4,000 applications, covering 7,000 to 8,000 objects of which they were apprised.

In the field of art export, what is of particular interest in the English system is how decisions are reached on licence applications for objects of national importance and details of the role of the Reviewing Committee on the specific export of such works of art. The Reviewing Committee is a non-statutory independent body set up to advise ministers whether a cultural object, for which an application for an export licence has been made, is of national importance

---

[1] See, further, Paul M. Bator, "An Essay on the International Trade in Art", (1982) 34 *Stanford Law Review*, 275–384.

[2] See, further, *Export Licensing for Cultural Goods: Procedures and Guidance for Exporters of Works of Art and Other Cultural Goods*, A Department of National Heritage Notice, 1997.

under certain established criteria outlined below. The Committee comprises eight members appointed by the Secretary of State for National Heritage who have expertise in one or more specialist areas such as manuscripts, furniture or paintings. We immediately notice that the Committee is not restricted to assessing only what are normally culturally recognised as "works of art". An object is appraised in accord with the following three "Waverley" criteria, named after the chairman of a 1950 committee that was appointed to consider and advise on an export policy:

(i) Is the object so closely connected with our history and national life that its departure would be a misfortune?
(ii) Is it of outstanding æsthetic importance?
(iii) Is it of outstanding significance for the study of some particular branch of art, learning or history?

Again, we observe that objects envisaged for assessment are broader than the merely artistic. The Committee expounded its interpretation of the Waverley criteria in its 1988–9 Annual Report:

"The first criterion is whether an item is 'so closely connected with our history or national life that its departure would be a misfortune'. This was originally intended to catch such objects as the Alfred Jewel or the manuscript of Gray's Elegy but we interpret it in a somewhat wider context to include items which are of major importance for local history, or which are part of collections which are of the greatest historical significance, or which are associated with significant historical events.

The second criterion refers to 'outstanding aesthetic importance'. There can be no definitive guidelines for judging whether an item is aesthetically outstanding, but we do not restrict this criterion to great works of painting or sculpture. We might, for instance, conclude that an exquisite snuff box met this criterion as well as a painting by Poussin. In the case of works by great artists it may be claimed that anything from the hand of Rembrandt is outstanding. We are not always swayed by such arguments and may take into account the condition or restoration to which it may have been subjected.

The third criterion is whether an item is 'of outstanding significance for the study of some particular branch of art, learning or history'. Almost anything could be caught under this heading: the worst works of the best artists (just to show that Homer nods), a poet's laundry list, a collection of seaside postcards. We therefore apply this criterion with rigour to objects which, in our view, are important for the study of some significant branch of art, learning or history; they have to be important for study rather than merely interesting to study. Many objects might provide attractive topics for a Ph.D. thesis but are not of wider significance for the study of the subject as a whole."

The Reviewing Committee is guided in its policy advice by the membership of the Advisory Council on the Export of Works of Art.

The Council is established to provide a forum for the discussion of the principles and operation of the export control system, and usually meets once a year in June or July. Museums and galleries, representatives of art trade organisations and various "heritage" bodies are represented on the Council.

Various non-art objects are excluded from the export control or licensed by virtue of the Open General Export Licence (Antiques) of 3 September 1993. If you intend to export an item which falls fully within one of the cited categories, an export licence application is not required for certain destinations. For example, postage stamps for any destination; birth, marriage or death certificates or other documents relating to the personal affairs of the exporter or the spouse of the exporter for a despatch to another European Union state; letters or other writings written by or to the exporter for a destination outside the European Union.

There are no restrictions on the import of cultural goods into the United Kingdom.

(b) *France*

Law No 92–1477 of 31 December 1992 on goods subject to certain movement restrictions imposes controls on the export of cultural assets and on the temporary exit of national treasures, whether involving items in intra-European Union exchanges or in transit to non-European Union states. This law introduces more liberal provisions than applied previously: higher value thresholds, and the abolition of the right of retention, i.e. a state's right to retain and purchase at the declared price items presented for export. It simplifies the application appraisal and certificate refusal procedures, and reduces the maximum period for the appraisal of applications. It gives the customs authorities new powers to act more effectively against illicit traffic in works of art and increases the penalties for such practices.

French legislation differentiates three categories of cultural assets: national treasures, cultural assets granted an exit permit and assets in free circulation. National treasures are subject to a blanket exit ban: these are national heritage items of major historical, artistic or archæological importance. They essentially comprise items belonging to public collections, items classified as historical monuments and cultural assets for which a certificate has been refused. With respect to cultural assets granted an exit permit, the sphere of application under French law is the same as in European Union legislation (see below). The items in question are assets of historical, artistic or archæological importance which fall within the categories defined by the Council of State Decree of 29 January 1993. The definitive or temporary exit from national territory of such assets and their export to a non-European Union country are subject to the production of a certificate issued by the Ministry of Culture attesting that they do not have national treasure status. When they are exported, a permit for their exit from European Union territory must also be produced. The category "assets in free circulation" covers all items whose declared estimated value is below the value and age thresholds listed in an annex to the Decree of 29 January 1993.

There are no restrictions on the import of cultural goods into France.

(c) *America*

Whereas most states attempt to prevent or limit the export of art works and other cultural property, the United States of America does not. However, in 1979 Congress enacted the Archæological Resources Protection Act (ARPA).[3] It applies solely to federal and Indian lands and prohibits excavation or removal of "any archaeo-logical resource located on public lands or Indian lands" without a permit. Nevertheless, the Act has enforcement provisions that tran-scend the confinement to federal and Indian territory. The basic pro-vision, section 2 of the Act, states:

"(a) The Congress finds that—
(1) archaeological resources on public lands and Indian lands are an accessi-ble and irreplaceable part of the Nation's heritage;
(2) these resources are increasingly endangered because of their commercial attractiveness;
(3) existing Federal laws do not provide adequate protection to prevent the loss and destruction of these archaeological resources and sites resulting from uncontrolled excavations and pillage; and
(4) there is a wealth of archaeological information which has been legally obtained by private individuals for non-commercial purposes and which could voluntarily be made available to professional archaeologists and insti-tutions.
(b) The purpose of this Act is to secure, for the present and future bene-fit of the American people, the protection of archaeological resources and

[3] See, further, J.H. Merryman and Albert E. Elsen, *Law, Ethics and the Visual Arts* (University of Pennsylvania Press, Philadelphia, Penn., 1987), Vol. 1 at 75–6.

sites which are on public lands and Indian lands, and to foster increased co-operation and exchange of information between governmental authorities, the professional archaeological community, and private individuals having collections of archaeological resources and data which were obtained before the date of the enactment of this Act."

To "sell, purchase, exchange, transport, receive or offer" any article removed in violation of the act is a crime. It is also criminal to traffic in items acquired in violation of "any provision, rule, regulation, ordinance, or permit in effect under state or local law". The Act could therefore feasibly be employed to prosecute individuals who sold or transported such material outside America. As leading commentators, Merryman and Elsen point out: "[i]t takes little imagination to see how the ARPA might be made the basis for a nationwide system of export controls indistinguishable from those in other nations".[4]

An instance of an import bar on art illegally exported from another state exists in the USA, i.e. a 1972 statute proscribing the import of pre-Columbian monumental sculpture and wall art.[5] It is fair to say that this measure gradually had a significant impact, diminishing the destruction of Mayan art, a circumstance of great emergency. It is only a shame that the United States of America did not seek to convince other art-importing states to enact likewise or to exhort Mexico and Guatemala to increase the efficacy of their export controls: two initiatives that would further have reduced the problem. Nevertheless, the US action does provide a model that other states may choose to adopt in similar contexts in the future. The primary law which provides the strongest protection against the importation of cultural patrimony from other countries is the US Convention on Cultural Property Implementation Act that enables US participation in the UNESCO Convention on the Means of Prohibiting and Preventing the Illicit, Export and Transfer of Cultural Property. The UNESCO Convention provides a framework for obtaining a US import restriction on certain cultural artifacts and any state party to the Convention may petition the USA for this form of protection. It is not automatically imposed.

---

[4] See, further, J.H. Merryman and Albert E. Elsen, *Law, Ethics and the Visual Arts* (University of Pennsylvania Press, Philadelphia, Penn., 1987), Vol. I at 75–6.

[5] N. I above at 287–8.

THE MOVEMENT OF ART IN THE EUROPEAN UNION

Article 30 of the EC Treaty provides:

> "Quantitative restrictions on imports and all measures having equivalent effect shall, without prejudice to the following provisions, be prohibited between Member States."

Article 34 applies a similarly-worded prohibition to quantitative restrictions on exports. Article 36 states:

> "The provisions of Articles 30 to 34 shall not preclude prohibitions or restrictions on imports, exports or goods in transit justified on grounds of public morality, public policy or public security; the protection of health and life of humans, animals or plants; the protection of national treasures possessing artistic, historic or archaeological value; or the protection of industrial and commercial property. Such prohibitions or restrictions shall not, however, constitute a means of arbitrary discrimination or a disguised restriction on trade between Member States."

Since both England and France are governed by European Union law, the present analysis examines the movement of art in that *sui generis* regime. Article 36 of the EC Treaty, pertaining to, *inter alia*, national treasures, is the key provision, specifying an exception for them from the application of Articles 30 to 34, which guarantee freedom of movement of goods. As the European Court of Justice has often stated in other cases decided under Article 36, the provision must be strictly construed, with due regard to the necessity and proportionality of any adopted protective measure. Article 36 apart, works of art traditionally enjoyed no special status under the EC Treaty, qualifying simply as goods within the meaning of Article 9(1) of the Treaty, namely "products having a monetary value [which], as such, may be the object of commercial transactions". However, the Treaty on European Union has produced amendments to the EC Treaty, placing more importance on the protection of cultural heritage. New sub-paragraph (d) has been added to Article 92(3) of the EC Treaty to incorporate and to promote culture and heritage conservation in accord with common market priorities, i.e. "where such aid does not affect trading conditions and competition in the community to an extent that is contrary to the common interest". New Article 94 facilitates Council Regulation exemption of certain previously undetermined conditions and categories of aid. Article G(37) of the Treaty on European Union introduces a new "Title IX—Culture" into the EC Treaty. Action is provided by Article 128 of the

EC Treaty to promote European culture in various instances including the conservation and safeguarding of cultural heritage of
European significance (Article 128(2)), co-operation with non-
member states and competent international organisations in the
sphere of culture (Article 128(3)) and the recognition of cultural
aspects of action adopted under other provisions of the EC Treaty
(Article 128(4)). The initiative in Article 128 of the EC Treaty, while
acknowledging the need to conserve and safeguard cultural heritage
of European significance, does not *ex cathedra* presume a common
heritage: it reinforces Article 36 of the EC Treaty whereby, as long as
national measures on the protection of cultural property have not
been harmonised, Articles 30 to 34 of the EC Treaty shall not apply
to prevent national treasure trade prohibitions or restrictions by
Member states unless such measures constitute a means of arbitrary
discrimination or a disguised restriction on trade between Member
States, and, as the preamble to Council Regulation 3911/92 and
Council Directive 93/7 expressly provide, it remains a matter for
Member States to define the category of objects to be adjudged
"national treasures" within the limits of those Articles of the EC
Treaty and the meaning of Article 36 of the same; the principle of
subsidiarity also galvanises Member States' responsibility in the protection of such treasures under Article 36 as well as Article 128(2) of
the EC Treaty.

The *Italian Art Treasures* case[6] on tax notwithstanding, the
European Court of Justice has not yet had the opportunity to consider practically the application of Article 36 to restrictions of the
trade in art works. Unhelpfully, whereas Article 36 refers to *national
treasures*, secondary legislation speaks of *cultural goods* (Council
Regulation 3911/92) and *cultural objects* (Council Directive 93/7).
Moreover, as a matter of definition, are *national* treasures only those
that originate in a certain state or have the most significant relationship with it, and what is a *treasure* and does it have to be *art*? The issue
is further confused by other relevant terminology that creeps into the
law because Article 36 is said to safeguard national *patrimony* or *heritage*. The meanings of all such terms presumably continue to fall to
be decided by the individual Member States, which is arguably an
abdication of EU legislative responsibility. In the area of trade in cultural objects both Regulation 3911/92 and Directive 93/7 strive to
harmonise Member States' labours under Article 36 of the EC Treaty

---

[6] Case 7/68 *Commission* v. *Italy* [1968] ECR 633.

to safeguard their national *patrimony* from illegal removal and theft.[7] The co-existence and virtually interchangeable use of various art and culture labels in European Union law can only ultimately lead to imprecision of regulation and harmonisation in this field, which is hardly a vote of confidence for legal clarity and efficiency.[8] It also augurs difficult territory ahead when Article 36 is practically used by the European Court of Justice.

CONCLUSIONS

Lyndel V. Prott and Patrick J. O'Keefe argue cogently that it is time to recognise that in law the term "cultural heritage" is rightfully superseding that of cultural property: there is no unified system of property law applying to all aspects of cultural manifestations.[9] What is equally clear is that in jurisdictions observed in this chapter art is not the legal *mot juste* in the context of the international movement of cultural assets/heritage. The reason is relatively simple: the term *art* is not broad enough to cover the multiplicity of valued products engaged in international movement. Nevertheless, there may be, notably in European Union law, a requirement that a national treasure has artistic content before it is classified as such: the matter is sadly obscured by the various different language versions of the Article 36 provision citing such works in differing ways. It would seem that the tendency of jurists to use the term "art" in the context of cultural works' more general international movement has also been transformed in the 16 years since Paul M. Bator's eminent treatise. Gradually, the legal world has transcended any need for an artistic criterion or content to determine protectable valued cultural status. Though this may be clear, it is lamentable that legal regimes and legal commentators persist in using a plethora of differing terms for such goods, since there is no obvious policy reason why such a variety is still extant. The term "cultural heritage" would seem to be the best to adopt in contemporary legal documents and paradigms,

[7] See, further, J.H. Merryman and Albert E. Elsen, "A Licit International Trade In Cultural Objects" (1995) *The International Journal of Cultural Property*, 15–16. The Reg. and the Dir. have the arguably regrettable effect of providing unconditional Community enforcement of the export controls of each of the Member States, favouring the nationalist image-endorsing of a cultural property regime.

[8] See Paul Kearns, "The Barrier of 'National Treasure' " in *European Brief*, Nov. 1994, Vol. 2, No. 2, at 11.

[9] (1992) 1, *The International Journal of Cultural Property*, 307–9.

given the increasing recognition of objects of cultural value beyond the merely artistic (at least in the "high" art sense of the word). There is no conclusive opinion, however, on the definitional ambit of the word "art", and it may well be that in the future an enhanced sense of it will reappear to cover all manner of created product fashioned by self-legitimising artists. This could be a natural result of the post-modernist tendency to self-legitimisation and eclecticism if in the long term the magic of the word "art" is durable enough to over-come competition from other categories of cultural import including a notion of heritage that has for the moment ousted it in the legal popularity stakes. This would involve the welcome permanent releasing of the concept of art from the charge of elitist hermeticism.

Art and the Customs Law of the European Union and America

INTRODUCTION

European Union (EU) customs law has evolved within the Customs Union and the Common Customs Tariff (CCT). The Customs Union regulates the common customs area's internal market and the CCT regulates the external trade of the EU, with the Common Commercial Policy (CCP) as a partner in this role. Articles 9, 13 and 95 of the EC Treaty eliminate customs duties within EU territory as is desired by any customs union. Article 9 provides the blueprint for a customs union, Article 13 prescribes gradual abolition of any customs duties on imports between Member States and Article 95 proscribes taxation which has a discriminating effect. By "customs duties", it must be remembered the framers of the Treaty meant not only pecuniary charges levied on imported goods but also those affecting exports.

In the United States of America, the 1787 Constitution removed the right from individual states to keep their own tariffs and currencies, and Article 10 proclaims that no state shall levy taxes or duties on imports or exports without the consent of Congress. Nineteenth-century state constitutions brought into the Union were compatible with the idea of achieving a united and free home market controlled by federal units, and an illustration of this is the extant Inter-State Commerce Commission established in 1887. In both the USA and the European Union, a degree of interaction between economic and political concerns has been inevitable, and the movement of art duty-free is a shared initiative with political as well as economic origins.

The presentation of something not *prima facie* ressembling art for customs duty assessment purposes sometimes leads to a dispute that is resolved only after careful legal consideration of the nature of art forms, exempted from customs duty, as specified in the relevant

customs regulations. The basic rule is that all art passes through customs control duty-free. This chapter treats case law that has accrued
following the practical difficulty of ascertaining what is, and what is
not, art. Art enters the USA duty-free and no duty is levied on art
within the European Community (hereinafter referred to as the EU).
As members of the EU, France and England combine with other
Member States in the suppression of customs duties *inter se* in accordance with EU law. EU law therefore complements the US model in
this chapter. In the customs law cases that follow, it is precisely the
definition of art that is called into question, because what is legally
debated is whether a given article is or is not one of the specified art
forms for customs duty classification purposes.[1]

Merchandise imported into the customs territory of the United
States is classified for duty purposes by officers of the US Customs
Service. A typical provision is 19 CFR paragraph 15211 (1985) which
provides: "[m]erchandise shall be classified in accordance with the
Tariff Schedules of the United States (19 U.S.C. Section 1202) as
interpreted by administrative and judicial rulings". Classification by
the Customs Service bears a presumption of correctness "having evi-
dentiary weight in and of itself".[2] The plaintiff has the burden of
establishing by a preponderance of evidence that the merchandise in
issue does not fall within such a classification. Tariff rates on specific
articles vary depending upon their classification. Items which fall
within the "works of art" classification may be imported duty-free.[3]
Within the EU, international trade in art benefits from, *inter alia*, the
suppression of customs laws and taxes of equivalent effect.[4]
Respecting "external" relations (such as with the USA), the common
customs policy nomenclature specified Chapter 99 to deal with, *inter
alia*, *"objets d'art"*. Its six sub-heads included the first three concerning art: pictures, paintings and designs (99.01); prints, stamps and
original lithographs (99.02); and sculptures (99.03); contained in
Council Regulation 2658/87.[5]

[1] See further, e.g., Paul Kearns, "Works of Art in EC Customs Law: The Problem of
Paperweights" in (1994) 3(1) *The International Journal of Cultural Property*, 115–20.
[2] It is not always to a given object's advantage to have (merely) an artistic element; for
example, there are higher duty rates for textile articles which are embroidered or orna-
mented in certain ways enumerated by para. 1529(a) of the Tariff Act of 1930. These rates
are retained today within the broad concept of ornamentation created under the Tariff
Classification Act of 1962.
[3] The USA places no restrictions on art exports.
[4] England and France have chosen to be obligated by the supranational law of the EC,
which body has external relations with, *inter alia*, the USA.
[5] [1987] OJ L256/1; D. Lasok in *The Customs Law of the European Economic Community*

THE TREATMENT OF ART CLASSIFICATION

Inconsistencies have arisen as a result of statutory and case law treatment of the works of art classifications. These result partly from the shifting nature of art with time (what is art tends to change according to epoque) but mainly from the variety of tests that have been legally employed to decide what qualifies as art. Courts have tended to focus on the occupation of the person producing it, the purpose for which the object is made, and, if the object is editioned, like certain sculpture or prints, the method of execution or number of pieces in the series.

In *Westfälisher Kunstverein*,[6] a distinction was made between products of graphic impression and original prints in the sense of category 99.02, and in *Volker Huber* v. *Hauptzollamt [Main Customs Office], Frankfurt Am Main-Flughafen*[7] it was held that exemption from customs duties for original lithographs under heading 99.02 of the Common Customs Tariff applies so long as the original plate has been made personally by the artist by hand, irrespective of the mechanisation of the actual reproduction process and of the number of impressions taken. A picture is deemed an original lithograph exempt from customs duties under heading 99.02 so long as it derives from an original hand-made by the artist. The original does not need itself to be on stone but may be a drawing on special paper which is then transferred to a stone and thence through multiple generations of transfer to the final plate from which the prints are taken. Although the number of prints taken from a single original design may be evidence of the non-original nature of the work, it does not in itself constitute a decisive criterion for the definition of an original lithograph for the purposes of customs exemption under heading 99.02.

(2nd edn., Kluwer, Deventer/Boston, Mass., 1990), 201 states that the Combined Nomenclature annexed to Reg. 2658/87 has been amended (by Council Reg. 20/89 [1989] OJ L4/19 and Reg. 1672/89) and Reg. 1672/89 ([1989] OJ L256/1), and Commission Reg. 646/89 ([1989] OJ L71/20) replaced the codes established on the basis of the CCT ("Common Customs Tariff") nomenclature in force on 31 Dec. 1989 with those established on the basis of the CN ("Combined Nomenclature") in certain regs. concerning the classification of goods. More recently, Commission Reg. 1734/96 of 9 Sept. 1996 has amended Annex I of Council Reg. 2658/87. Like every other legal text, says Lasok, Reg. 2658/87 is subject to judicial interpretation, and since it simply continues the life of its predecessors much of the case law appears still relevant for the practice of today.

[6] Case 23/77 [1977] ECR 1985.
[7] Case 291/87 [1988] ECR 6449.

Although the technical definitions of art that emerge from court interpretation for customs purposes reflect political and economic concerns divorced from æsthetics, in deciding what qualifies as art for the purposes of determining tariff rates or exemption on imports the courts have nevertheless often focused heavily on the appearance of the object. This disadvantages art that has the appearance of a merely functional object, such as an example of *art nouveau* or *kitsch*, or art that imitates a functional object (such as in the form of a ladder).[8] Sadly, customs arts appraisal is frequently, but perhaps ineluctably, a step behind seemingly esoteric, particularly contemporary, definitions of art, not least because of the enduringly static nature of the guiding written legal policy or statute. The law in this area ideally requires consistent rapid revision.

The customs tradition in America of creating barriers to the duty-free entry of items which are not in a traditional art form began with *United States* v. *Olivotti & Co.*[9] In *Olivotti*, the court addressed the problem of whether or not a decorative marble font was a work of art. The court held that the reliefs on the item were only ornamental and, though beautiful, could not be considered fine art. It concluded that Congress did not intend to include all æsthetic items in the customs definition of fine art but, instead, that only sculptures which imitated natural objects (human and otherwise) and represented them in their correct proportions would be considered fine art and thus enter the United States duty-free. The *Olivotti* standard became known as the representational test. With the emergence of more modern and postmodern schools of art, definitional conflicts were inevitable. It will be seen that these mainly result from law being insufficiently activist; although *United States* v. *Brancusi*[10] expanded the customs definition of art to include more abstract art, the more liberal stance did not receive legislative codification for nearly 30 years. So, whereas in *Brancusi* the court concluded that one of the artist's bronze sculptures evocative of a bird in flight was indeed a work of art notwithstanding the fact that it did not look any-

---

[8] Marcell Broodhaers, the Belgian surrealist (1924–76), is famous for sculpture using everyday objects that could be mistaken for everyday objects rather than sculpture. What might have been a workman's ladder piled up with some bricks fetched £132,000 in Christie's in the summer of 1992.

[9] 7 Ct.Cust. App. 46 (1916). The author is grateful for the scholarship of Leonard D. Duboff which, in various learned writings, helped profile useful American case law in this field; in general Prof. Duboff's art law studies have been seminal and highly important in American law.

[10] 54 Treas. Dec. 428 (Cust. Ct. 1928).

thing like any bird with which the court was familiar, in *United States v. Wanamaker*[11] materials were considered determinative of artistic status and reproductions of tapestries were held to be merely manufactures of wool, and therefore dutiable.

In the *Onnasch* case,[12] the European Court of Justice had to consider whether a three-dimensional work in polystyrene was to be classed as a sculpture under heading 99.03 or simply as plastic material. In contrast to *Wanamaker*, the court adopted a sensible post-modern stance: the expression "sculpture" must be understood as designating all three-dimensional art-works irrespective of the techniques and materials employed.[13] It is significant, though, that in *Onnasch* the defendant did not deny that the object was a work of art; it did deny it was sculpture. It is easier for a court to decide for the plaintiff's claim as to the form of the art if the defendant has conceded that it certainly is art than it is for a court to impose a notion of what art is when that is disputed.

In *United States v. Ehrlich*,[14] ornamental glass objects were treated as glassware instead of art, and a duty imposed under American law. Similarly, in *Firma Farfalla Flemming und Partner v. Hauptzollamt München-West*[15] the European Court ruled that glass spheres having a flat base, decorated with two- or three-dimensional motifs and described as "paperweights", which are executed entirely by hand in limited series and signed by well-known glassware artists, are to be regarded, for the purposes of tariff classification, as being works of a commercial character and, consequently, classified according to their constituent materials.[16]

In *Peters v. United States*,[17] it was held that although a collage was an original work of art, it was not a painting in one of the media enumerated by Congress and thus could not enter the United States duty-free. This again shows the limitation of set criteria for duty exemption in the realm of art. The 1959 Customs Law

---

[11] 19 CCPA 229 (1931).

[12] Case 155/84 *Reinhard Onnasch v. Hauptzollamt Berlin-Packhof* [1986] 2 CMLR at 456–64.

[13] While sculpture is no longer required to be representational in order to enter the USA duty-free, it must be produced by a *professional* sculptor. (*Tariff Schedules of the United States*, Sched. 7, Pt. II, Subpt. A, Item 765.15). This category includes a graduate of a course in sculpture from a recognised art school, or an artist who has held a public exhibition, or one recognised by arts critics or perhaps, even, his peers.

[14] 22 CCPA 1 (1934).

[15] Case 228/89 [1990] ECR I–3387.

[16] See, further, Paul Kearns, n. 1, above, and the summary of the case, below.

[17] 41 Cust. Ct. 195 (1958).

Amendments[18] attempted to resolve some the problems that had surfaced in the case law. At paragraph 1807, the language "in any other media" was added to the definition of fine arts to extend its range to include collages, lithographs, prints, and original mosaics, as well as other modern and postmodern art forms. Sculpture "made in any form" was admitted duty-free to end the problems engendered by the representational test. It had certainly been inconsistent, for example, to require that sculpture be representational given that abstract paintings had been allowed duty-free entry under the Tariff Act of 1913. The law showed here a preference for medium as opposed to style as a means of distinguishing the dutiable and the non-dutiable.

The particular injustices created by legal definitions of art being behind the art world's definitions of art by an inordinate period can also be witnessed in the contexts of contemporary "ethnic" or "primitive" art, art used for non-artistic purposes, and photography and photography-related art.

Most so-called "primitive"[19] objects that are considered art happen to take the form of sculpture (masks, carved statues etc.). The American Tariff Schedule for works of art permits duty-free importation of "original sculptures and statuary . . . all the foregoing made in any form from any material as the professional productions of sculptors only . . .". To qualify as a duty-free work of art under the "professional production of an artist" standard, a sculpture must be created by an artist who is "a graduate of a course in sculpture at a recognised school of art (fine art, not industrial art), or . . . [is] recognised in art circles as a professional sculptor by the acceptance of his works in public exhibitions limited to the free fine arts". Unfortunately, the "professional productions of an artist" standard does more than exclude objects made by non-artists; it also excludes many old-world works of sculptors. An old totem pole was assessed to duty because the sculptor was not identified,[20] and Canadian Indian masks have also been assessed to duty.[21]

The purpose of the professional productions standard and the test used to apply that standard is to enable US customs officials to distinguish between the works of genuine artists and the works of crafts-

[18] 19 USC para. 1201, 73 Stat. 549 (1959).
[19] "Most people who care much about art find that of the work that moves them most the greater part is what scholars call 'primitive' . . . In primitive art you will find no accurate representation; you will find only significant form" (Clive Bell). See, further, Clive Bell, "The Aesthetic Hypothesis" in *Art* (Chatto and Windus, London, 1931), 3–30.
[20] CIE 334/66.
[21] CLA 2: RRUSC 061749 TMP, 16 Jan. 1980.

men or so-called artisans. In *Mayer, Osterwald & Muhlfeld Inc.*,[22] the court concluded that a cut diamond was the product of an artisan rather than an artist because there was no pre-conceived artistic idea resulting in an æsthetic expression of the cutter in the cutting of the stone, and in *United States* v. *Oberlaender*[23] the court found hand-painted porcelain plates to be the work of non-artists since the items could have been made according to explicit instructions from the buyer. From this context it seems that it is artistic concept or inspiration that makes art and which provides the reason for its fiscally-privileged importation. The EC regulations also distinguish craft from art, suggesting a conceptual art basis of differentiation.[24]

Paintings, sculpture and other items that may traditionally be defined as works of fine art within the art world's art classification may under present American and European law nevertheless be excluded from the art classification if these objects are being imported for "industrial use" or are "articles of utility". These exclusions arguably unnecessarily restrict the importation of *bona fide* works of art and should be deleted from the works of art classification. Artistic merit and functionality/utility are independent characteristics that need not cancel one another out. Functional art, even if applied for a non-artistic purpose, is no less artistic in origin and creation than is non-functional art.

The American case of *T.D. Downing Company* v. *United States*[25] illustrates the unnecessarily harsh results of the utility limitation: the plaintiff imported six carved door panels which the court chose to consider not as sculpture by a recognised artist but as intrinsic parts of church doors without which the church doors would be incomplete and ineffectual. The court adopted utilitarian rather than artistic spectacles, which is an inappropriate perspective when treating a works of art classification: the matter of utility is second here to the matter of art and should be treated as such.

The somewhat arbitrary nature of the utility criterion is apparent in cases such as *H.W. St. John & Co.* v. *United States*[26] and *Kobata* v. *United States*.[27] In *H.W. St. John*, two imported stone capitals

[22] 18 CCPA 117.
[23] 25 CCPA 24 (1937).
[24] The stone-carver Eric Gill was not alone in considering art and craft synonymous, and any distinction between them made in customs law is for legal reasons. See, further, "A Stone's Throw from Greatness", *The Sunday Times*, Art, 6 Dec. 1992 at 12.
[25] 321 F Supp. 1036 (Cust. Ct. 1971).
[26] Cust. Dec. 4141, 65 Cust. Ct. 577 (1970).
[27] 326 F Supp. 1397 (Cust. Ct. 1971).

possessed ornamentation that could not be art, simply because the capitals were of utility; in *Kobata* v. *United States*, hand-painted Japanese screens were accepted as wall-hangings (and therefore art) and not as room-dividers (and therefore "utilitarian") simply because they had hanging devices attached to them. Unsurprisingly, Japanese screens are now habitually shipped with hanging devices. Law in this small way invites the undesirable duplicity of non-artists.

The American Tariff Schedules also exclude any article intended for industrial use. In *United States* v. *J.E. Barnard & Company*,[28] the industrial use criterion was not employed to determine whether the object was art or not, but to determine whether it was being put to some art-extraneous commercial use. In addition, articles made even partially by photochemical processes are denied the duty-free status of the works of art classification.[29] This is astounding given the contemporary acceptance of certain photographs as art and would presumably exclude, *inter alia*, art such as Man Ray's "rayographs". It is a sad comment on law that it is the slowest societal unit to recognise some artistic development that is commonly accepted by even the least expert sector of the general public. More importantly, such backwardness amounts to a reckless abuse of the power to regulate others' lives, in blatant disaccord with community-accepted values and conceptions.

TWO EU LAW PARADIGMS:
PAPERWEIGHTS AND PHOTOGRAPHS

(a) *Paperweights*

In *Farfalla Flemming und Partner* v. *Hamptzollant München West*,[30] the European Court of Justice denied presented "paperweights" classification as "works of art, collectors' pieces, and antiques" under Chapter 99 of the common customs duty policy of the European Community. It held, *inter alia*, that works of craftmanship do not fit the requirements of that chapter and are classified in a non-art chapter covering merely their consistent material. The Court considered that the relevant customs duty headings could not be interpreted by reference to subjective and indeterminate criteria for reasons not least

---

[28] Cust. Dec. 887, 33 CCPA 166 (1946).
[29] 19 USC para. 1201, sched. 7, pt. 11, Subpt. A, headnote 1(iii) (1978).
[30] Case C–228/89 [1990] ECR I–3387.

of legal certainty. Artistic quality is so defined and the fact that a "paperweight" may be recognised as being of an artistic nature does not necessarily determine that such an item is to be classified under Chapter 99. Moreover, the items in question were, according to the Court, goods of commercial character by courtesy of their ostensible characteristics and properties. The Court so held despite evidence that the "paperweights" had been executed by famous glassware artists, by hand, and painted in a way not dissimilar to traditional painting. The Court further held that the price of the items was not an appropriate criterion for Common Customs Tariff purposes; neither was the actual use to which the items would be put. The Court's approach was inconsistent in this regard with its approach in *Reinhard Onnasch v. Hauptzollamt Berlin Packhof*,[31] where the Court emphasised the need for the headings in Chapter 99 to be liberally interpreted. The Court saw fit not to classify the "paperweights" as "collectors' items" under Chapter 99, despite accepting evidence that the objects were collected in the same way as paintings and exhibited as collectors' pieces in celebrated venues such as the Chicago Art Institute. This militates against the ordinary meaning of "collectors' items" and therefore calls into question that label's practical usefulness as a Common Customs Tariff heading. Since the Court espoused the view that customs officials could not spend undue time assessing æsthetic or artistic merits, an inappropriate superficial analysis of the items was conducted. A point not considered by the Court, *a fortiori*, is that some works of art happen to resemble purely functional objects and others are designed to imitate such objects. In addition, an object should not be categorised as a commercial object *per se* simply because it has a certain commercial significance. All art has a potential commercial importance. In disregard of such observations, the exquisite "paperweights", more appropriately called art in glass, were denied their rightful artistic status for non-dutiable passage through customs.

(b) Photographs

In the European Community law case of *Raab*,[32] the legal question centred on whether certain art photographs by the late Robert Mapplethorpe were to be classified for Common Customs Tariff purposes as simple "photographs", or as "original engravings, prints

---

[31] Case C–155/84 [1985] ECR 1449.
[32] [1989] ECR 4423.

and lithographs" or "artists' screen prints" as Mrs Raab, an art gallery curator from Berlin, claimed. The practical effect of such a distinction was the concomitant relief from customs duty if the items fell into the category Mrs Raab prescribed.

Mapplethorpe's photographs were taken from an artistically prepared original plate and only existed in a limited number of copies. They were of significantly greater value than the price of the materials used. Consequently, Mrs Raab argued, as graphic art they rightfully belonged under heading 99.02 of the Common Customs Tariff, "original engravings, prints and lithographs". Alternatively, she contended, they should be favourably classified as "artists' screen prints"; Mrs Raab proffered that "artists' screen prints" had been temporarily exempted from customs duties; artistic photographs should be so categorised in the spirit of that exemption. The Court held that the Mapplethorpe art-work failed to fall into either of the non-dutiable categories mentioned. Photographs were not wholly executed by hand, it pronounced, and so could not come under the ambit of heading 99.02's "original engravings, prints and lithographs". Such reasoning was also applied to the "artists' screen prints" contention: the original design to be reproduced, the Court held, was executed by hand by the artist in the case of "artists' screen prints"; photographs were therefore outside this classification.

The Court's judgment runs against the postmodern acceptance of art photographs as works of art rather than as ordinary *sui generis* items. Moreover, it is unjust if a work of art has a customs duty imposed on it according to its full value at the rate laid down for the material used, when the price of such material is negligible in contrast to the computed financial value of the object as art. Culturally, it is also demoded to consider the use of a camera as evidence of the absence of personal artistic style in a photograph's creation. The current customs law provisions as judicially interpreted also have a "chilling effect" on all art photographers' creativity, discouraging art production by financial penalty.

CONCLUSIONS

Since art has been subject to lower import duties than other items, there has been much litigation over its definition when used in this particular context, and it is evident that customs law often penalises innovative forms. "Works of art" in a customs tariff sense also refers only to the fine arts, *not* the useful, mechanical, industrial or commercial arts.[33]

In determining whether an item may be considered a work of art, the courts have not only concerned themselves with whether its appearance meets some definition of one of the fine arts but have also looked at:

(a) the *occupation* of the person producing it, and/or
(b) the *purpose* for which it was made.

Customs courts, generally, will not classify an item as a work of art if it is the product of an artisan (or craftsman or mechanic) rather than an artist,[34] or if it is designed primarily to serve a utilitarian purpose.

The customs approach can sometimes be overly strict in favour of a commercial characterisation of an object as opposed to tending to favour an artistic designation.[35] An item may meet all of the tests for classification as a work of art but still not be eligible for duty-free entry if it is imported for a commercial use: since the commercial art market is limited, the imported piece might displace one created by a national of the state receiving it. Whereas pop art—the use of commercial art (merely) as subject matter in painting—clearly transcends the commercial character barrier, paperweights, for example, do not. There is an habitual unfair customs mischaracterisation of art objects that, on superficial analysis, resemble functional objects, and also art objects that are designed to imitate the appearance of functional objects, resulting in the denial of their rightful classification as art objects in contradistinction to the ordinary utilitarian ones they only resemble.

All art-works have an incidental commercial potential because their artistic worth gives them the possibility of commercial signifi-

---

[33] Mistaken identity sometimes occurs. e.g., customs officers in Philadelphia discovered three buckets welded together with a sealed metal lid in a package that looked suspicious. They drilled holes in the buckets and tore off the lids. In so doing, they destroyed a £12,100 work of art, namely "Third Hand" by Richard Wentworth. See *The Independent*, 4 Sept. 1991, at 1.

[34] Compare American customs procedure whereby the invoices accompanying works of art must give the name of the artist if the item is to proceed duty-free, if the artist is known. Other proof that the object is art may otherwise be required. Such proof would normally take the form of expert certification, which may not be readily available, especially if the artwork is highly contemporary and its precise origin anonymous.

[35] When the Harmonised Schedule was adopted in the USA in 1988, the customs definition of art was accordingly transmuted in order to comply with international law. This Schedule embraces international product definitions to which all prominent American traders adhere. Goods classification as art, for example, should acquire greater accuracy based on a uniform scheme of description.

cance. If an item can be regarded as a work of art, any concomitant commercial potential, either in its character or in the light of considerations of economic competition, should not defeat its being placed under the works of art heading for customs classification purposes. A contrary interpretation renders the purpose of customs duty exemptions applicable to art unjustly jeopardised by the giving of inappropriate weight to factors inimical to the fiscal privilege specifically designed to be conferred on art and art-related objects beyond the normal commercial *raison d'être* for customs duties.

9

A Short Miscellany

The general scope of this work has been dictated by delimiting criteria including time and space. Nevertheless, in this brief excursus some more residual information may be found of use to the reader. Art law is not confined, of course, to the subject areas covered by this book's more substantive chapters, but they most effectively demonstrate law's problems when faced with defining and appreciating artistic works and concerns. Here, I mention the omissions and a brief summary of three extra fields that have addressed the art–law relation.

First, the omissions. Forgery and "art crime", in general, including insurance, have not found a place in this book because they are specialisms of some magnitude in themselves, on which a considerable amount has already been written. Likewise, revenue law is omitted, not least because of the limited lifespans of most tax laws. Artists' moral rights do not find a place in this text because, although they support artists, they add little as a subject to the discussion of what the law regards as art. Although *The Legal Concept of Art* examines the law–literature relation, it does so more indirectly than the works of those involved in the law and literature movement, including Fiss and Fish. Contract law presents no extensive specific art law difficulties, so is omitted, together with the aspects of the law of trusts that do not operate on art in particular. Many other subjects simply do not have any relation to the art–law problematic. Below, aspects of jurisprudence, the law of armed conflict and freedom of expression are noted as having a sufficiently significant art–law relation to warrant mention in this text, albeit residual attention given the acknowledged constraints on the production of this particular monograph. In the cases of jurisprudence and freedom of expression, the reader will perceive obvious connections between these subjects and the abiding themes of the text. Auctions, galleries, museums and dealers do not feature prominently in the text because of their incidental character in relation to the prevailing scrutiny of the work, focusing not least on the law/art culture clash.

JURISPRUDENCE

It is beyond the ambit of this book to analyse art in the non-legal context of æsthetics, but the search for the definition of art within law naturally prompts various jurisprudential insights that could profitably be more fully explored.

It is not easy to set the bounds of art. In his famed work *Natural Law and Natural Rights*,[1] John Finnis identifies æsthetic experience as a basic component in our human flourishing. It is a corollary of this that works of art are particularly valued. Finnis writes within the natural law tradition but his work is not pre-eminently deity-based or non-analytic, characteristics sometimes associated with natural law treatises. Æsthetic experience, he maintains, is of self-evident, basic objective value; and a personal submission is that such an approach need not involve a leap of faith over rationale, though the acknowledgement of the power of religious, sacred or spiritual art may well involve more than the faculty of pure reason. Natural law should not be confined to principles immanent in nature but should also reflect the spiritual significance of the products of human creativity: to alter Hume's maxim, one derives an "art" from an "is".[2] It may also be necessary to identify what could be called the natural laws of art since the alleged autonomy of art suggests special treatment. Does art comprise its own moral universe? Do works of art come from a level of inner truth that transcends sexual difference? In what ways is artistic ontology "higher" than that of "mere" fact? Can we make any connections between artistic virtuosity and the virtues of sainthood? Such considerations may affect the legal regulation of art and have yet to be comprehensively identified. What is clear is that art analysis for legal purposes is long overdue in these and other areas: art law cases are hard cases and hard cases make bad law. Perhaps strands of legal positivism as well as natural law could alleviate this situation by paying especial attention to art, with its own unique system of creative elements and processes, that currently so afflict the inner certitude of legal mechanisms.

---

[1] (Clarendon Press, Oxford, 1980.)
[2] David Hume is famous for his positivistic dictum that you cannot derive an "ought" from an "is".

THE LAW OF ARMED CONFLICT

Cultural Heritage, Cultural Property and Art

A convention was signed in The Hague on 14 May 1954 concerning the protection of "cultural property" in the event of armed conflict. Its preamble refers in its second paragraph to damage to "cultural property" damaging the "cultural heritage" of all mankind. These concepts are challenging to define, but it is clear that "cultural heritage" embraces movable property including artistic works. There is no single concept of "cultural heritage" and various UNESCO instruments provide different definitions.[3]

UNESCO adopted the specific term "cultural heritage" in a collection of recommendations, notably the Declaration of the Principles of International Cultural Co-operation adopted by the General Conference of UNESCO at its fourteenth session in 1966.[4] These are eclectic documents specifying all cultures as an aspect of the "cultural heritage" of mankind. The 1970 Convention emphasises, in particular, national heritage. In the context of the 1972 Convention for the Protection of the World Cultural and Natural Heritage, a sharper definition was advanced.[5] As part of "cultural heritage", works of monumental sculpture and painting, and architectural works, of "outstanding universal value from the point of view of history, art or science", are featured. This is stated in the Convention's Article 1.

Beyond this, the idea of "cultural heritage" has also been evolved in the European Cultural Convention of 19 December 1954, and the European Convention for the Protection of the Archæological Heritage of 6 May 1969, which both emphasised it as a particular responsibility of European states. A different Western responsibility has been built into the Convention on the Protection of the Archæological, Historical and Artistic Heritage of the American Nations, signed on 16 June 1976 in San Salvador.[6]

The definition of "cultural property" adopted by the Hague Convention of 1954 was deliberately designed to be utilised by the majority of states and was therefore of average standard, as far as such

---

[3] See, further, Jiri Toman, *The Protection of Cultural Property in the Event of Armed Conflict* (Dartmouth/Unesco, Aldershot, 1996), 40.

[4] *Ibid.*, 41.

[5] *Ibid.*

[6] *Ibid.*

a judgement is feasible. Throughout the conference a more general definition was proffered by certain states, including France. Other states favoured a listing of elements technique; such states included the USA. The English delegate advanced that any list of examples should be short and indicate only principal categories. Of origin, ownership and value of "cultural property", value alone was ultimately considered appropriate for arrival at a definition. Works of art were broadly defined to include both the decorative and graphic arts. Interestingly, these terms also embraced exhibitions of works of art, galleries, art museums and all productions of a period or country in the arts.[7] The Hague Convention of 1954's final definition of "cultural property" reads as follows and is contained in its Article 1:

> "For the purposes of the present Convention, the term 'cultural property' shall cover, irrespective of origin or ownership:
> (a) movable or immovable property of great importance to the cultural heritage of every people, such as monuments of architecture, art or history, whether religious or secular; archaeological sites; groups of buildings which, as a whole, are of historical or artistic interest; works of art; manuscripts, books and other objects of artistic, historical or archaeological interest; as well as scientific collections and important collections of books or archives or of reproductions of the property defined above;
> (b) buildings whose main and effective purpose is to preserve or exhibit the movable cultural property defined in subparagraph (a) such as museums, large libraries and depositories of archives, and refuges intended to shelter, in the event of armed conflict, the movable cultural property defined in subparagraph (a);
> (c) centres containing a large amount of cultural property as defined in subparagraphs (a) and (b), to be known as 'centres containing monuments'."

FREEDOM OF EXPRESSION

Freedom of artistic expression in a human rights dimension tends to be protected under the general canopy of free speech, especially at national level. This can lead to inaccuracies because not all art can be protected as "symbolic speech" if that term implies a cognitive or propositional content. Abstract art, for instance, seldom communicates a knowledge-based idea but, more often, an implicit feeling based on artistic structure or colour.

There are various philosophical rationales that underpin freedom of expression, such as the arguments from truth, democracy and self-

---

[7] N. 3 above, at 51.

fulfilment. In which of these areas can freedom of artistic expression, in particular, be best supported? Cognitive art can be seen to challenge pre-existing supposed truths; it can serve as a catalyst for discourse on the verity of a particular belief. The chances of truth being established in or via art clearly militate in favour of freedom over repression. With respect to the democracy argument, art has a culturally-acknowledged role in helping to shape individual and public opinion; cognitive art can also be a direct expression of such opinion and confront its audience with the major issues of the day. It is debatable, though, whether one can identify art as a politicised vehicle when its *raison d'être* is essentially of an artistic order. President Roosevelt of the USA once said:

> "The conditions for democracy and for art are one and the same. What we call liberty in politics results in freedom of the arts."[8]

Politics and art, therefore, have a common basis in freedom and liberty, which latter terms can, of course, be seen as synonymous. The argument for freedom of artistic expression from self-fulfilment predicates art, not as a means to an end, but as an end in itself. What is protected here is not merely an individual artistic idea but the whole process of artistic thinking as intellectually common. As the artist Jean Jacques Lebel has commented:

> "in order to survive socially you hold things back. And you hold them back and hold them back and hold them back till finally you get to a point where you are holding so many things back that you are not yourself anymore. Talk about 'depersonalization' . . . .".[9]

Censorship is, we perceive, the enemy of the free artistic spirit, that needs to spread its wings well beyond the proprieties of polite society, in order to gratify its ontological inner nerves and heart.

---

[8] See H.M. Clor (ed.), *Censorship and Freedom of Expression: Essays on Obscenity and the Law* (Rand McNally, Chicago, Ill., 1971), 17.

[9] See E. and P. Kronhausen, *Erotic Art* (W.H. Allen, London, 1971), 45.

10

Some General Conclusions

Legal systems produce their own elements as legally relevant units. Though closed systems of the norms they create,[1] they are nevertheless receptive to facts of the general environment they work on, which facts become objects of their discourse and, consequently, contained: hence, for example, the forging of art as a legal concept in various legal contexts such as those discussed above.

Legal concepts of art are shaped by the presiding policies of the legal subject area art finds itself in. Sometimes such policy is a more general policy of the national legal systems. Proscription of the obscene, for example, traverses many legal subject areas in which art sometimes features. If art is deemed obscene, copyright protection can be withheld, passage through customs control prevented, charitable status denied, public funding withdrawn, defamation augmented, as well as prosecution for obscenity instigated under obscenity and other public morality laws.

The way law treats art is on the whole unsatisfactory. Art's distinctive ontological autonomy is unrespected.

In the context of obscenity law, for example, there is no legal presumption that what is displayed in an art gallery by an artist is art.[2] Neither is there any legal recognition that art is a large specialised cultural unit whose difference from other items should be acknowledged from the outset. Instead, in English law, for example, art is first treated as any other offending object and, if deemed obscene, subsequently defensible as being of artistic merit.[3] Artistic factors are therefore only secondary in the application of the legal rules of what is to be proscribed, whereas artistic character should indicate *ab initio* that

---

[1] See, further, N. Luhmann, *A Sociological Theory of Law* (trans. E. King and M. Albrow, Routledge & Kegan Paul, London, 1985), especially at 283.

[2] See Paul Kearns, "Five Simple Steps to Art Appreciation", Letters, *The Independent*, 9 Dec. 1992, 24.

[3] Artistic merit is used here as a relative moral value that can outbalance a charge of sexual or other immorality.

the intent of the work, for example, is different from that of a non-art object. Art should be differentiated from other objects in a primary legal step in accordance with art's distinct innate character and distinctive cultural *modus operandi*. Presently, on the contrary, within the legal concept of obscenity is reinforced a concomitant concept of obscene art; and yet art, *per se*, is incapable of being obscene.[4] At the moment, English law finds obscene content in the art communication then deems it either legal or illegal according to a test of merit. The binary code[5] result (either lawful or unlawful) does not reflect gradations of taste inherent, for example, in artistic judgements. The legal non-recognition of the ontological autonomy of art leads to unwanted confusion within the legal mechanism. The calling of art experts to defend mistakenly entitled "obscene art" could be avoided by the legal recognition that ill-informed response to art or non-informed response to art, rather than art itself, is the source of any obscenity. Art requires a sober observation and, ultimately, an appropriately sober contemplative response. To say that "art upset me" is to say something in the realm of personal response rather than to say something of art's inadequacy or culpability. An appropriate subsequent response to the reaction "that art upset me" is "it must have been meant to shock" (reflective) rather than a call for inappropriate (outside) legal action to redress a temporary emotional imbalance in the viewer that the latter should place in the appropriate context of art–viewer relation.

In defamation law, artistic originality is often unrecognised as a category separate from the original sources of artistic inspiration. An artistic creation of an imagined character based on a real-life model is then mistaken by law to be a factual presentation. The fully legitimate character of fiction and the cultural category known as fiction are thereby ignored and fiction's right and class of very being are jeopardised. Artistic originality is a new birth, not a re-birth of the life model.

The law gives less recognition to art than to other values in some of its legal balancing processes. For example, in defamation law personal reputation is given priority over art as a protectable value and in obscenity law a concept of public morality is enforced by law over art's claim to differentiation from the sphere of objectionable obscenity.

Law also gives less weight to art than to other justifiable pursuits not at odds with it. In the law of charitable trusts, for example, the

---

[4] See Appendix, Essay 2, below.
[5] The author is grateful to Niklas Luhmann for this terminology.

advancement of education is favoured as a charitable purpose over the promotion of artistic enterprise. Political speech is favoured over artistic expression as constitutionally protectable, especially notice-ably in America. Political statements are also given privileged status in certain appropriate politically-relevant or politically-necessary contexts (such as the English Parliament) so as to exclude the possi-bility of successful actions for defamation otherwise sustainable, whereas art never enjoys such privilege against charges of libel even when in one of its own specialised appropriate contexts such as in an art gallery.

Sometimes legal tests simply do not fit art. For example, in the law of defamation art cannot be said to be either fact, opinion or com-ment, and yet the legitimacy of allegedly defamatory art is based on its being classed as "opinion" rather than "fact", or defensible as fair "comment". Occasionally, as in the international movement of art, art competes with other terms like "cultural property" or "cultural heritage" for prominence.

Sometimes the mischaracterisation of art as non-art can have dra-matic financial repercussions. In customs law, mischaracterising art as an ordinary object comprising simply its constituent material can lead to particularly unjust fiscal results. An object not recognised to be art by customs officials has a duty levied on its constituent material. If the value of the object is accepted as the price accorded to it by the sender, who considers it an art object, an astronomical duty can, in theory, be unjustly levied: the price accorded to the item as art is applied to its contrary assessment as merely its constituent material. The mischaracterisation of art as libellous fact can also lead to possi-bly huge financial loss by the artist depending on the particular cir-cumstances of the case. Adverse financial consequences also occur for the artist when art is unrecognised in copyright law, in terms, for example, of the non-receipt of royalties. If art is deemed of non-charitable status in the law of charitable trusts, there is non-exemption from certain types of taxation otherwise avoided. Conviction of an artist following an obscenity charge can lead to a fine or imprisonment, and the destruction of the offending art, and the non-granting of public funds to the best candidates (on purely meritocratic grounds) can lead to the premature termination of potentially prosperous artistic careers.

Where there is poor discretion exercised on art matters within cer-tain established legal categories of the operating legal system, law does not provide for it to be exercised otherwise. Veiled as well as open judicial suggestions are part of the legal system and very important for art, as revealed in the context of obscenity law in Chapter 2. The individual tastes of judges are reconstructed as law as their impression within the legal arena is transmuted from the merely personal "psychic" realm to the socio-legal (including their sometimes weighty influence, for example, on a jury). There is no legal control of the lack of judicial deference to art expertise when the judge's opinion is at variance with it. The exercise of discretion in the field of the public funding of the arts also requires additional legal regulation.[6] The law should provide that arts policy is based solely on artistic considerations, and that it is unjustifiable, for example, to restrict funding to one visible or other minority group in any circumstances. The artistic spirit, itself exercised by a minority, is independent of gender, race, religion or sexual orientation, and arts funding should not be permitted to deal in unmeritocratic non-artistic discriminations. In the public funding of the arts, law should provide that assessors for publicly-funded grants give reasons for their decisions which are publicly available. This reassures the public that justice is being done in grant allocation of public monies, and the candidates for the grants are reassured that decisions solely on merit have been made.

Obscenity law cases involving art reveal judges to be arbiters of taste. Non-observance of the legal principle that judges should not be arbiters of taste goes unchallenged in the legal systems examined in this text. The inevitable exercise of taste in art-based legal problems suggests the establishment of special art tribunals to consider art law matters, where unsubjective judicial assessments expected by law can be appropriately modified. This would shift the art–law interface to a more specialised legal setting with improved techniques for the specific treatment of art issues (as demanded by the persistent problems that arise in the unspecialised treatment of art). Such tribunals could provide for the greater legal significance of what are now considered non-legal aids, particularly art experts. In such tribunals, the legal personnel would be specifically chosen as particularly competent in art appreciation and assessment of art–law relations.

Traditional legal structures enforce "accepted"[7] morality. Art, as a

---

[6] At issue here are methods of determination of what is the best art rather than what is art or meritorious art.

[7] The Utilitarians distinguished the morality accepted by a given social group from the general moral principles used in the criticism of actual social institutions including accepted morality. H.L.A. Hart has called such general principles critical morality: *Law, Liberty and Morality* (OUP, Oxford, 1963), 20.

vehicle of "critical"[8] morality, is disfavoured by the legal moralism[9] perpetuated by law's conservative tradition. Art has its own moral scheme aside from law's contemporary narrow preoccupation with sexual morality, for example, and presents all images, sexual and other, within its own order, to which the society of extra-artistic "accepted" morality often chooses to do violence[10] via existing legal moralism. The law does not embrace the idea of critical morality or moral advance except very slowly, which puts the immediacy of the morality picked up by artistic antennae at a considerable legal disadvantage, and increases the vulnerability[11] already inherent in art's new, sometimes iconoclastic, ideas.

The way the legal system processes art is not in accordance with cultural equality: law regulates art without due attention to its rela-

---

[8] *Law, Liberty and Morality* (OUP, Oxford, 1963), 20.

[9] Hart permits self-development outside the enforcement of established morality. The searching for new moralities is arguably a natural facet of the ontogeny/ontogenesis of artistic genius. The results could be termed æstheticised moralities. Schelling sees art as a phase preceding philosophy and religion, and Dewey views art as experientialism as a condition, not only as a stage of development. Because art is ontologically heuristic, it cannot conform to all received moral and ideological norms except with discomfort. Law is a framework in which Man can peacefully achieve things that he could not in disorder, and art is one of the enduringly recognised higher achievements possible. Art's ontology should therefore receive appropriate treatment by law in accordance with its specialised needs and value and, from a legal standpoint, aberrations. An interesting question is the degree to which transgression is an ineluctable part of the artistic mechanism/psyche. Space does not permit its full treatment here. The artist tends to look outside or beyond immediately surrounding social mores: not in a specious experimental way but in a search for "truth" in a less social context-dependent sense i.e. sometimes, unfortunately for the artist, that to which contemporary law tends to be shackled or adhered.

[10] Art and artists are clearly in need of the protection of the law of human rights. The incorporation of the European Convention on Human Rights and Fundamental Freedoms, for example, into national law gives citizens the right to petition their own courts if their rights are denied. The Convention is a set of internationally agreed *minimum* standards that were established at the end of the Second World War. Although these have brought many positive benefits, they have not provided for the specific and specialised protection of art and artists. Freedom of expression under Article 10 protects speech including "symbolic speech" (it has been held), but the latter term is inaccurate for art's protection because not all art is symbolic and not all art is cognitive. For "symbolic speech" cases, see Eric Barendt, *Freedom of Speech* (OUP, Oxford, 1989), 43–8. Art. 10(1) of the European Convention on Human Rights and Fundamental Freedoms provides: "[e]veryone has the right to freedom of expression. This right shall include freedom to hold opinions and to receive and impart information and ideas without interference by public authority and regardless of frontiers. This Article shall not prevent states from requiring the licensing of broadcasting, television or cinema enterprises."

[11] Consider more general vulnerabilities of the artist, such as the difficulty of making a living from art, even if he or she is relatively acclaimed. Could artists be exempted from paying income tax? See, further, R.A. Posner, *Law and Literature: A Misunderstood Relation* (Harvard University Press, New Haven, 1988), 326.

tive vulnerability. Art is a dynamic force whose mechanisms are sometimes noticeably antithetical to law's conservatised practice based on precedent and tradition[12]; hence art and law might be caricatured as mutual threats rather than as simply different elements in rich cultural systems of which they are but two major components. To assign positive value to differentness is to recognise alternative modes of identity in a very plural stucture. The current arrangement of legal categories is arguably too undifferentiated to attribute to art its own important cultural identity for legal purposes.

Without attempting a partial cameo of this identity, it can be readily understood why law finds art difficult to accommodate with unspecialised legal mechanisms. An idea behind art is to elevate the mind above literal fact, be a stimulus to cast light on real issues. This valuable role requires protection at least equal to that of political communications, for example, because art transmutes identities into artistic identities, whereas politics identifies its real-life targets unambiguously. The world of art is once removed. Art is a type of metaphor or symbol or impression or abstraction beyond meaning at a factual level, richer than literal sense. The honesty of art is the sincerity of the imagination, and only the authentic voices of art, rather than their maker, can be malicious, for example, in art, because artistic character transports all "statement" into the artistic dimension aside from life.

The public funding of the arts is an area that reveals deficiencies in adminstrative perspective towards the permanent arts in particular. The orientation of Britain's "Ministry of Fun"[13] is lamentably consumerist, with under-emphasis on the funding of the discreetly performed creative processes, such as creative writing and painting, that produce national heritage. What is mainly promoted is not the creation of new art work but public enjoyment of what already exists, be that established opera or museum priorities or even comparative but more sensational trivia. There is a parallel lack of concern for the actual welfare of artists in the course of creation of future heritage. The public interest is ultimately best rewarded not by immediate gratification but by the promotion of excellent art-work for the

---

[12] Even in legal scholarship, there is the internal expectation within the society of legal scholars that a legal text contains a majority of recognisably legal elements according to established legal scholarship discourse or tradition. However, any necessity for reference citation in set modes, for example, can be a hindrance as well as a help in the swift communication of good ideas on legal development within, as well as outside, legal circles.

[13] A meretricious title espoused by the once Minister for National Heitage, David Mellor.

future. With such little emphasis on the subsidising of artistic creativity in the form of non-motion visual art and creative literature, the prospects for the accumulation of national heritage are bleak unless the majority of such artists struggle on under their own steam (a cliché situation for artists that the modern invention of the public funding of the arts was designed to go a long way to alleviating, which motive contrasts markedly with present consumerist priorities).

A legal area inadvertently crystallises a theory of art for itself in accordance with its legal policies. Copyright law protects original as opposed to imitative art, and customs law favours only the fine arts (not the useful, mechanical, industrial or commercial arts). The extent to which art becomes a distinct legal category in each area depends on the prominence of art as an object of its attention. Whatever the area, quality standards tend only to be implicit, but become more obvious in copyright law and customs law, for example, where art objects are individually assessed for an economic end. This is also the case in the law of charitable trusts. In the case of the public funding of the arts, the criteria by which individual art-work is selected for funding remain unavailable to the public, so laudable quality tests alone cannot be assumed.

In the realm of the definition of art, it is noticeable that for legal purposes it is the definition of particular art forms that is most commonly addressed. Copyright law has formulated very successful definitions of a photograph,[14] for example, because photographs have readily scientifically-discernible characteristics. These definitions have evolved and altered according to scientific as well as artistic developments. Legal definitions of art forms should be regulated and updated where necessary, in accordance with such developments. The 1988 Copyright, Designs and Patents Act provides for many diverse art forms, reflecting new artistic developments, but does not include video art or installations as specific art forms. However, although definitions of art forms are inherently short-lived, or developments are too rapid to include them in new legislation, they are nevertheless useful, as proven in copyright law; and the lack of them has been unhelpful in customs law, for example, where lengthy litigation and court proceedings have occurred directly because of the

---

[14] Consider the succinct definition of a photograph in s. 4(2) of the Copyright, Designs and Patents Act 1988: "photograph means a recording of light or other radiation on any medium on which an image is produced or from which an image may by any means be produced, and which is not part of a film". A still, however, may infringe copyright in a film (s. 17(4)).

lack of definitions of art forms, including, *inter alia*, debate over the meanings of "original lithograph"[15] and "paperweight"[16] in artistic and legal terms. Ideally, what should develop is an "art legal" vocabularly to accommodate the specific definitional and other problems peculiar to art law. The lack of provision of art legal definitions protracts proceedings because the question of the definition of a given art form has to be attempted *ab initio* by both parties and the court(s). Some art-forms create fewer difficulties for identification of their members than others. In copyright law, works of artistic craftsmanship, for example, are more difficult to identify than paintings. The latter are produced using a much more limited number of basic materials, and each example is more easily identifiable as a member of a distinctive class. The term "works of artistic craftsmanship" embraces a broader variety of types of item within a less obviously recognisable class.

The classic division of art and nature acknowledges that art is somehow apart from the general stream of human action. In this book I have tried to indicate the nature of art's autonomy even though the precise nature of art remains blurred at the edges, given the protean quality of the bounds of art as a cultural category and the bounds of each acknowledged art form within that category. What is clear is that art is a catalyst for the civilised discursive realm only, in a sense culturally "abstracted" from the more violent interactions of life. It is not exertion of the will that its images or ideas result in action; and in this sense it could be called non-conative. To moralise about the contents of an artistic work from a standard of accepted morality is to miss the point of one of art's roles, which is as an aspect of critical morality for society's moral, and other, stimulus, and for corresponding adjustment of society's demoded or wrong "accepted" morality. When art is seen as symbol or signal rather than threat, vehicle for interesting stimulus and perhaps enlightenment, its critically moral role will find approval in the mechanisms of law as well as the art-interested community, and those appreciative of purer and higher things than society's often compromised mores.

Art achieves order within its own world. E.M. Forster, the novelist, claimed that order *only* existed in art.[17] With this in mind, it seems

---

[15] See Case 291/87 *Volker Huber v. Hauptzollamt, Frankfurt Am Main-Flughafen* [1988] ECR 6449.

[16] See Case 228/89 [1990] ECR I–3387.

[17] Within art, there is the internal regulation as prescribed by the artist: the art contains itself. See, further, E.M Forster, *Two Cheers for Democracy* (E. Arnold, London, 1972) and *Aspects of the Novel* (E. Arnold, London, 1974).

ironic that it should be further ordered by legal regulation: to regulate its relation with other facts of existence when it itself is ordered and orderly. It is, of course, a different type of order from law's active ordering purpose. Law achieves order by reductivist simplifications because it is specifically designed to achieve particular and practical results: "just" conclusions from legally honed discourse and definitions.

Processed within the legal environment, art becomes a legal semantic artefact[18] only partially or temporarily. This is why rapid legal development is imperative to keep step justly and efficiently with art's perpetual self-modification. No form of coercion can bring about conclusive definition of its general or particular categories or alter its basic identity to conform to mechanisms external to its own ontology. The interface of art and law within law cannot be one of equality, and the emergence of a neutral arena to solve questions of art law is desirable in the interests of both art and law. It is ineluctable that law will not give art full exemption from the operation of existing legal mechanisms unsuited to its treatment until the difficulties art presents for law are fully appreciated and the law changed accordingly. However, in the meantime, it should be recognised that those systems which are most widely accepted as defining meanings for the whole of society are in a much more powerful position than others. Law probably shares this prominence today with politics, science and economics. With a vested interest in maintaining its own inner consistency and self-reproductive capability, law must pay due attention to the particular nature of all distinct cultural units and systems it internally processes, including art. Art has the peculiar capacity to transcend logical boundaries and the designing of law adequately attuned to it is a major intellectual challenge.

[18] The author is grateful to Günther Teubner for this terminology.

Appendix

ESSAY 1: POSTMODERNISM: A CRITICAL GUIDE

Postmodernism is the era covered by the greater part of this book, and it is important that the anticipated legal readership, in particular, becomes acquainted with this epoque's central artistic themes, to comprehend the nature of the artistic process on which the law is here seen to be operating, and any associated art-law interfacial problems.

Postmodernism, treated here as the sum of the prevailing tendencies after Modernism,[1] presents at least the following 30 traits:

(1) The meaninglessness of all higher truths.

(2) The constant collaging of fact and fiction, images and reality.

(3) The purported favourable treatment of "other" (alternative) cultures and minorities.

(4) The dominance of market forces.

(5) Consumerism.[2]

(6) An ethic peculiar to the first world.

(7) Emphasis on service industries.

(8) The purported parity of voices and forms and irrelevance of status.

(9) Emphasis on the mass media and information technology.

(10) In art: (a), a desire to dissolve Modernism's founding oppositions: high against low art, authentic against inauthentic, art against commerce; and (b), nostalgia without anguish: a happy and rather passive mode of creativity, involving the collection of motifs from the past, especially classical culture.[3]

---

[1] Modernism is a term that has been applied to the period c.1890–1940, allowing a subsequent distinction between itself and postmodernism.

[2] On 7 June 1991 the Pope declared in Warsaw, "Do not let yourselves get caught up by the civilisation of desire and corruption". See, "Pope Rails against the 'Sensual' West", *The Independent*, 8 June 1991, 11.

[3] A phenomenon particularly conspicuous in the architecture and décor of certain fashionable night-clubs.

(11) Apparent lack of a coherent *"Zeitgeist"* and corresponding lack of a solid *"Weltanschauung"* on the part of its living subjects.
(12) Eclecticism.
(13) De-centred individuals impressionable to, and prone to, quick change of stimulus.[4]
(14) A fondness for surface image: the cosmetic.
(15) Simulation.
(16) Circumspection (wariness) on the part of people.
(17) A manifestation of the Western European metropolis.
(18) The absence of a native culture.
(19) Promiscuity (including sexual).
(20) Miscomprehension or ignorance of the symbolic relation of art to life.
(21) A refusal to specify *a priori* moral goods or evils.
(22) Self-legitimation.
(23) In poetry: (a), importance of form over content with notable emphasis on the visual shape of the piece; and (b), lack of emphasis on intrinsic beauty.
(24) Relative unimportance of the Christian God and a lack of emphasis on individual importance, spirit and soul.
(25) A concept-labelled social discourse: "gay", "black", "environmentally friendly".
(26) Oblique and ironic statement; reverence of "clever-cleverness"; pseudo-sophistication.
(27) Self-consciousness.
(28) Technological depersonalisation; limited real human contact.
(29) The attempted assimilation of vastly different cultural sectors (homogenisation) despite;
(30) Respectful differentiation of self-classifying units.

Postmodernism is an extension of liberal secularism[5] and its lack of one cohesive moral fabric invites a tendency to nihilism on the part of citizens. The era is the product of an over-emphasis on economic and political thinking and development and a concomitant lack of emphasis on the arts and religion as central values. There is a purported respect for all self-classifying collective units of a plural society (feminists, gays, blacks, the Far Right . . .) but a practical lack of

---

[4] The "switch-kid" of Fredric Jameson (n. 5 below).
[5] See, further, F. Jameson, *Postmodernism, or, The Cultural Logic of Late Capitalism* (Verso, London, 1991).

real freedom for the expressive individual whose needs are sacrificed to the demands of ideology via the political enforcement of this purist creed,[6] which silences voices against it, and against its attempted process of homogenisation of possibly irreconcilable cultures. The postmodernist ideal is unitary multi-dimensionality. Arguably impractical and tyrannical, a notion of "political correctness" censors voices hostile to its probably well motivated intent of harmonious co-existence of varying interests.

Postmodernism is founded on the assumption that there are no foundations.[7] This means it is a precarious condition: a reflex to what has gone before, and arrangement of it, but providing no new substance of its own. There is little entirely "native" to postmodernism (except in a purely temporal sense). Postmodern products in the realm of the arts are often characterised by their unimportance (because only oblique parodies or commentaries on something else) and lack of strong individual integrity illustrated often by the gathering of material and style from outside the self. There is a paucity of postmodern artists who have a truly original deep distinctive artistic voice[8] that will pass the test of time except, perhaps, those who will be discovered retrospectively, who will be considered unrepresentative of postmodern times because of their more genuinely artistic status.[9]

The postmodern era has to deal with a plurality of cultures that now happen to co-exist within what was once a more cohesive homogenous unit (especially premodernism when the white

---

[6] Via, *inter alia*, the movement termed Political Correctness (known simply as PC). The political initiative behind it was to make certain "sensitive" ideas, words and actions "off limits". Consequently, the University of Connecticut, for example, outlaws "inappropriately directed laughter" and "conspicuous exclusion of students from conversations". Doubt is cast on the validity of arts criticism by whites of black works. The main forces behind PC are special interest groups including feminists; no reference is welcome, for example, to higher achievement by men over women that is not attributable, or said to be attributable, to discrimination. Though evolving within a liberal society, PC can be seen as a very Orwellian idea not far removed from "Goodthink" and "Newspeak". See further, e.g., "Campus Newspeak" by Barbara Amiel, *The Sunday Times News Review*, 16 June 1991, Section 2, 1.

[7] See D. Harvey, *The Condition of Postmodernity: An Enquiry into the Origins of Cultural Change* (Blackwell, Oxford, 1990).

[8] See, e.g., Bryan Appleyard, "Books", *The Sunday Times*, 30 June 1991, 7: "After Four Quartets and Auden's last golden phase in the immediate post-war period, British poetry publishing lost interest and decided to invest in mediocrity".

[9] See Peter Abbs, University of Sussex, letter, *The Independent*, 13 June 1991, 24: "real art matters because of the meanings it aesthetically represents, not because of the symptoms (of the historic period) it displays". The writer is the editor of the *Falmer Press Library on Aesthetic Education* (Falmer Press, London, 1988).

Christian conformist ethic was strong, and various overt and politically enforced cultural prejudices acute). The state now houses a variety of relatively equal voices of sometimes conflicting cultures, and
government is at pains to say that minorities are at least as well-treated
as the majority. However, this is usually only at the level of abstract
politics (and gender and race classification), whereas in everyday living tolerance or benefit is rarely bestowed on the "eccentric"[10] individual. In this way, a type of unification is broadcast and advanced,
whereas the reality is the persistent lack of common identity, and
maintenance of old prejudice.[11] A tension results between what is
said to be happening and what, in effect, is. Aiming at harmonisation
necessitates a degree of integration, and this is difficult when societies
within society so often tend to cultural self-containment. The traditional government framework in England for example, with the
absence of a more appropriate scheme of coalition, is incompatible
with the nature of a plural society with the interests of one society
(currently the Labour) allowed to dominate for at least five years at a
time.

Eclecticism is a central characteristic of postmodernism: why this
should be so is complex. The history of its origin can be construed as
follows.

Postmodernism resulted from an impasse. The Modernist *avant-
garde* petered out under the unassailable momentum of commercial-
ism.[12] This produced an abrupt de-Romanticisation, a de-centring
from the individual whose outlook became almost inevitably nihilist
since he applied the relative unimportance of individual vision to his
own vision of himself, negating self-worth and self-belief. Hence
postmodern subjects turn to the collection of things external to self
in an attempt to compensate for deficit of creative initiative (stem-
ming from lack of inner cohesion and security that was once provided by an unfragmented moral vision or God). A new artificial
vision is thus collaged: a blended, ambiguous and inoffensive picture
that is unrebellious. Images are drawn from the past and from immediate stimulus, the passivity or laziness of approach a reaction to
Modernists' *angst*. Energy in postmodern man is reserved for an
extra-artistic activity, solipsistic creativity now demeaned as demod-

---

[10] In the original sense (Gk) of "out of the centre".

[11] The Commission for Racial Equality said in its second review of the Race Relations
Act 1976 (published 12 June 1991): "Direct discrimination is generally covert, and indirect
discrimination [where minority groups are disadvantaged by employment practices] a product of ordinary practices not recognised unlawful by those who operate them".

[12] See, further, n. 7 above.

edly egotistic, and exhausted, becoming, instead, a form of self-conscious play. In a broader context, artistic eclecticism can be seen as a means of styling the very fragmentation of the contemporary context to off-set a type of schizophrenic collapse. It vernacularises, too, to project as much security as possible by form. This is to counter postmodern man's perceived substantive disorientation.

Other facets of postmodernism include its city-focus, habitual sexual promiscuity and indifference to paradox in important areas, including matters of justice and principle. The metropolis is postmodernism's exercise-ground, the provinces on the fringes of its influence (reached by the media but lacking the variety of facilities that a typical eclectic postmodern experience pre-required). Habitual sexual promiscuity (tempered only slightly by the fear of AIDS) is a social facet of the postmodern view of the human condition as ephemeral, discontinuous and eclectic. In religious matters, in Britain at least, it would seem that although the Christian God would, ideally, be phased out of the picture (too absolute for postmodernism's momentum of "amoral" fluidity), it is part of postmodernism's paradoxical ethic that a non-Christian ("other") concept of God must nevertheless be respected even to the point of eradication of the freedom of the individual (the paradigm case being that of the novelist Salman Rushdie), a freedom that postmodernists purport to ensure absolutely. The retention of the law of blasphemy as only protective of the Christian God displays further inconsistency, demonstrating law's adherence to a pre-postmodern (and, indeed, premodern) value scheme, further complicating the postmodern problematic.

One face of it is æsthetic. In poetry, there is a trend (in tone) to the oblique and ironic and (in content) the commonplace. There is noticeable experimentation with form, and inordinate importance seems to be attached to the visual shape of the poem. It tends to avoid the objectives of beauty and truth (in the sense of profundity). There also seems to be a relatively small clan of acknowledged poets who appear to self-perpetuate in a quasi-masonic way (and who sometimes inter-refer by way of replies or responses to one another in "poetic" form). By traditional standards, most of the work would appear more prose-like than poetic, except for its continued arrangement in stanzas of one kind or another.[13] A typical postmodern poem would contain the almost obligatory occasional use of highly unusual (pseudo-sophisticated) vocabulary. Straightforwardness is exceptional.

---

[13] The semblance or simulation of the art is the dominant feature.

Atypical in the latter two respects was Philip Larkin, but his detached voice, deflecting away from self in neutral tones, hints at the postmodernist self-consciousness and self-abnegation that was to be more explicitly manifested in later postmodern verse. A lack of jubilance is a feature of contemporary verse in general (a consequence of the disapproval of innocent expression). The institutionalisation of creative writing in the form of degree courses in the activity emphasises postmodernism's lack of reverence for inspiration in favour of an art that can be learnt like any other trade (*tekhne*).[14] This re-affirms the postmodern stance that art is unspecial. The exceptional inspired talent with the personal and beautiful voice goes unregarded. The angel has gone: no-one wants him. And no-one believes in him. There can be no such thing as native untutored quality which traditionalists would agree is the hallmark of an artist. His presence would embarrass the profitable scheme of "let's pretend we're poets" and the philosophy that anyone can be recognised if well-connected yet (by demoded more objective standards) talentless. For, without criteria for quality, everything is possible, and in the spirit of a postmodern policy that encourages belief in sameness, everyone is to be (falsely) considered equally capable of everything (and the same things), without sufficient scope for the possibility of genius or the voicing of the possibility of talentlessness (especially if the work is that of a member of a minority or alternative culture). Politics dictate a lot in the area that should be free from it.

Art-forms that would once have cancelled each other out now harmoniously co-exist: the cartoon is received with equal dignity as the painting. We also witness an experimentation with what art is, sometimes intended trivially but treated with utmost gravity by arts critics. These are not necessarily unhealthy developments.

More disconcertingly, within postmodernism art is denied its distinctive relation to life. It has lost the security of its own category. This is most noticeable in the case of *The Satanic Verses*[15] where the apolitical essence of art, whatever its subject matter, is ignored, and a novel treated as a political document (not even just as any other datum).[16] It makes writing a novel giving insight into reality a painful task if the novelist is subsequently charged with the sexism or racism or other alleged offensiveness his art's reflection of reality presents.

---

[14] The main practical advice is how to "package" your writing properly so that it *appears* creditable/publishable.

[15] Salman Rushdie's controversial novel.

[16] "A novel is an impression not an argument" (Thomas Hardy). Art is more imagination than assertion.

Moreover, it leads to the impoverishment of "art", which, in the end, by autocensorship, will display nothing that can feasibly offend according to current criteria (that curb freedom of expression), which will make it inert for purposes of enlightenment and edification. "Art" will be made to be merely a reflection of an imposed political idea.

A peculiarly little-noted phenomenon is postmodernism's political over-seriousness, oversensitively eradicating whole areas of humour, including the xenophobic joke common to most cultures. When, for example, Prince Philip of England suggested to some English students in China that if they stayed much longer they may become "slitty-eyed", he drew attention to a fact of differentness. It is puerile to interpret such light-hearted humour as maliciously racist and stupid to attempt to disregard facts in favour of one of postmodernism's distortions i.e. that we are all exactly, even physically, the same (rather than simply equal).

Jean Baudrillard sees the passage to postmodernity as characterised, *inter alia*, by a "loss of the real": a pervasive domination of the representation of reality over reality itself.[17] Through the media, objective reality has become a membrane of simulacra[18] stretched over the real. It binds us to our own precarious social realities by making them appear external to ourselves. Some are even tempted to forget reality completely in a new artifically fabricated world known as "virtual reality" (by donning a high-tech head-piece and living in a videoscape). Bureaucratisation is also a facet of postmodernism's favouring of appearance over reality: we are happy to see that things are simply seen to be done. These are rather immature aspects of a somewhat inchoate ethic that may develop positively with time.

There is potential in postmodernism for the dynamic equilibrium of different identities. However, if the separate identity of one category (for example, art) goes unacknowledged, it incurs not only a lack of affirmation as a positive quality but disadvantaging treatment as well. Postmodernism should develop to accept differentiation and not to expect assimilation. At the moment, there is a tendency to recognise and respect difference but somehow, idealistically, expect unification. It is as if in an attempt at equalisation there is a vain hope for sameness from all different categories, to satisfy a traditional need

---

[17] See, also and further, Jean-Michel Roy, "The French Invasion Of American Art Criticism" (1989) 2(2), *The Journal of Art*, 20.

[18] The word "simulacrum" means a copy of which there is no original.

for homogenisation of a type a state is used to. There should be a shift in focus from the hope of unification to an ideal of equivalence.

Equivalence involves a compelling claim to equal significance and respect. Within the legal construction, for example, all elements should enjoy equal compositional value. Those in minority classifications, in particular, should be recognised, since their more unusual situation is most obviously jeopardised by non-recognition of their fundamental difference. Moreover, each constituent—the homosexual, the artist, the child—should be treated according to the qualities of her own identity. All different elements are thus given positive compositional value in the legal picture. Sadly, postmodernism's current response to the "unlike" amounts to little more than a cosmetic tolerance. Law should ensure that there is no reality of isolation and, in effect, give depth to postmodernism's surface ideals.

ESSAY 2: A CRITIQUE OF THE OBSCENE IN ART, PORNOGRAPHY, LAW AND SOCIETY

The art experience is not a passive one, but requires the active participation of the audience. Obscenity is a possible property of the viewing of an object out of context. Only when the object is responded to in an æsthetic context can a work of art result.[1] Only when not can obscenity be achieved. Ignoring this results in a legally canonised art with the tempering of artistic ardour to the point of its silence.

There is contextual importance too for the English defence to obscenity of artistic merit, because it is a *legal* artistic merit, the product of obscenity law. It is basically a device to balance the factor of sex in art, the "good" in a work that is weighed against the "bad": this role differentiates it from non-legal artistic merit, the function of which is altogether less delimited. Sex is considered by law somehow undesirable in art, and legal artistic merit constitutes simply an operation whereby art containing sex may be excused.

It is not only in England, France and America that there has been a taboo on artistic representations of lust or love-making; the attitude of censure pervades the whole Christian West. One could hypothesise *ad infinitum* on the conscientious objections that led to this. The objection on grounds of indecency is one of social mores, often reinforced by law. Beneath this, however, more fundamental human considerations have probably played a part: there may have been a feeling that sex has a mystique and that much of the pleasure in it is dependent on that; less artistically and more reverentially, it may at some time have been felt that the honour in which some hold the action would be undone by its representation. Those who applaud the sexual act may have thought that doing would be replaced by a sterile beholding, love-making witnessed rather than performed. Others may have resented an important action being made vulnerable to power over it inherent in re-creating it.[2] These singular human attitudes apart, the origins of the law of obscenity, so entwined with those of blasphemy, suggest that mass rejection of sex represented in art emanated from notions of "good" and "bad" shared by the main

---

[1] See Abraham Kaplan, "Obscenity as an Esthetic Category" in (1955) 20 *Law And Contemporary Problems*, 544.

[2] Wayland Young, *Eros Denied* (Weidenfeld & Nicolson, London, 1965), 101.

corpus of society or, rather, in our less democratic condition, by the ruling oligarchy.

It is not inconceivable that the anachronism of restraining representation of sex in an allegedly developed civilisation directly emerged from the governing classes' wish to restrain, rather than protect, the "people", in any matter not totally reconcilable with their concept of order. Obscenity law can be seen as a relic of the days when the rulers needed to grip power tightly and proscribe any activity, particularly emotive, that could feasibly inspire disorder. The obscene matter needs a human partner for such inspiration to arise. Art needs more: all art is essentially ambiguous in the sense that the interpretation it calls for includes an imaginative aspect. Art cannot occur without room in an object's reading for our own creative viewing activity, making us its internal co-creators. It requires an uncarnal aspect of meditation, *inter alia*, and a contemplative reaction.

The law has difficulty in regulating this realm with exhaustive formulae. Judge Woolsey has made use of *"l'homme moyen sensuel"* as a standard. He must not be equated with English tort's "reasonable man". It is doubtful whether sexual sensitivity has a logic that corresponds to the "reasonableness" of reasoning.[3] Moreover, the judge may identify with *"l'homme moyen sensuel"* and inadvertently replace the latter's judgement with his own. Any justification of obscene matter by reference to artistic merit is open to abuse in a somewhat different way. In legal practice, artistic merit becomes no more than a neutralising agent to negative certain passages' obscenity: neither art nor sex is valued for itself and an unrealistic dichotomy is established whereby sex and artistic merit do battle (the artist's equivalent of the old "trial by ordeal"). Treating artistic merit as this functional neutralising legal tool denudes it, of necessity, of controversial content, particularly sexual (its opponent); artistic merit is drained of its sensual colours and becomes a pale reflection of its lay cousin which has become no such bland half of a legal balancing technique.

Where is the commonsensical recognition that treatment of sex may in itself be artistic and meritorious? *A fortiori*, sex is very difficult subject matter for an artist to present successfully and accomplished responses to this challenge should arguably be highly praised; any quality of response should arguably be treated indulgently rather than be the victim of a legal fist. The technical difficulties about representing two people making love, as opposed to having sexual inter-

---

[3] See, further, Kaplan, n. 1 above, at 547.

course *per se*, include the consideration that possibly only exhibition-ists will be happy to make love for an artist's purpose and only a voyeur artist will want to capture the act.[4] Whereas it is possible for a voyeur to draw two exhibitionists, what is the likelihood that he will be a very good artist and that they are genuinely very much in love? As it happens, the greater part of established Euro-American "erotic" art does not portray heterosexual intercourse; more fre-quently, the artist has turned to the love-making of two women in the tradition of Rodin's "Bacchantes" and Courbet's "Sleepers".[5] It has never been popular to present the love-making of two men except in ancient civilisations, but the second half of the twentieth century has seen more public acceptance of such portrayals: Plato's "The Symposium" is no longer one of the very few classics treated seriously on the subject. Sexual orientation may have not only an incidental relation to art and heterosexually-based legal mores.

Unlike pictorial art, creative literature avoids technical problems in the presentation of love-making. The painter cannot manage his audience as effectively as the writer can—in a few sentences, a writer can declare that it is love that is presented rather than have to reply on the viewer's perception of the love feeling allegedly presented in the graphically visual presentation without an accompanying title. A writer can have a private word with his reader; a painter cannot[6] (unless, as in many postmodern exhibitions such as that of Chagall in 1986 at the Royal Academy, London, the paintings are supplemented with the artist's explanations or philosophical comment[7]). The point remains that painting *per se* can explain less than writing, whose con-tent is discourse. What a painting says is never as verbally clear and therefore, from a legal standpoint, not as easy to accuse precisely. Lack of degree of clarity also explains the toleration of a greater erotic content in music: the imperceptive do not feel it and cannot see it.[8]

It may be a sad truth that only a frightened and insecure culture has to promote withdrawal of vision from anything at all; proscription of sex in art indicts a culture as unable to integrate reality and commu-nication, honesty and society. The corruptive effect of obscenity is only alleged, and, even if it were conclusively proven, such effect could never emerge from an æsthetic experience which requires an

---

[4] Young, n. 2 above, at 101–2.

[5] *Ibid.*, at 103.

[6] *Ibid.*, at 105.

[7] This can be seen as an aspect of the self-consciousness of postmodernism. See, further, Appendix, Essay 1, above.

[8] *Ibid.*, at 106.

element of distance in the mind of the viewer: art presents scenes for contemplation, and what the viewer feels is a type of imagined feeling based on a medium which removes him from real experience and therefore works against his turning into action what he does not receive from action but from art. It is not a case of feelings being sublimated but of feelings being presented by art and appreciated as art's feelings not as the viewer's own. To ignore this element of psychic distance, intrinsic to the æsthetic experience, is to make art promotional which, unlike advertising, it is not. In the realm of obscenity, it is pornography not art that promotes. Society is said by law to decry, in general, this promotion, and art and pornography are set in strange opposition by law without careful attention to any quality that divides them.[9] This is particularly the case where there is simply the detestation of the pornographic: the prejudice is so firm that even prosecuted artists frequently furnish censors with ammunition when, in the course of defending their art against a charge of obscenity, they are forced to condemn pornography in order to show how it contrasts with their relatively "inoffensive" work. The legal system tends to shoulder everyone to a commitment that pornography is intolerable. Art saves itself at the expense of pornography and the law promotes this unnatural, and arguably unnecessary, conflict.

This is not to forget that pornography is different from art in important respects not often accurately articulated: unlike art, pornography aims to satisfy as a stimulus to action and the release of a compelling urge.

In English law there is no formal defence for pornographers—only when something feasibly approximates to recognised merit is a defence available. Why is it unlawful to publish matter which may influence people to commit an act which is not in itself unlawful? This anomaly renders the law inequitable and intellectually unacceptable. Very few "good" books are prosecuted these days for obscenity—artistic merit's cause is virtually won.[10] What is needed is a defence for that which is considered unmeritorious by the legislature. Without it, we deny the value of honesty and promote hypocrisy—an inconsistency between what happens in private and what is wished to be said to happen by the society that makes law. Is the presentation of sexual intercourse so undesirable to witness? Or is

---

[9] From a Buddhist standpoint, such distinctions are only the result of a discriminating mind, and inessential. From a Christian standpoint, they have become unhealthily imperative.

[10] D.F. Barber, *Pornography and Society* (Skilton, London, 1972), at 111.

it simply that it is undesirable that it should be enjoyable to witness? Is it so harmful that it is necessary to legislate against it and deprive the individual of exercising his own judgement about whether he views it? Is this paternalism really simply promoting the "scruples" of its exponents rather than the happiness of people law is designed to preserve?

Is the main socio-moral limitation on artists dealing with sex a habit of feeling in our culture about the subject represented perpetuated simply by a sort of inertia? If other facets of life are regarded with disapproval, one might assume, quite logically, that the same would apply to representations of them. The uninhibited representation of dishonesty and theft (amongst other undesirable things) in the graphic arts emphasises the bizarre nature of the sex taboo. And sex is not a crime! However, an explanation does exist for this seemingly ridiculous state of affairs. The obscene in art threatens conformity not morality: it is a matter of propriety. The representation of what some consider the "lower" feelings distresses decorum—most often the decorum of "polite society" of which, by contrast, our legislators tend to be representative. Obscenity law is a product of the sex-tabooing convention of the governing class of people reinforced by general neurosis about sexual matters. It could be called bourgeois if it were not so pernicious.[11]

Art is distinguished from pornography according to its mode of operating; the legal is distinguished from the illegal according to the juridical mode of operating. Whether we like a certain mode of operating is a matter of taste; but sometimes that is imposed on us, law being a certain type of ultimate authority. Moreover, in the contest of social realities in postmodern systemic independence in pluralism, it is unsurprising but lamentable that formal legal enterprise is so resistant to the necessarily rapid acceptance of new sensuous artistic versions of reality.[12]

[11] Note the immediate political misfortunes of Mr Gary Hart and Mr Jeffrey Archer following media revelation about their alleged extra-marital affairs (USA and England, 1987). Contrast the success of Mr John F. Kennedy who made the most of the solid beauty of his marriage in his campaign for the US Presidency against Mr Richard Nixon. The appointment of Ilona Staller, pornography star, as an Italian Member of Parliament indicated just how irrelevant the stigma of sexual activity can be. The author ventures to suggest she would not have been appointed in England, America or France.

[12] Consider the dilemma posed by the following: on 17 Apr. 1998, artist Angela Marshall planned to paint a work in the presence of the purchaser but to sell each painting conditional on the particular purchaser having sex with her during the process in order for the art to be fully consummated in the purchaser's presence.

ESSAY 3: ART AND DEFAMATION: A COMPARATIVE MORAL PERSPECTIVE

This appendix essay could be said to be about competing goods, the right to reputation and the right to create artistically, in a context where they clash. This would be so if the author could think of reputation as a good, which he cannot.[1] He can see it as of societal and economic use but cannot conceive of it as having intrinsic moral worth; it only has worth contingent on (and only is) the opinion of others, and this is not moral worth. For good reputation is only a brand of rumour, a particular kind of rumour beneficial to the plaintiff,[2] but only a rumour nevertheless. It is not a fact and not a value, except for the ego and to aid the societal advancement of the plaintiff in a society where reputations matter. The latter consideration makes a good reputation socially and economically worth having if you happen to live in that sort of society and you look at things pragmatically; but there is nothing morally good about social advancement. There may even be something ignobly egotistic, even hubristic, about a concern for reputation for one's own petty human ends. Art, by contrast, has intrinsic value in itself, and for others. It is not rumour but value: it is of creation and in it is the spirit of creation, i.e. it is a good thing.[3] It cannot be art if its conception is destructive, for art is of creation. The assumption when faced with an art-work must be that this, created, was, of necessity, created with creative intention. A malicious motive does not negate creative intention implicit in the creation. What is significant for our purposes is how a malicious motive manifests itself as a negative effect of a created work and whether there should be legal redress for those "harmed" by the negative effect. There are instances, too, of negligent causation where, for example, a name used in creative fiction corresponds to the name of a real person the creator did not know. The artist should oblige in changing the name when alerted to the error, and the error should be made public if the victim desires.

---

[1] I am influenced by the New Testament in making such a judgement, bearing in mind, in particular, Christ's disdain for status-consciousness. See, for example, Matthew, XXIII, verses 5–7 (New International Version): "[e]verything they do is done for men to see: they make their phylacteries wide and the tassels of their prayer shawls long; they love the place of honour at banquets and the most important seats in the synagogues; they love to be greeted in the market places and to have men call them 'Rabbi'."

[2] In a defamation action understood.

[3] Creativity builds and beautifies.

Naming someone in a work whom you do in fact know, and continuing to use a name you know to belong to someone in (factual) reality, in the absence of consent, invites enquiry as to malicious motive, for you, the creator, have for some reason decided in this instance not to transmute life to art in a matter which seldom, if ever, substantially affects the creative integrity of such a work i.e. simply changing the names of your characters.

More difficult is the case of caricature, which relies heavily on a real-life image—indeed, cannot be without it. It is creative imitation of life. If accepted as such, as an art, it cannot harm if treated as art. In the same way as the public accepts, through routine, that unflattering cartoons in the national press are to be treated as other than fact, should it not be educated and encouraged to interpret art as art, thus removing the possibility of art being used as a tool for generating harm for those portrayed?

Indeed, defamation by art is only possible with the agency of an ignorant audience which has misinterpreted art as fact and perpetrated harm by acting negatively towards their victim who was only art's model. The public, the audience, should be educated to treat art appropriately—as art, i.e. never to be interpreted as fact for them to use to another's detriment. Art offers insights as artistic insights, not factual ones. Art is not opinion; it is an assembly of artistic ideas. If art offers truth, it is artistically synthesised truth and any meaning is an artistic construct. Nowhere is there fact. Given an educated and accordingly civilised audience, art can never be abused as a tool for harm because the audience comprehends that it is receiving art, not fact. Art and artists must not be the scapegoats for society ignorance and its harmful effects. When something is art, it is aside from life, near it, reflecting from it and on it, but not factually. This is a simple lesson to teach and to know and its promulgation would culturally enrich society and preclude ill-conceived lawsuits. Since creativity is such a good thing, it should be promoted and not inhibited by audience ignorance of how to treat it, and consequently supported by law. Plaintiffs who bring an action against allegedly defamatory art (in the unideal uneducated society) should be made to question if they are not being just a little over-serious about themselves, a little philistine and, perhaps, humourless. They may prove themselves to be all these things by bringing such an action. They may not mind so long as their cause is fulfilling for them but, if so, they are somewhat immoral, art being a higher value than reputation not least because it gives to others, care for reputation being a more selfish concern.

Dealing as we are with the unideal society containing the art-ignorant, defamation law, in all its complexity, accommodates uncomfortably a concept of defamation by art, not as a distinct category but as one of many undistinguished modes of defamation.[4] However, a conceptual framework of defamation law is possible that effectively exempts the bulk of art from its operation; the example taken here will be fiction though similar appropriately-amended considerations also apply to other art forms.

Defamation should be founded on accusation. Is fiction (art) an accusation of real person X? The standard argument now is that defamation should be defined in terms of an utterance's illocutionary force (which relates to its intended force) rather than, as traditionally, a perlocutionary act which relates to the effect of the utterance on the hearer. The (contrary) tradition has caused much injustice, the classic case being *Jones* v. *E. Hulton & Co.,*[5] where the total absence of fault on the defendant's part was considered immaterial: the effect of his published statement was in fact to injure the plaintiff. In the much earlier case of *Villers* v. *Mousley*,[6] clear poetic intent was disregarded, defamation construed. The roots of inattention to intent as central to defamation are deep-set in both French and Anglo-American defamation law traditions. This in part explains the difficulties the law faces when art is defendant: the law has no tradition of considering art's purpose (intent) as a necessary consideration; intent is peripheral, effect central to the concept of defamation the law enforces and the weight of centuries and concomitant legal inertia reinforces.

Some traditional defamation law tests are framed in a way that is prejudiced against individuals and eccentrics[7] (in the true unpejorative sense of the word). This is surprisingly the case in the three plural "democratic" states treated here, whose political ideology is allegedly aimed at the protection of the individual, of minorities as well as the majority (who, *a fortiori*, arguably do not need as much legal support, being a majority). Artists and writers are of necessity individual: what we appreciate is precisely the manifestation of their highly individual

---

[4] It is the author who separates art from the rest, a job which law reform committees should arguably have done a long time ago. The author sees art as a particularly life-enhancing entity in accordance with our creative function as created beings; in more atheistic and artistic terms, we emulate creative processes we witness about us with the peculiarly human capacity for a consciously artistic mode of creation—the human being's particularly refined and fine contribution.

[5] [1909] 2 KB 444.

[6] 95 ER 886, 886 (KB, 1769).

[7] The word "eccentric" derives from the Greek "out of the centre".

creative voice. Their individuality (singularity) is the source of what makes them particularly valuable and distinctive. Nevertheless, defamation law enforces at root the notion of violation of community norms; it is precisely one of the (valuable) roles of artists to keep society alert to the useful reassessment of such norms,[8] to doubt them. If a community considers art with indifference (as exemplified by the traditional conception of defamation that does not accommodate art satisfactorily as a distinct cultural unit), and subjects art to rules it is simply of essence unable to obey, a vast programme of re-education of the community (to improve its norms) and massive reform of the law should take place. For an utterance to have the propositional content of an accusation, the community has to find the conduct reprehensible; if the community were taught to view art as a culture of creative ideas unintended and ungeared for the consequences of real-life accusation, defamation law would have to become correspondingly more sophisticated. However, comprehension of the ultimate value of art and its value over comparatively petty, egotistic and ignoble concern for one's own "honour" is not a current community priority. Is this a good reason for law to ignore art's specific cultural mechanism?

An analogy can be made with homosexuality.[9] In postmodern society with its plural scheme of living, general community appreciation of diverse modes of sexual lifestyles as being not just tolerable but useful for a richer society is still an ideal. Defamation law, demoded as it undeniably is, further retards community enlightenment and development. If it can be defamatory to say of someone that he is gay, what does that say about the way the formers of defamation law view homosexuals? Moreover, defamation law promotes regional prejudice by framing its community standard test according to regional mores and not according to the guidelines of, for example, the law of human rights.

It is true that France has been traditionally less oppressive towards sexual minorities than England and America, and in this regard can be congratulated for being more cultured. All three states, however, in setting such store by honour and reputation (as exemplified by their defamation law) freeze respect for these intractable notions and, co-extensively, general intellectual development, to the sacrifice of

[8] I am grateful to Martin Greig for information on the conscious effort of the Dada movement in this regard.

[9] Art and homosexuality have an uncanny historical alliance. My own attempted explanation for this is probably too esoteric to be regarded as scientifically viable.

(and under-promotion of) intrinsically superior values such as the value of artistic endeavour. The adherence to a regional community standard for testing the defamatory nature of a comment's effect panders to parochial prejudice and does nothing to improve such society. Despite the fact that all these states emphasise taking into account the context of the allegedly defamatory statement, there is insufficient legal awareness of art's unique contextual framework; more generally-directed legal provisions often simply cannot apply to art's distinctive mechanism without grave violation of legal respect for a different culture.

What defamation law does at present is to pander to (often irrational) community reflex without considering the merits of that reflex. If the audience is viewing art and understands it in a defamatory sense, it might be useful for the law to promote the knowledge that even if art is a reflection of life, art does not reflect back on life other than as art. Moreover, at a more general level, is there not something radically wrong (something intrinsically cruel) about a society that shuns because of "disgrace" as a result of defamatory art?

Defamation law distinguishes fact and opinion, but not art and fact or art and opinion. The law tends to assume that art is either (usually) opinion and cannot be defamatory or fact (rarely) and can be. There seems to be no legal awareness that art is neither opinion nor fact but an assembly of creative ideas. This makes art's position particularly precarious in traditional defamation law—it has to be fitted uncomfortably on one of the two sides of a dichotomy (fact or opinion) and does not fit at all on either. The difference between art and fact and art and opinion is not of nuance but essential. Art is a totally different entity and is consequently treated unfairly by defamation law which makes no attempt to recognise its intrinsic difference from opinion and fact. The structural basis of defamation ("is it fact or is it opinion?") simply does not accommodate the extra consideration, "or is it art?". Instead, art has to be found some sort of subsidiary defence based on fair comment or (feasibly but rarely) justification or, as in French law, judged as any other statement in issue save for individual judicial discretion on the art aspect.

Art intends to evoke a particular type of mental state in its audience. It invites contemplation. Unlikeable characters in a novel invite a quasi-moral awareness on the part of the reader, the object not being to accuse any real life model for the unlikeable protagonist (for he is distant from the picture portrayed and irrelevant for artistic purposes) but in some way to use the traits to illumine or edify and enhance inner life for the reader. If the novel is *à clef*, then the improving impact may be even stronger because straight from experience: a tale is told to make aware not accuse, proof of which is not least that the reader, not the model for the character, is the object of its attention. Art addresses itself to a general audience who choose to view it, only incidentally to the plaintiff (who may himself be improved by it). Art is crafted information with a large amount of imaginative input: it is a construct. Art is not opinion[10] but creation, not false but created. Art is not representing something as an actual state of affairs: it is a construct of experience of fact and creative imagination. Not to see it thus is a mistake and a mistake that defamation law makes and perpetuates.

Unless a novel is total fantasy (and if so arguably of inferior quality for lack of verisimilitude), it does profitably emerge directly or indirectly from forms of fact as the novelist (with all his singular creative powers) has perceived them. The novelist transmutes experience impressions into an artistic creation—any subsequent effect is too oblique to be accusation[11] (notwithstanding the other reasons why art cannot be accusation). A destructive motive (uncreative) cannot produce art (creative).

Those with a particular reverence for the highest forms of culture Man produces ("the arts") could pose the following considerations to whet the legal appetite. First, judges can accuse by virtue of their position: why cannot novelists? A judge is permitted to accuse to fulfil certain practical (prosaic) societal needs, including the need for societal order. Should the artist be privileged to accuse in the course of his noble attempt to improve the life of Man in a pleasing intellectual, spiritual or mental-stimulating way? If the law is entitled privilege, why not art? Secondly, should timeless personalities be insulated from petty transient legal processes and mores to enable them to fulfil better their untime-contingent artistic duty? The work of art exists beyond or despite time; the law adapts with time. Laws are of the moment; art endures intact. What right has law to restrict permanent expression according to more transient tools i.e. laws?

Defamation law must recognise the independence of art, a little to the side, if you like, of life and fact and distinct from opinion. Art

---

[10] "Opinion" (likewise, *a fortiori*, "opinionated") is charged with a political implication on the part of the holder. Such implication is not an identifying characteristic of an artistic product.
[11] Contrast bald factual accusations whose sole unambiguous object, negative, is the causing of harm.

embodies value (created); it can, and often does, reflect facts, but these are artistically synthesised, as are life's truths; art intends to be received as art and reflect back on life only as art. Art is for the nourishment of the audience, not to harm. Incidental negative functioning of the audience having been exposed to art is not art's intent (creative) and not art's fault.

With these considerations in mind, the defamation law of art could be reformed either by excluding art from its ambit or, failing that, following the ensuing guidelines when art is alleged to defame.

There must be a legal presumption that a novel (art work) is not an accusatory form, and it must be for the plaintiff to prove that it is. In the light of the above critique, this should prove difficult. If, by some means, it is achieved, the plaintiff must then show that (a) the art was designed to harm him and (b) it has in fact harmed him. If he satisfies these requirements, the court must decide which is the greater value to society, to have and promote the novel in society or to have the reputation of harmed "victim" X preserved. If the court decides for the plaintiff, the novel should be removed from public view, for it is deemed harmful and negative. With this decision the law de-artifies it and reifies it. The object is no longer value but (harmful) fact; artistic status is removed. Any protest against such injunction should be greeted well by those who admire culture. Under no circumstances should damages be payable by the defendant and the work be allowed to carry on in circulation: the law cannot be seen to compromise its values like this. Having only the option of an injunction against art forces society to consider whether art should be the victim of law which the mere payment of damages by the artist does not reveal as patently or painfully to society.

ESSAY 4: ON THE NATURE OF ART AND LAW

Art is not necessarily logical, and there is always something in it that escapes definition; one could venture that if complete definition is possible, the article under consideration is not art: a pile of bricks is a pile of bricks. Art is creative; it does not destroy. It is the antithesis of destruction, created and communicating. It promotes ideas suggestively and cannot be violence, even though it can communicate it. Art is not reason, though it may be understandable; in a way, too, it is like faith—it exists for the subjective mind; unlike faith, it always has a concrete externally discernible form. Art, then, is not as unidentifiable as faith but more readily communicable; art is less essentially reasonable and rational than law. Art, if you like, is the mid-point between material and spirit: a thing, but not a thing. It is more than a thing. The law deals with facts though accommodates feelings. It appreciates order and its executors, particularly the judiciary, are esteemed for their logical minds. The law scrutinises facts and arranges them in orderly fashion to which to apply the relevant rules. The essence of law is order. It is not allowed the same freedom as art, for its purpose is to regulate people with as much consistency as possible. The *raison d'être* of law is that it is a socially necessary mechanism on which people can rely for them to be secure. Art is one of their indulgences once secure; art presumes security and survival. Law attempts to provide order via rules on which people can rely: it values objectivity and attempts to be predictable though bombarded from all sides by subjectivity. Artistic ego meets functional lex.

Select Bibliography

ADAMS, L., *Art on Trial* (Walker & Company, New York, 1976).

ANDERSON, N., *Liberty, Law and Justice* (Stevens & Son, London, 1978).

ASHTON, D. (ed.), *Twentieth-Century Artists on Art* (Pantheon Books, New York, 1985).

BARENDT, E., *Freedom of Speech* (Clarendon Press, Oxford, 1985; reprinted with additions 1987, 1989).

BECKETT, W., *Art and the Sacred* (Rider Books, London, 1992).

BÉCOURT, D., *Livres Condamnés, Livres Interdits* (2nd edn., Cercle de la Libraire, Paris, 1972).

BILGER, P., and PRÉVOST, B., *Le Droit de la Presse* (Presses Universitaires de France, Paris, 1989).

BOYD WHITE, J., *The Legal Imagination* (The University of Chicago Press, Chicago, Ill., 1973, abridged edn. 1985).

BRITTAIN, V., *Radclyffe Hall—A Case of Obscenity* (Femina, London, 1968).

CALDER-MARSHALL, A., *Lewd, Blasphemous and Obscene* (Hutchinson & Co. Publishers Ltd, London, 1972).

CHAFEE Z., JR., *Free Speech in the United States* (Harvard University Press, New Haven, Conn., 1946).

CHERPILLOD, I., *L'objet du droit d'auteur* (CEDIDAC, Lausanne, 1985).

COLOMBET, C., *Propriété Littéraire et Artistique (Et Droits Voisins)* (3rd edn., Dalloz, Paris, 1986).

CORNISH, W.R., *Intellectual Property: Patents, Copyright, Trade Marks and Allied Rights* (2nd edn., Sweet & Maxwell, London, 1989).

COPINGER, W.A. and SKONE JAMES, E.P., *Copinger and Skone James on Copyright* (12th edn., Sweet & Maxwell, London, 1980).

CRAWFORD, T., *Legal Guide for the Visual Artist* (Hawthorn Books, Inc., New York, 1977).

DAVID, R., *French Law*, 1972 (Louisiana State University Press, Baton Rouge, Lou., 1972).

DICEY, A.V., *Introduction to the Study of the Law of the Constitution* (10th edn., Macmillan, London, 1964).

DUBOFF, L.D., *Art Law* (West Publishing Co., St Paul, Minn., 1984).

ECO, U., *Art and Beauty in the Middle Ages* (Yale University Press, Princeton, NJ, 1986).

EDELMAN, B., *Ownership of The Image* (trans. E. Kingdom, Routledge & Kegan Paul, London, 1979).

ELIOT, T.S., *Notes Towards the Definition of Culture* (Faber and Faber, London/Boston, 1948, 1983 reprint).

FELDMAN, F. and WEIL, S.E., *Art Law* (Little, Brown & Company (Canada) Ltd., Boston, Mass., 1986), 2 vols.

FORD, B. (ed.), *The Cambridge Guide to the Arts in Britain* (Cambridge University Press, Cambridge, 1988), vol. 9.

FORSTER, E.M., *Two Cheers For Democracy* (E. Arnold, London, 1972).

FRASCINA, F., and HARRISON, C., with the assistance of PAUL, D., *Modern Art and Modernism: A Critical Anthology* (Harper Row Ltd., London, 1982).

GODAMER, H.-G., *The Relevance of the Beautiful and Other Essays* (Cambridge University Press, Cambridge, 1986).

HAIMAN, F.S., *Freedom of Speech* (National Textbook Company, Stokie, Ill., 1978).

HART, H.L.A., *Law, Liberty and Morality* (Oxford University Press, Oxford/New York, 1963, 1982 reprint).

HARVEY, D., *The Condition of Postmodernity: An Enquiry into the Origins of Cultural Change* (Blackwell, Oxford, 1990).

HOFSTADTER, A., and KUHNS, R., *Philosophies of Art and Beauty* (The University of Chicago Press, Chicago, Ill., 1964).

HOLLANDER, B., *The International Law of Art* (Bowes and Bowes, London, 1959).

HYDE, H.M., *A History Of Pornography* (Heinemann, London, 1964).

KAUPERT, P.G., and BEYTAGH, F.X., *Constitutional Law: Cases and Materials* (5th edn., Little, Brown and Company, Boston/Toronto, 1980).

KITARO, N., *Art and Morality* (The University Press of Hawaii, Honolulu, Hawaii, 1973).

KOESTLER, A., *The Art of Creation* (Hutchinson & Co. Publishers Ltd, London, 1976).

LAHAYE, N., *L'Outrage aux Mœurs* (Publication no 9 of the Centre National de Criminologie, Brussels, 1980).

LEHMANN-HAUPT, H., *Art under a Dictatorship* (Octagon Books, New York, 1973).

MACCORMICK, N., *Legal Right and Social Democracy* (Oxford University Press, Oxford, 1982).

McEWAN, R., and LEWIS, P., *Gatley on Libel and Slander* (7th edn., Sweet & Maxwell Ltd., London, 1974).

MERLE, R., and VITU, A., *Traité de droit criminel; droit pénal spécial* (Editions Cujas, Paris, 1982).

MERRYMAN, J.H., and ELSEN, A.E., *Law, Ethics and the Visual Arts* (University of Pensylvania Press, Philadelphia, Penn., 1987), vol. 1.

MITCHELL, B., *Law, Morality and Religion in a Secular Society* (Gerald Duckworth & Co., Ltd, London, 1977).

MOFFAT, G., and CHESTERMAN, M., with DEWAR, J., *Trusts Law: Text and Materials* (Weidenfeld and Nicolson, London, 1988).

The New Testament

POSNER, R.A., *Law and Literature: A Misunderstood Relation* (Harvard University Press, New Haven, Conn., 1988).

REMBAR, C., *The End of Obscenity* (André Deutsch Ltd, London, 1968).

ROBERTSON, G., *Obscenity* (Weidenfeld and Nicolson, London, 1979).

ROKEACH, M., *The Open and Closed Mind* (Basic Books Inc., New York, 1960).

ROLPH, C.H., *The Trial of Lady Chatterly, Regina v. Penguin Books Ltd.* (Penguin Books, Baltimore, Mld., 1961).

ROOKMAAKER, H.R., *The Creative Gift: The Arts and the Christian Life* (Inter-Varsity Press, Leicester, 1981).

ROSENBAUM, A.S., *The Philosophy of Human Rights* (Aldwych Press, London, 1981).

ROSENBERG, N.L., *Protecting the Best Men: An Interpretive History of the Law of Libel* (University of North Carolina Press, 1986).

ST. JOHN STEVAS, N., *Obscenity and the Law* (Secker & Warburg, London, 1956).

VATIMMO, G., *The End of Modernity: Nihilism and Hermeneutics in Post-Modern Culture* (Polity Press, Cambridge, 1989).

WILDE, O.F.O.W., *The Picture of Dorian Gray* (ed. P. Ackroyd, Penguin, London, 1985).

YOUNG, W., *Eros Denied* (Weidenfeld & Nicolson, London, 1965).

Index